Strangers IN Paradox

EXPLORATIONS
IN MORMON
THEOLOGY
~

Strangers ▊IN▊ Paradox

EXPLORATIONS
IN MORMON
THEOLOGY

~

by
Margaret & Paul Toscano

Signature Books
Salt Lake City
1990

Cover Illustration: "Strangers in Paradox" by Carol H. Norby, collage, 1990.

Cover Design: Julie Easton

ILLUSTRATOR'S NOTE:

The cover illustration to *Strangers in Paradox: Explorations in Mormon Theology* represents the Toscanos' eclectic approach to their subject through a variety of symbols.

The all-seeing eye represents God's omniscience.

The ministering angel is a messenger of good tidings whose wings suggest flight through time and space and between the celestial and earthly realms.

The cross is the Christian symbol of atonement.

The lion is a king, a ruler, and an ancient Christian symbol of strength.

The handclasp (ca. 1300 A.D.) represents friendship and love. The clasped hand is trusting, welcoming, and free of weapons.

The oak leaf and acorn are symbolic of human potential for spiritual growth.

The figures of Adam and Eve are adapted from the work of Albrecht Dürer, from the sixteenth century. Eve holds a candle in one hand, for light and knowledge, and a lily in the other, for purity. The golden drapery represents the sacred trust of motherhood. Adam holds an apple signifying the Fall. Adam and Eve lean toward one another representing their interdependence.

The hand of God lifts the veil that separates the earth (the foliage) from the celestial worlds. The arch is placed between the veil and the foliage to show entrance into life on earth from a previous existence.

LIBRARY OF CONGRESS CATALOGING-IN-PUBLICATION DATA
Toscano, Margaret Merrill, 1949–
    Strangers in paradox : explorations in Mormon theology / Margaret Merrill Toscano, Paul James Toscano.
        p.   cm.
    ISBN 0-941214-98-2
    1. Mormon Church—Doctrines. 2. Church of Jesus Christ of Latter-day Saints—Doctrines.
I. Toscano, Paul James, 1945–
II. Title.
BX8635.2.T67   1990
230′.93—dc20   89–27210
                                                              CIP

For our daughters
Angela, Elizabeth, Mary, and Sarah

I am the resurrection and the life: he that believeth in me, though he were dead, yet shall he live: and whosoever liveth and believeth in me shall never die.
—JESUS

Were it not for our transgression we never should have had seed, and never should have known good and evil, and the joy of our redemption, and the eternal life which God giveth unto all the obedient.
—EVE

Thy mind, O man! If thou wilt lead a soul unto salvation, must stretch as high as the utmost heavens, and search into and contemplate the darkest abyss...
—JOSEPH SMITH

When I leave this frail existence,
When I lay this mortal by,
Father, Mother, may I greet you
In your royal courts on high?
Then, at length, when I've completed
All you sent me forth to do,
With your mutual approbation
Let me come and dwell with you.
—ELIZA R. SNOW

CONTENTS

Introduction   xi

Part I: First Principles

Chapter 1. Cornerstones   3
Chapter 2. Keystones   14

Part II: Godhead

Chapter 3. Holiness to the Lord   29
Chapter 4. The God of Flesh and Glory   37
Chapter 5. The Divine Mother   47
Chapter 6. Jesus Christ and the Mormon Pantheon   60
Chapter 7. Beyond Matriarchy, Beyond Patriarchy   71
Chapter 8. The Marriage of Time and Eternity   98

Part III: Redemption

Chapter 9. Divinity and Humanity   107
Chapter 10. Bringing Good Out of Evil   111
Chapter 11. The Case for Grace   116
Chapter 12. Metaphors of Salvation   130

Part IV: Priesthood

Chapter 13. The Nature and Purpose of Priesthood   143
Chapter 14. Priesthood in the Book of Mormon   154
Chapter 15. Women and Priesthood in the Bible   167
Chapter 16. A Kingdom of Priestesses   179
Chapter 17. The Oath and Covenant of the Priesthood   198

CONTENTS

Chapter 18. Women, Ordination, and Hierarchy   209
Chapter 19. Zion: Vision or Mirage   221

Part V: Sex Roles, Marriage Patterns, and the Temple
Chapter 20. Sex Roles   237
Chapter 21. Monogamy, Polygamy, and Humility   250
Chapter 22. Rending the Veil   265
Chapter 23. The Mormon Endowment   278

Bibliography   293

INTRODUCTION

This book is about religious ideas. Our objective is to explore the landscape of our religion and to share our discoveries with others, who like us struggle with the primary questions of life, who find themselves thinking about divinity and humanity, good and evil, justice and mercy, male and female, substance and form, the sacred and the secular.

This is not a systematic theology, nor is it reflective of mainstream Mormon thought. We do not provide complete discussions of or final answers to the questions we address here. Rather, our approach is personal and subjective. In these chapters we invite further discussion and reassessment. Our goal is to be clear and thought-provoking without being strident or dogmatic.

This work is based in large measure on our experiences as Mormons and our studies of the history and doctrine of the Church of Jesus Christ of Latter-day Saints. We hope that none of our readers will find this objectionable or offensive. It cannot be helped. Throughout these chapters we deal with the ideas, teachings, and revelations of Joseph Smith, whom we love and admire. We do not shy away from his most controversial contributions: sexuality, materiality, magic, polygamy, eternal progression, and continuing revelation. But this book is not meant to be a description of his teachings or a restatement of Mormon theology. We do not see either his period or our own as a golden age. For us Joseph Smith's teachings, like those of every other prophet, constitute not the final word but a point of departure.

We are guided in many of our discussions by concepts and precepts of Christianity and to some extent by Judaism and other religious traditions ancient and modern. We feel a profound kinship with many men and women in these other traditions, people we have come to respect deeply, who have given us much in the way of insight and inspiration. But we also realize that we have some profound disagreements even with those whom we quote extensively. We are aware that religions, while they share much in common, differ on important questions. We believe that there is good in both what is common and uncommon in them and that people who are interested in religious ideas and a religious life can benefit by reflecting on the spiritual insights and experiences of others, even of those with whom they disagree.

Though our primary audience will undoubtedly be LDS, we hope those of other faiths will find our ideas stimulating. This approach, however, presents us with a problem. How are we to deal with both groups at the same time? In most cases, we resolve this by addressing the LDS reader directly and assume the non-LDS reader to be an interested onlooker. Because of the diversity of our audience and the particularity of our own world view, we have provided explications of the basic assumptions and interpretive principles that underlie this book. These appear in the first two chapters. Here however we must say a word about our employment of pronouns and references to deity. Traditionally God has been pictured as a male, and therefore scriptural language has reflected this masculine bias. This bent, we believe, must be counterbalanced, but without either arbitrarily negating or rewriting our historical religious texts or being slaves to their deficiencies. The simple solution is to employ gender neutral references where possible. But this is more difficult than it sounds because there are not many words in English that can be used in this way without sounding archaic or cumbersome (i.e., "the Most High," "the Eternal," "Eloheim," etc.). The other technique is to alternate pronoun references to deity between "he" and "she." This solution is not always workable for those like us who believe that most scriptural references are to Christ. On the other hand if, as we believe, there is a female counterpart to Christ, then all references to him, except in a particular historical context, are references to her as well.

We have done our best to resolve this problem, but our resolution is inadequate. This is because every reference to deity invokes a deep, complex, and unresolved theological question about the nature, number, and character of the godhead. Thus our references reflect our own imperfect and incomplete understanding of the divine nature. We wish therefore to clarify that when we use the masculine pronoun to refer to deity, we do not mean to deny the reality, importance, or equality of the female; and when we make reference to the female, we do not wish to slight the traditional view of God.

A number of chapters deal with the female divinity and require appropriate references to her. The word "Goddess" is offensive to some because it sounds pagan. On the other hand the exclusive use of the term "Heavenly Mother" emphasizes nurturing and mothering while neglecting other attributes. For this reason we use both of these appellations as well as the terms "female deity," "Divine Lady," "God the Mother," and "female God." Unfortunately none of these is as personal as the name Jesus. But this failing arises from the absence of a clear and universally accepted revelation of the identity of the female, which no lexical or grammatical legerdemain can correct.

Finally we must acknowledge that many of the ideas contained in this book have been gleaned from and refined through conversations with friends to whom we owe much. In gratitude we would like to name them all but will not, primarily to refrain from burdening anyone else with the responsibility for ideas and concepts they may not share.

Strangers IN Paradox

EXPLORATIONS
IN MORMON
THEOLOGY
~

PART I

First Principles

~ CHAPTER ONE ~

CORNERSTONES

We believe Joseph Smith was referring to the concept of paradox in his 5 June 1844 letter to L. Daniel Rupp, author of *An Original History of the Religious Denominations At Present Existing in the United States*. After praising Rupp for letting each sect tell its own story, Joseph stated that "by proving contraries, truth is made manifest" (HC 6:428). In other words by examining various, even contrary views, new truths may be revealed.

The gospels, as we know, contain many paradoxical statements of Jesus: "Whosoever shall exalt himself shall be abased; and he that shall humble himself shall be exalted" (Matt. 23:12). "He that is greatest among you shall be your servant" (v. 11). "He that findeth his life shall lose it: and he that loseth his life for my sake shall find it" (10:39). "Blessed are the meek; for they shall inherit the earth" (5:5). These phrases are so familiar that we sometimes fail to appreciate their basic internal contrariness.

How can we be exalted by being abased? Or find our lives by losing them? Or expect through meekness to triumph? Reason and ordinary human experience tell us that those who abase themselves will usually find that others stand ready to abase them even further. The greatest have usually served no one but themselves, while those who seek their lives go on living and those who lose their lives go on dying. As for the meek, the lyrics of a song cynically remind us that it is not the earth they inherit but "the dirt." And when the meek do inherit anything, they either fritter it away forthwith or they make an abrupt break with meekness.

In spite of all this, many of us still accept the paradoxes of Jesus as statements of profound spiritual insight rather than nonsensical rubbish. We do this because we are willing to accept that there is more to the world than what is visible to our senses and understandable to the human mind, that there is a place, unlike this earth, where the loving, the selfless, and the sacrificing are blessed. If we accept the larger paradox that the universe is made up of a spiritual world and a temporal one, then the smaller paradoxes make sense. It becomes clear why the meek of the earth may inherit the glories of heaven or how the humble here may be exalted hereafter.

This suggests that paradox is a device which invites us to change our perception of reality. When we first perceive a paradox, its contrary elements seem utterly incompatible. We are tempted to think that either one or the other element is false or that both are false. It is not easy to see how both can be true. However, if we accept the truth of both propositions and change our frame of reference, the rival statements of the paradox may suddenly appear to be compatible truths which tend to validate our new found perspective. This process encourages us to sacrifice traditional concepts, to take risks, to make leaps into the dark, to reassess our assumptions. It encourages not just a change of mind but a change of heart, which is repentance in its most basic form.

In order to grow spiritually, we must be willing to change our views again and again so that our understanding of the world and of God will mature. One of the basic premises of this book is our belief that by accepting as true the contradictions manifest in the person, the story, and the teachings of Jesus Christ, the highest and holiest truths may be revealed to us.

THE PARADOX OF JESUS: GOD AND MAN—MALE AND FEMALE

Nearly every symbol, ritual, teaching, and text of the Judeo-Christian tradition can be interpreted either from a legalistic perspective or a spiritual one. In this book we take a decidedly non-legalistic view. For us God is not inflexible and demanding but loving, humble, and willing to sacrifice to save us. Paradoxically God is also fiercely passionate and possesses an unpredictable holiness. God's love is sometimes terrifying and exacting. Nevertheless we do not see religion primarily in terms of moral commandments but of spiritual birth and growth. Instead of seeing the teachings of Christ as dogmas, we see them as touchstones for the further expansion of our beliefs. For us genuine religious community cannot be dominated by a hierarchical power structure of competitive, ecclesiastical athletes. It must be a body of interdependent believers of whom the greatest of all is the servant of all. Rather than seeing the religious life in terms of meetings or fund raising or institutional management, we see it as love, hope, art, imagination, religious feeling, and contact with the divine. This view, we believe, is mandated by the revelation of God in the person of Jesus Christ.

Undoubtedly the most fundamental assumption of this book is that Jesus Christ is God and the initial truth of our religion. For us Christ is the way, the truth, and the life — the principal historical revelation to us of the divine nature. His cross is the linchpin of our salvation, the cosmic bridge that connects the human with the divine.

But we must say at once that Christ, as the revelation of God, is a paradox — the supreme paradox. Rather than reinforce our fantasies, our philosophies, and our formalisms, Christ calls us to leave the confines of our human limitations and enter into a new and marvelous country replete with the unexpected and the unforeseen. The religion of Jesus calls us to accept the paradox lying at the heart of nature, supernature, and divine nature. It calls us to accept as truth what seems at first to be foolishness or error.

Thus, from the perspective of paradox, it was no mistake that the creator stepped into his creation. Through God's incarnation, we are called to accept as eternal realities the paradoxical elements of the spirit and the flesh. Nor was it a mistake that God was revealed to us as a white, Jewish male. These very specifics of his incarnation challenge our egocentricity and our arrogance, our inability to accept God in terms other than those we dictate. If we reject Jesus because he was white, are we not racist? If we reject him because he was a Jew, are we not anti-semitic? If we reject him because he was male, are we not sexist? And by the same token, if we accept him only because he was a white Jewish male, or because he meets our definition of God in some other way, are we not narrow-minded or elitist? The paradox of Jesus calls us to transcend the particularities of his incarnation without obliterating them. It not only requires us to see that we can be made in God's image without being white, Jewish, or male, it also asks us to see that we cannot relate to God as a person unless we accept the revelation of God's personal characteristics. Thus, in his incarnation, Jesus calls us to love him unconditionally even as we wish to be loved unconditionally by him.

From the perspective of paradox, it was no mistake that God was revealed as a person. Divine personhood reinforces the eternal reality of human personhood; divine materiality, human materiality; divine sex and sexuality, human sex and sexuality. In these ways we are summoned to accept the interconnectedness of human and divine, male and female, and to acknowledge that God needs humanity as much as God is needed by humanity.

From the perspective of paradox, it was no mistake that Jesus preached only to the Israelites and then sent his gospel to Gentiles and pagans. In this he showed us that, although God may be best experienced through the specific myths and rituals of a given religious tradition, such a tradition, whatever it is, should not serve as a basis for a narcissistic denial of the validity or holiness of other traditions.

From the perspective of paradox, it was no mistake that God became man or that the Father made of himself a son. In this way the transcendent was made accessible to us. Nor was it a mistake that God is described as both beginning and end, author and finisher, creator and creation, or that the temporal is the womb of the eternal, or that the eternal is the seed of the temporal. Nor was it a mistake that the alpha and omega is also the everlasting, or that the living God is the dying God, or that the greatest of all should become the servant of servants.

Perhaps the chief paradox of Christianity, however, is that Jesus, as the manifestation of the one God, beckons us to worship not only the Father, but to receive the Son and the Holy Ghost as new god figures. Christ, by repeatedly comparing himself to a bridegroom in many of his sayings, also suggests the existence of a female counterpart that is to be joined to him. By this usage, he opens the way for the revelation of a female divinity of equal stature with the other members of the Christian godhead. This suggestion resolves a problem many find troubling: the absence in Christian theology of a female divinity.

Of course, this void has been partially filled in Catholicism by the Virgin Mary, who is seen as the Queen of Heaven, and in Mormonism by the tradition of Heavenly Mother as the counterpart to Heavenly Father, both of whom are distinct, personal deities yet mystically united. Though such concepts are promising, they are unsatisfying for at least two reasons. First, the male divinity was manifest to us in the light of history in the person of Jesus, while the female divinity is available to us principally in the shadowy and more unfamiliar realm of myth. Second, the scriptures in both content and language are heavily biased in favor of the male God. To correct this imbalance we must retrieve, retell, and reevaluate in terms of the Christian revelation the myths of the

Great Goddess, while simultaneously reinterpreting the scriptures to eliminate, wherever possible, the masculine bias. Part of the work of this book is dedicated to these ends.

THE PARADOX OF MALE AND FEMALE

This leads to another of our principal assumptions. We see the sexes as necessary opposites of equal dignity and value. For this reason we believe that women are the spiritual equals of men and ought to have full access to all of the privileges, keys, rights, offices, callings, and gifts that have been available to men in the church. This idea echoes the teachings of Joseph Smith, who was the initiator of Mormonism and enunciator of its deepest and most enduring doctrines — doctrines which have given Mormonism its shape and character, doctrines which were forged into the foundational texts and early history of the church. Imbedded among these is the idea of religious and political equality for women.

In our view Joseph Smith was also the initiator of Mormon feminism. It was he who gave the stamp of approval to the organization of the Female Relief Society of Nauvoo. It was he who told its earliest members that he intended to make of that society "a kingdom of priests" (WJS, 110). It was he who defended women's right to heal the sick and cast out devils (ibid., 115–17) and the promise that they would come into possession of all the privileges enjoyed by male priesthood holders (ibid., 117–19).

Since those days Mormon feminism has fended for itself, living on its own within the culture of the Latter-day Saints, most often surviving in obscurity in the hearts of certain activists of the nineteenth and early twentieth centuries and, more recently, in the hearts of some modern Mormons as well. The resurgence of Mormon feminism has occurred, we believe, in response to certain troubling conditions in the modern church, including the disenfranchisement of women from church governance and the exclusion of women from the exercise of spiritual gifts. It must be noted, however, that the negative effects of patriarchal authoritarianism have not only led to the oppression of women but to a larger and growing spiritual malaise, marked by a lack of inner life, by a sense that we have somehow strayed from our religious mission, that we have borrowed too much from the male world of business and commerce, that we have become too narrow, too self-righteous, too legalistic and judgmental. The paradox of male and female demands that we respond to these concerns. But this demand is much more than a claim for equality within Mormon culture or for power within the ecclesiastical or priestly hierarchy. It is more than a plea for cultural and social change. It is a call for the fundamental spiritual revitalization of our entire religion. Because the paradox of male and female lies at the heart of the gospel of Jesus Christ, the feminist theme forms one of the recurring motifs of this book.

By stressing these concerns, we wish to emphasize that the central gospel message is that God's love is without bounds or conditions, that God is no respecter of persons, that the sexes, the families, the races, and the nations are one through the blood of Christ, and that men and women are in God's sight equal in value and dignity. For us Mormon feminism is but another form of the call to accept the fullness of God's grace — a call to all Mormons, male and female, to reject the primacy of male-dominated institutional power and to embrace instead the powers of the spirit under conditions where men and women share equal responsibility for the welfare and governance of the church.

In stressing this point we are not attempting to create a new gospel but rather to point up ideas that resist the institutional tendency to move away from the spiritual and egalitarian teachings of the restored gospel and toward the materialism, corporatism, and elitism of the modern world. In this book we attempt to reexamine and reevaluate our traditional interpretation of Mormonism to see where we may have become entangled in cultural biases. At times we introduce new perspectives on the revelations with the aim of providing an alternative to the views of those who see our scriptures as authorizations for oppression rather than for liberation.

Though some of our discussions emphasize the problems and suffering of women, our ultimate concerns extend beyond this focal point to embrace ideas that tend both to reform and reaffirm important aspects of our religion. As Mormons we must recognize the concept of a democratized priesthood in which members are valued as much for their God-given spiritual gifts as for their ecclesiastical offices. We believe in a true lay priesthood composed of both men and women joined together as equals in a general assembly of priesthood-holding believers. We argue that God is not a single male person but a duality: God the Female and God the Male. We accept the concept that the Bridegroom is not without the Bride, that the feminine is an integral part of the Christian revelation of God, and that the essential equality and mutual interdependence of male and female in the priesthood is a revelation of the true image of God as the union of the divine female and male.

The godhead seen in this way makes possible a redefinition of priesthood, not as an earthly structure of individual or corporate power but as the spiritual power of God bestowed by grace in equal dignity upon males and females alike. In this light it is possible to assert that the revelation of the fullness of the priesthood to males and females was Joseph Smith's crowning revelation to the church.

THE PARADOX OF HISTORY AND MYTH

Another of our chief assumptions grows out of the paradox of history and myth. In our view the mythical approach to understanding religious ideas is as useful and valuable as the historical method. We enjoy reading history and admire the work of religious historians. However, the methodology we employ here is not principally historical, though we employ historical data in some chapters. We are more interested in theology, ritual, symbolism, and myth. This book reflects that orientation.

Because Mormon historians have held center stage in our intellectual community for almost three decades, their influence is now so strong that any writing failing to treat Mormonism from a strictly historical and empirical perspective runs the risk of receiving a second-class welcome. For this reason we wish to justify our approach.

The modern world for the most part thinks of myth as a false story, the product of a primitive, superstitious mind without the benefit of science to explain how the world works.[1] History is often characterized as the opposite of myth because history deals in the scientific discovery of verifiable facts and events while myth is seen merely as the product of imagination. The modern, objectivist world prefers history and often denigrates myth. But we see a relationship between these approaches. Each has an indispensable function, and each has a valuable contribution to make to our culture and our understanding of the world.

History is essentially story-telling. But good history is more than mere narrative in that it relies on documents and artifacts. In a histor-

---

[1] The recent attention given to Joseph Campbell's work through Bill Moyer's television series, "The Power of Myth," has done much to reverse this tendency. Of course scholars have recognized the importance of the mythic view for some time. See, for example, *Myth: A Symposium* (Sebeok 1955) and *Sacred Narrative* (Dundes 1984).

ical narrative, people, places, things, and ideas actually existed and are identifiable, demonstrable, and verifiable. It is because history relies upon this type of evidence to tie events to particular sectors within a known chronological framework that we see history as reliable. For most people history is the truth about how the present came to be.

History, however, is not the past. It is a partial retelling of selected pieces of inter-woven incidents whose causes and effects the historian wishes to understand and illuminate. Most past incidents are disregarded because they illuminate and explain nothing: a baby is born, a volcano erupts, a cow moves in its stall. But some of these incidents seem to be important to our story. They are events. Not any baby but Elizabeth Tudor is born. Not any volcano but Mount Vesuvius erupts. Not any cow but Mrs. O'Leary's cow moves in its stall.

History is not only empirical and selective, it is sequential. The primary arrangement of historical material is that of cause and effect. Facts are seen as causes which lead to effects, which in turn become causes that lead to other effects, and so on. The problem with causation, of course, is determining the proper interpretation of what causes gave rise to what effects. This is particularly difficult in the context of religious history, where historical events are sometimes preceded by claims of supernatural causes. For example, Joseph Smith visits the Shakers and later writes a revelation on economic communalism. What caused this revelation? God? The visit to the Shakers? The creative mind of Joseph Smith? Some of the above? All of the above? None of the above? It is perhaps difficult to say with certainty. The more committed to empiricism a historian is, the more likely she or he will dismiss the supernatural as the cause of historical events. The willingness to seriously admit the supernatural into an historical analysis is perhaps what distinguishes sacred from secular history — neither of which is necessarily unreliable or white-washed history.

In either case, causation lies at the heart of the historian's task to understand what events influenced later people to say and do what they said and did. It is this feature which gives history its essentially linear shape. When most people think of history, they envision a continuum stretching from the present back into the past. The more sophisticated a person's historical sense, the more this image becomes cluttered with parallel lines, by-ways, loops, detours, and signposts. This linear paradigm is popular, satisfying, and useful.

But we see equal value in the mythical, symbolic, and theological approach to understanding the past, the present, and the future. Where history attempts to reconstruct the past fact by fact, myth attempts to see the meaning of the facts as they relate to one another and to the whole fabric of human knowledge and experience — past, present, and future. To quote William Irwin Thompson: "mythology . . . is interested in paradoxes, opposites, and transformations — the deep structure of consciousness and not the surface of facts and sensory perceptions" (1978, 120).

This is not to say that objective fact is unimportant. It is extremely important that hypotheses and theories be tied to reality, to actual experience, lest we construct world views of delusion which lead people to deny their real feelings and experience. Myth then is not whitewashed history but an acknowledgment that facts, like salamanders, are slippery things, that objectivity is also a point of view, and that data is usually determined by what individuals perceive.

For us myth is not a false story; nor is it a story that is historically false while remaining emotionally or morally true. For us myth is a story whose truth is set forth symbolically and is so basic it serves as a pattern which enhances our understanding and sometimes calls for emulation. This is why myth can serve as a road map to help us get our bearings on our spiritual journey. The mythical method does not deny the truth or importance of history. It only serves to superimpose on the historical paradigm another pattern. If history is represented by a horizontal line, then myth may be represented by a vertical line bisecting it. Myth is not primarily concerned with the horizontal axis of cause and effect but with the vertical dimension of microcosms and macrocosms. The mythical approach accepts history but sees it also as a symbol or set of symbols through which the mind may perceive or intuit unknown or dimly perceived truths. Thus from the mythical perspective, the event of Moses leading the people of Israel through the wilderness, through the waters of the Red Sea, and eventually into the promised land may or may not point to a historical Hebrew epic, but it can serve as a symbol of the journey of the soul through the wilderness of sin into the waters of regeneration and out again into the abundant grace of God.

This approach, although employed more in the past, is not unfamiliar. We usually use it to deny the historical reality of some of the supernatural events of the Bible while stressing their significance as representations of theological or ethical propositions. By this means the universal flood, the story of the confounding of language at the tower of Babel, the virgin birth, and the feeding of the five thousand may be rejected as history but retained as allegories of moral or spiritual truth. Nowadays most of us tend to segregate our religious symbols from our realities. We can accept, for example, the Garden of Eden as a type more easily than as a real place. Or else we tend to think of commonalities such as the ocean, the mountains, the old oak tree as realities but not as symbols.

Yet what most of the great religions of the world ask us to do is to see both common objects and mundane events as microcosms patterning or revealing a more significant or enduring spiritual reality. Thus a piece of broken bread is no longer a scrap of food but the broken flesh of the dying god. A goblet of wine is not simply to slake our physical thirst but our moral and spiritual thirst for justice, for an answer to the pain and the evil in the world, for the blood which God freely gives in taking responsibility for the shortcomings of creation. The washing of feet, once an ordinary hospitality ritual, becomes the symbol of the imputation to us of God's divine righteousness which replaces our inferior human righteousness. Religious ritual represents perhaps the clearest and most familiar manifestation of the mythical approach, which transforms the ordinary into the sacred.

For us history and myth are essential elements of a paradox. History helps us understand the causes shaping the present. Myth helps us understand the meaning of the present and its relation to the past, to the future, and to the divine. For the historian life is a chronicle. For the mystic life is a poem. Historians must continue to tell us what happened and how that effected what happened later. But theologians, poets, artists, and mystics should be respected for their attempt to see events as parables and to extract from them the meaning of realities not seen or experienced directly.

To those who are deeply committed to the empirical historical approach, what we have to say may at times be reminiscent of the work of soothsayers studying the entrails of birds to augur the intention of the gods. Nevertheless, we think there is considerable intellectual and spiritual rigor in the theory that the pattern of the eternal is to be found in the temporal and that the structure of the whole is to be found in the patterns displayed in the parts.

One reason for the negative reaction toward myth, in Mormonism, is that it has demonstrated an historical perference for the pragmatic and a distaste for the philosophical or intellectual. As Mormons, we tend to distrust any idea that cannot be directly applied to our daily lives, perferably with immediate and verifiable results. For this reason, myths, which deal more with the metaphysical than the practical, usually strike us as obscure, irrelevant, or nonsensical. The most that can be said for them by many people is that they are entertaining.

This, in our view, is an unhealthy sign. It means that we, like other elements in Western culture, cannot readily accept the paradox of the secular and the sacred. We seem to have lost the ability to respond to the world except in a linear and practical way. We tend to secularize every department of life. As secular individuals we shun the transcedent and look for all meaning in the here and now as we create it. We do not readily recognize how our own existence in the modern world fits in with the larger, mystical patterns of creation. By seeing our lives only in terms of probabilities and molecules we have made possible, even probable, the rejection of all meaning. Those who cannot intuit the purpose of life will find no reasons to exist. Such people are all around us. They wander homeless in the streets. They aggregate in gangs to do mischief. They buy up profitable companies, siphon off the assets, and leave the rinds behind. They build cartels to supply the demand for cocaine in all its forms.

Even as we write, great changes are taking place throughout the world as one secular totalitarian government after another falls before the demands of diverse peoples for personal liberty and democracy. How strange that the greatest effect this worldwide shift may have upon the West is to reveal our spiritual bankruptcy. Karl Marx said that religion was the opiate of the people. Ironically, we have come to see, in the late twentieth century, that in the absence of spirituality, opiates become the religion of the people. If we have no myth to live by, there is no reason to say "no" to drugs—no reason to live.

~ CHAPTER TWO ~

KEYSTONES

No literate person can escape interpretation. This is especially true when it comes to sacred texts manifest in the form of religious symbols, rituals, writings, or oral communications. Even people who believe in divine revelation still find the need for interpretation. Every act of listening or reading involves an interpretive process.

In this book we employ what we have called the mythic interpretive approach. Its purpose is to explore theological possibilities, to make symbolic connections, and to examine the import of religious ideas in the present. But our reliance on subjectivity does not mean that we disparage objectivity. Anyone serious about understanding a particular religious tradition must carefully examine its primary texts for provenance and historical context. But such texts also call for personal response. People with religious feeling cannot and should not repress such a response. For this reason we attempt to see texts both objectively and subjectively. Objectivity can serve to correct our false notions about the original purpose, context, and content of the text, while subjectivity can help us see what the text may mean for us and our world.

Paul Ricoeur, the French philosopher and phenomenologist, says that interpretation involves a process of "appropriation" or making "one's own what was initially 'alien.'" For Ricoeur, "the aim of all hermeneutics is to struggle against cultural distance and historical alienation. Interpretation brings together, equalizes, renders contemporary and similar. This goal is attained only insofar as interpretation actualizes the meaning of the text for the present reader" (185). However, Ricoeur also warns against what he calls the "illusion of the subject" or, in terms borrowed from Freud, the "narcissism of the reader." Interpretation as appropriation should not simply be the "projection of the prejudices of the readers." Thus a text should not be a prisoner of the meaning ascribed to it by its original author or its original audience, nor should it become the exclusive property of its present critics. If it is to continue to be vital, it must have a life of its own.

Both extreme subjectivity and extreme objectivity can be avoided if we can both reinterpret a text for the present and also be drawn into the world of the text (what Ricoeur calls "letting go"). By thus "appropriating" a text while simultaneously "relinquishing" our own biases, we can be changed by the text and receive through it, not simply a reaffirmation of our old prejudices, but a new capacity for self-knowledge. The end product of this process is a new interpretation that becomes an extension of the text, a new version of the myth. In this way some interpreters can also become myth-makers; and through each new version of a myth, there can be created both a departure from and a continuity with tradition.

In this book, for example, we have made a genuine effort to understand the life and thought of Joseph Smith objectively, as it fits in its historical context, and subjectively, as it relates to our present condition. The problem with the objective approach is the illusory nature of all knowledge. How can we ever reconstruct the past? Though we have tried to enter the world of Joseph Smith in order to understand his ideas, can we ever really retrieve and be certain of the original intent of his theological statements? In contrast the problem with the subjective approach is the relative nature of opinion. Why should our view be any more valid than any other? The task of understanding the past or the present seems impossible, but we have found that in making the attempt, illumination does come. In spite of this conviction, we bear a burden of doubt about our conclusions. And we reserve the right to change our minds, even on fundamentals.

Having said this we wish to present several keystones for the interpretive method we employ throughout this book. We do this to make our approach clear and to demonstrate how the richness of a given text, myth, or symbol may be developed and reevaluated.

Principle 1: Because we cannot approach a sacred text with complete neutrality and objectivity, we must recognize and acknowledge the religious, cultural, and intellectual biases we bring to the text, and we must accord to the belief-structures of others the same dignity and respect we reserve for our own.

We are all predisposed in various ways by our different educations, upbringings, and experiences. The more deeply our predilections run, the more likely we are to be oblivious to them. We cannot and should not rid ourselves of all of these. But we must at least admit them and compensate for them as we engage in the interpretive process.

In our own case, for example, we must face the fact that our interpretations of sacred texts (whether Mormon or otherwise) will be heavily influenced by our belief that Jesus Christ is God, that "God is no respecter of persons" (Acts 10:34; Gal. 3:28), that our divine parents are good and would not give their daughters or sons stones when they need bread (Luke 11:11), and that the godhead can and does intervene in human affairs. This decidedly religious outlook could be attacked or dismissed as disabling or invalid. But we are convinced it is no more so than an "unbelieving" point of view. We are none of us neutral observers, and it is no use pretending we are. Our divergent world views cause us to draw various meanings out of a given text.

Of course we understand that the interpretive process can be genuinely limited or even frustrated by closed-mindedness. But this can manifest itself both religiously, as rigid literalism or fundamentalism, or non-religiously, as an uncompromising attachment to naturalism or positivism. In our view, however, God speaks to all people through human experience, in dreams, through myths, symbols, and rituals, not just in the words of holy writ. God speaks in the ironies of life and of history. We are by no means presented with a consistent picture. God has not spoken the final word or given the *whole* of divine truth to any person or people or institution (cf. 2 Ne. 29:6–14). Further, God's mind and will are not easy to discern. Genuine revelation is usually paradoxical and ambiguous and, therefore, susceptible to multiple interpretations. Finally, we do not believe God speaks in only one voice. Divine communication comes to people "after the manner of their language," and these people receive and record their revelations according to their understanding and "weakness" (D&C 124:24; 1 Ne. 19:6; 2 Ne. 31:3; 33:4, 11).

That our renditions of texts tend to favor our convictions does not automatically invalidate our conclusions. If our convictions are not narcissistic and unbending, they may allow us to better understand the convictions of others. Thus, to fully appreciate the richness and complexity of the meanings associated with a given text, we must be willing to bestow equal dignity and weight upon the belief structures of others and, thus, transcend the limits of our own cultural prejudices.

Principle 2. For us God's voice is one of the voices in a sacred text; when speaking to one, God speaks to all through paradigmatic symbols.

Though God speaks to women and men in their own language in terms of their own cultural, ideological, and historical perceptions, it is nevertheless legitimate to look for the divine voice among the human voices in a sacred text. We have found that the ironies of a text, which can appear as contradictions, competing view points, changing frames of reference, or anomalies, are often manifestations of the different timbres of the divine voice. A reference to the development of the Mormon temple endowment may illustrate this point.

We know that in many ways the endowment was a product of Joseph Smith and the nineteenth century. Joseph Smith and his associates were well aware of what many have been eager to point out in recent years, namely parallels between Mormon and Masonic rites. However, even more important may be the many differences between the two rites. One of the most significant of these is that women were forbidden to participate in Masonry, while Joseph Smith accorded them equal access to the temple endowment. Because of our concern with the elements of gender inequality we detect in the temple, we can fail to see how radical it was for Joseph Smith to include women in the temple ritual at all. This fact alone suggests that Joseph Smith was not simply reflecting a nineteenth-century world view of women in the temple revelation. If the endowment ceremony were either in part or in total a product of divine revelation, then its meaning would probably go beyond the intentions of Joseph Smith. In other words the temple ceremony would not only echo nineteenth-century voices but the voice of God as well. This is not to say, however, that whatever we find in the revelations of Joseph Smith attributable to nineteenth-century American culture is only the voice of Joseph Smith; nor does it mean that whatever can be shown to have been alien to the nineteenth century is automatically to be understood to be the voice of God, or that originality was not one of Joseph Smith's characteristics.

Our point is that when God speaks to prophets in a way comprehensible to them and to their culture, God still may put something more into the revelation than can be understood by the person or culture receiving it. This is not only possible but likely because of the highly symbolic nature of revelatory language. Anyone who has ever consciously used symbols in the creative process knows that it is common to communicate unconsciously with these symbols various levels of meaning which nevertheless fit into the overall theme of the work. This idea finds support in the framework of the Book of Mormon, which tells us that while speaking to one age, God may be speaking simultaneously to another, since the past, the present, and the future are all present at once in the divine vision of reality (D&C 130:7; Morm. 8:35). Often in communicating with us, God draws upon symbols of common experience such as water, oil, fire, minerals, plants, animals — symbols which are accessible and can communicate to vast numbers of human beings regardless of the age or culture in which they may have lived.

The divine voice can be found in sacred texts, often by way of these universal symbols which serve to hide and to reveal simultaneously. This is why Jesus is said to have spoken in parables (Matt. 13:9–14). The greatest divine truths are not set forth as factual propositions or explanations but are conveyed in the more timeless language of symbols and myths. Because of their flexibility and adaptability, such symbols and myths are more suitable for the transmittal of ideas which are complex, subtle, and paradoxical.

Principle 3. Because many different meanings can be derived from a text, reinterpretation of a text by each culture and generation is inevitable and desirable.

The ongoing reinterpretation of God's words is not only unavoidable, it is legitimate and appropriate.[1] Each age (and each person) must work through the texts for itself, revisiting the symbols and extracting from them the riches hidden there. In fact this is an important part of the prophetic calling — one that Joseph Smith saw himself fulfilling as evidenced by his revision of the Bible. Unfortunately the priestly class often sees itself as guardian of the status quo and refuses to allow for even modest manifestations of reinterpretation of sacred texts. Rosemary Radford Ruether comments on this situation: "Received symbols, formulas, and law are either authenticated or not through their ability to illuminate and interpret experience. Systems of authority try to reverse this relation and make received symbols dictate what can be experienced as well as the interpretation of that which is experienced. In reality, the relation is the opposite. If a symbol does not speak authentically to experience, it becomes dead or must be altered to provide a new meaning" (1983, 12–13). Reinterpretation is not a sign of disbe-

---

[1] Jacob Katz in an article about tradition and change in Jewish communities argues that there is "no society that does not change." The difference between a traditional society and a modern society is not change, since that is inevitable; rather traditional societies do not "aspire" to change and like to think of themselves as static, whereas modern societies do aspire to change and see themselves as progressive (36–39).

lief. It is a sign that a religion is still vital to its adherents. Only dead languages, dead religions, and dead symbols no longer change.

Religious texts by their very nature require corrections, expansions, and readjustments in the interpretation of the past. In this way the generation receiving the revelation cannot claim an inalienable title to it.[2] As possession of the text passes down through the ages, the divine voice can continue to speak a living and ever-fresh message to each rising generation, whose own experience with God and the world will prepare them to hear in the old stories something new, something tailor-made for them. As we mentioned, this is not to dismiss the need to examine a sacred text from the point of view of the historical period which produced it. In fact such work is crucial if we are to understand and expand our view of God's dealings with human beings. Since the tyranny of the present is as real a threat as the tyranny of the past, it is essential to dig into history lest we become prisoners of our present world view and of the destructive and arrogant assumption that nothing in the past can be as important as anything in the present. Moreover, examining the historical context of a sacred text can demonstrate how received traditions usually differ as well as grow out of the text's original meaning, thereby suggesting both the inevitability of changing views as well as some possibilities for reinterpretation. Retrieving lost meanings from the past can revitalize the present. The believing community must ask itself how both the text and the received tradition throw light on God's present relationship to them. In other words we must have latitude to explore how God is speaking to us through the old texts about our present situation.[3]

Principle 4. Because people and cultures are religiously similar, it is possible to transcend the boundaries of time and place in searching for new meanings of a text; however, because people and cultures are also dissimilar, such searching cannot establish a text's historical meaning.

This is perhaps the most controversial principle of the seven. For example, in interpreting the face veil worn by women in the Mormon temple, we may not only draw upon that symbol's uses and associations within the context of nineteenth and twentieth century Mormonism, but we may also range across cultural and temporal boundaries in

---

[2] Ricoeur paraphrases Gadamer: "the letters of Saint Paul are not less addressed to me than to the Romans, the Galatians, the Corinthians, etc." (192).

[3] In the past few years, a new school of biblical criticism has attempted to examine the important relationships among text, tradition, and community (Sanders 1984).

search of interpretations of the same and similar symbols in order to construct a complete catalogue of possible meanings.

This principle assumes that in spite of the differences among the cultures and societies which have existed all over the world throughout the long and complex history of humankind, there exist certain common elements, which allow the symbols, rituals, myths, and dreams of one group to illuminate our understanding of those of another. This relation among symbols is often expressed by the Jungian term "archetype," which refers to "any of a number of prototypic phenomena (e.g., the wise old man, the great mother) which form the content of the collective unconscious and which are assumed to reflect universal human thoughts found in all cultures" (Bullock 1988, 48). It is argued that archetypes exist in part because of the similarities in the bodies, minds, needs, longings, fears, and common life experiences of all people.

Of course it is also argued that the dissimilarities in our experiences, assumptions, perceptions, aspirations, and spiritual world views require our interpretations to be limited strictly to those meanings attributable to the time, place, and culture in which the given symbol was employed. Otherwise the process of interpretation will tend to disintegrate into a muddle of free associations in which the symbol can mean anything and everything the interpreter wants it to mean. But in our view, religious symbols have meanings that transcend their cultural usages and manifestations. Such symbols can and do recur through history in one culture after another, and they can and do appear simultaneously in one or more unconnected cultures. Further the symbols themselves are outward projections, which represent different spiritual and psychological states common to most people. So it is legitimate, we think, to look for the meaning of a symbol or text beyond its historical context.

We can do this and still avoid the problem of free association by tying our interpretation to the literary framework or mythological structure in which a given symbol or idea appears. For example, in Genesis we encounter the symbol of the serpent in the garden of Eden. Later in the biblical text, we encounter the same symbol; but this time we see it placed by Moses on a pole and held up before all the people of Israel. To determine what the serpent symbol means in these two instances, we can range across cultures and epochs in order to catalogue as many meanings of this symbol as we can. This search will reveal that the serpent can symbolize death or life, good or evil, God or the devil. One of the peculiarities of religious symbols is that most of them carry simultaneously both "negative" as well as "positive" meanings. To determine which meanings apply in a particular story, we must see how the symbol is used in a specific context. In the Garden of Eden, the serpent symbol is set in opposition to God, linking the serpent with death and evil. However, when the same symbol is set by Moses on a pole as a means to heal the sick, the mythic structure links the symbol to life and health.

But what should we make of the story of the confrontation between Moses and Pharaoh's priests? The priests turn their rods into snakes; but so does Moses. Then Moses' serpent devours the serpents of the priests. Here the same symbol is used in a single context to represent both good and evil. But why? Why not use opposing symbols, such as the serpent and the dove? One possible reason is that this story through its symbols is meant to suggest a complex set of ideas which defy a clear, lucid, and linear explanation: good and evil are somehow ever in flux; the face of evil and the face of good are similar; God and the devil and good and evil are more interlinked than we might suppose — an idea also implied in the story of Job.

Our point here, however, is not to discuss these interesting texts but to observe that because human beings and human cultures not only disagree profoundly but agree in many religious matters, it is sometimes legitimate to go beyond the world view of the culture producing a text to search for possible meanings. If our interpretation is tied to the literary and mythic framework in which the symbol appears, we can come to a fuller understanding of the text's transcendent religious meaning. But we cannot by this method learn its historical significance. Whether we tie our interpretation to a text's historical setting or to its literary constraints will depend on whether our goal is primarily to acquire historical accuracy or religious insight.

Principle 5. Sacred narrative and ritual can best be understood through the lens of a sacral world view.

In interpreting any sacred communication, we must understand that it will remain largely meaningless to us unless we can put aside for a time our secular outlook and enter into the world of the sacred. The concept of the sacred informed the experiences of many ancient societies, but it is quite foreign to modern culture. Though most of us have a feel for the distinction between these two world views, it may be helpful to detail some of the ways in which they differ.

The sacral world is interested in the transcendent, the supernatural, and the symbolic meaning of events; the secular world is interested in the here and now, the physical, and the natural causes and effects of events. The sacral society sees nothing as happening by chance or accident; the secular society believes in the random occurrence of events. The sacral world is holistic, and all aspects of life are viewed as connected on a spiritual continuum; the secular world is compartmentalized, and life is seen in terms of the subject-object dichotomy. The sacral world sees history as recurring cyclical patterns; the secular world sees history as linear and often in terms of social progress. The sacral world is organic; the secular is mechanistic. The sacral society assumes there is meaning inherent in things; the secular society says that meaning is what we ascribe to a thing. The sacral society believes in becoming one with God and nature through ritual; the secular society believes in the control of nature through technology. Mircea Eliade, the historian of religions, makes a similar comparison between what he calls religious and nonreligious man. Eliade says that the religious man

> always believes that there is an absolute reality, *the sacred*, which transcends this world but manifests itself in the world, thereby sanctifying it and making it real. He further believes that life has a sacred origin and that human existence realizes all of its potentialities in proportion as it is religious—that is, participates in reality. The gods created man and the world, the culture heroes completed the Creation, and the history of all these divine and semidivine works is preserved in the myths. By reactualizing sacred history, by imitating the divine behavior, man puts and keeps himself close to the gods—that is, in the real and the significant....
>
> Modern nonreligious man assumes a new existential situation; he regards himself solely as the subject and agent of history, and he refuses all appeal to transcendence. In other words, he accepts no model for humanity outside the human condition as it can be seen in the various historical situations. Man *makes himself*, and he only makes himself completely in proportion as he desacralizes himself and the world (1959, 202–203).

This is not to say that the sacral world view is superior to the secular or that we should simply replace one with the other. Each has its positive and negative characteristics. For example, secular societies tend to emphasize the importance of human achievement, humanitarianism, individualism, and freedom, whereas sacral societies tend toward dogmatism, authoritarianism, and denigration of naturalistic experience. But sacred cultures are more conducive to spirituality, meaning, and community, while secular cultures are susceptible to materialism, superficiality, and alienation. In our view a healthy society has the best elements of both the secular and the sacred acting as counterweights to each other. However, since our present society is predominantly secular, our argument here is that we need an infusion of the sacred in order for us to experience the reality of the spiritual world through myth and ritual.

Though Mormonism shares with the sacral world view the belief in the supernatural and the sacred origin of humanity, still it views religion mostly from a secular perspective, as evidenced by its pragmatic approach to salvation, its literal interpretation of scripture, and its general aversion to symbols and ritual.

Principle 6. From a sacral perspective, one of the purposes of a sacred text is to connect the natural and supernatural worlds; therefore, sacred texts, symbols, and rituals can serve as a conduit for actual spiritual power and as a means of revealing heavenly patterns.

If we are to understand a religious text, we must not only receive it as such, we must also treat it the way a sacral society would. In a secular society we use symbols as metaphors. We connect an object, event, or person with something to which it is not literally or logically related to suggest a comparison and thus create a vivid description. A sacral society uses symbols as types or shadows of the spiritual realm and of future divine acts. Symbols are not chosen arbitrarily but rather grow out of the nature of the symbols themselves and the nature of whatever it is they point to, so that the symbols have inherent meaning apart from what they symbolize and yet are in a sense part of what they symbolize too. This idea can be illustrated with a symbol familiar to Mormons. The priesthood undergarment has a meaning growing out of its function. It physically "covers our nakedness"; but it also draws meaning from what it points to. It symbolizes the death of Christ. The garment, we are told, was originally made out of the skin of a sacrificial animal representing Christ. By wearing the garment we take upon ourselves Christ's death, his sacrifice, his righteousness, his love. In other words, we take upon ourselves his image and are covered or washed in his blood. The sacral society uses symbols in this way to point our minds to the spiritual realm, to help us see in everyday processes and objects the patterns of eternity.

The secular society, on the other hand, uses symbols to point us toward the earthly realm, to compare some everyday processes and objects with others. Where the religious society uses symbols to sacralize experience, the secular society uses symbols in a profane way because it fails to see in the world the image and pattern of the divine. Thus the secularized version of the garment is that it symbolizes or reminds us only of the need to be modest.

Positioned between the sacral and the secular approach to symbols is the magic world view. From this perspective the priesthood garment is seen as a literal protection against bodily injury. It is a magic suit of sorts. The magical world view is similar to the sacral because both see symbol and ritual as conduits for spiritual power. However, the sacral approach is broader because it also sees ritual as a means of revealing heavenly patterns and for experiencing inner spiritual transformation. In the sacral culture those who participate in imitating the divine through re-enacting the stories of the gods, particularly the creation stories, are re-created in the image of the divine. Magic practices may include an emphasis on symbolism and inner transformation, but not necessarily (Quinn 1987, ix-xxii).

Joseph Smith is an example of one who embraced the sacral world view, though his early emphasis may have been on magic. In Doctrine and Covenants 128, for example, he discusses the ordinance of baptism for the dead and explains that it should be performed in such a way as to reveal the pattern "of the resurrection of the dead in coming forth out of their graves" (v. 12). Joseph Smith goes on to explain that for this reason "the baptismal font was instituted as a similitude of the grave, and was commanded to be in a place underneath . . . to show forth the living and the dead, and that all things may have their likeness, and that they may accord one with another — that which is earthly conforming to that which is heavenly" (v. 13). A similar idea is expressed through Joseph Smith in Moses 6:63: "And behold, all things have their likeness, and all things are created and made to bear record of me [i.e., the Lord], both things which are temporal, and things which are spiritual; things which are in the heavens above, and things which are on the earth, and things which are in the earth, and things which are under the earth, both above and beneath: all things bear record of me." These ideas imply that, in the creation of the world, God planted in it natural objects and processes which can be drawn upon and used as microcosms, representations, or reflections of eternal objects and processes. Though this idea is both foreign and obscure to the secular world, it is intrinsic to the sacral point of view and, perhaps, necessary for understanding sacred texts and rituals.

Principle 7. Neither a literal nor a figurative interpretation of a text should be favored; religious texts are best seen from both perspectives simultaneously.

In interpreting any religious symbol, it is well to avoid the literal-figurative dichotomy. The figurative mode of interpretation is analogous to the spiritual dimension of human nature. Symbols like the spirit serve to unify and provide coherence. They enable us to see relationships and make connections. They allow a given experience to serve as a universal paradigm. Symbols give us access to inner as well as outward reality. They help us see the meaning of things. If we look at reality and only see what is visible, we are not seeing the full picture. Things are not only what they appear, they also represent other things. Anything can be a symbol or a pattern of anything else. Thus the visible world is a window into the invisible.

However, there is a drawback in always viewing things symbolically. If our symbols are not anchored to something real, if they only refer to a totally other that lies beyond all that can ever be known, then our sacred texts mean nothing. And all religious communication is just babble. As Joseph Smith said, "That which is without body or parts is nothing" (WJS, 60). The literal mode of interpretation is analogous to the elemental or bodily dimension of life. Just as Joseph Smith argued that our physical bodies give our spirits greater scope and power, it may also be argued that a literal interpretation of scripture adds substance, relevance, and focus to our understanding. We see this most clearly when the words of a sacred text are anchored to a historical context. Jesus as a symbol may have value, but Jesus as an historical being, as God made man, makes the concept of redemption real and speaks to us at various levels of our experience. Not all scriptural passages can be taken literally of course. But by the same token, to interpret all passages only as symbols is to deprive the texts of poignancy and power and to reduce them to ethical fiction or fraud.

Of course a strictly literal approach also has its drawbacks. If applied narrowly and blindly, literalism can imprison us in a single, rigid, and often elitist world view. It keeps us from perceiving how all our descriptions of reality are never the same as the thing itself but are always constructions of language, as modern theorists tell us. Everything we experience begins to reinforce our viewpoint. Nothing challenges us to look beyond our own interpretations. We become trapped because we cannot see how reality may serve as a representation or pattern of what is not immediately available to us. A narrow literalism can prevent us from seeing beyond our own culture or personal experience. Strict literalism closes the window to the unknown and can lead to the false assumption that our pictures, images, or models of God are complete and final. This view is extremely damaging because it forecloses inquiry and with that further knowledge.

Our own approach is to accept whenever possible both a literal and figurative interpretation. Thus for us the Garden of Eden may be a place — an undoubtedly inaccessible place — as well as a type. The cross was not only a real wooden structure that featured prominently in the penal system of Rome but is also a symbol of the intersection of the human and the divine in the person of Jesus of Nazareth. Obviously some symbols defy a literal interpretation, while some realities may serve as relatively trivial symbols. Nevertheless we believe it is insurance against prejudice to avoid any tendency toward a systematic rejection of one approach in favor of the other.

These interpretive principles and the assumptions set forth in the previous chapter have guided us in the discussions that comprise the balance of this book.

PART II
Godhead

~ CHAPTER THREE ~

HOLINESS TO THE LORD

Some years ago two of our friends told us of their intention to leave the Mormon church for a Protestant group. This was a big step. Why, we wondered, were they doing this? They told us they were leaving Mormonism because they could no longer accept Joseph Smith. He was offensive to them. Not only did he not fit the ideal of a pious, consistent man of God, but his doctrines appeared to them to be heretical. Our friends claimed that his biggest mistakes were his teachings on polytheism and his involvement in polygamy and magic.

Like many Mormons our friends had grown up believing that Mormonism was an ideal religion, that it provided answers to the major questions of life, and that it promised certainty where other religions created confusion. It was perfectly understandable our friends believed these things. As a church we promote this view in our manuals, our visitor centers, our public relations messages, and through our missionaries. For the modern church perfection is static, righteousness can be recognized in fixed categories of behavior, goodness is respectable, good people will always speak and act consistently and acceptably, the revealed voice of God will always be clear and distinguishable from other voices, God will not call prophets who are flawed or embarrassing, his chosen ones will not be allowed to err in significant ways, we can know with certainty good from evil, truth from error, light from darkness, and the church's motives will always be pure and its actions defensible.

But as many of us dig into our sacred texts and our history, we discover how difficult, inconsistent, murky, troubling, and sometimes embarrassing our religion can be. This awareness can be traumatic, especially for those who do not suspect that complications lurk behind the appealing simplicity of popular teachings. What we seem to want is an ideal religion. What we have is a human religion and a God who is holy. This difference between the expectation of the ideal and the reality of the human and the holy is a source of constant discomfort and disillusionment.

In our view idealized expectations are arrived at not through revelation or experience but through reason. The ideal God is a projection of our own concepts of perfection. Ideal doctrines are a creation of our own sense of what is true. And the ideal ethic is an invention of our own notions of right and wrong. An ideal religion is burdened with our limitations and must inevitably fail or disappoint us.

In contrast holiness is not so much a concept as an attribute of God understood through mystical experience. We do not arrive at holiness by conscious thought but by contact with the divine. A religion which is holy is not simply the projection of human ideas of truth but the revelation of divine truths we could never have suspected. Holiness is goodness as God sees goodness, righteousness as God sees righteousness. It is God as God is, not as we wish God to be. For this reason holiness is paradoxical, unpredictable, unsettling, and often seems undesirable. It may contradict our common-sense notions of what the universe should be like.

In a 31 August 1842 sermon to the women's Relief Society of Nauvoo, Joseph Smith said: "Do you think that even Jesus, if he were here would be without fault in your eyes?" (WJS, 130). Because we tend to idealize and inflate our expectations of God, Joseph Smith warned, we might be offended and disheartened by the reality of God. He apparently could see that Mormons no less than others might reject revelations not consonant with ideal theological and ethical predispositions. Latter-day Saints too could be threatened by new and unfamiliar ideas. We too want God to give us certainty and stability and are frustrated when God gives us revelations and experiences that challenge the status quo. Perhaps this is why we would rather serve than think and why we are more concerned with being "active" than being "devout." Joseph Smith commented on this problem: "But their has been a great difficulty in getting anything into the heads of this generation it has been like splitting hemlock knots with a Corn doger for a wedge & a pumpkin for a beetle, Even the Saints are slow to understand I have tried for a number of years to get the minds of the Saints prepared to receive the things of God, but we frequently see some of them after suffering all they have for the work of God will fly to peaces like glass as soon as anything Comes that is Contrary to their traditions, they Cannot stand the fire at all" (ibid., 319).

In Joseph Smith's time and in ours, the penchant of people in and out of the church for the ideal and their distaste for the holy and the human has been manifest by a stubborn insistence on an idealistic picture of God. It is hard to say exactly where this idealized God concept comes from. The early Greeks, for example, did not have it. Their gods were sexual, anthropomorphic, and unpredictable. But as philosophy came into prominence, this ancient religion faded. By the fifth century B.C., Greek intellectuals, if they believed in God at all, believed in a supreme ideal. This same process occurred in the Jewish tradition. Yahweh was first presented as personal, anthropomorphic, and tribal but was later idealized by rabbinical teachings influenced by Hellenistic thought.

In Christianity Jesus was first accepted as a real individual with body, parts, and passions. But he too was later idealized. Jesus so offended common sense, philosophical wisdom, the deeply rooted sense of bodily shame, and the lofty aspirations of the intellect and reason that the early church fathers were compelled to depersonify, disembody, and unsex him. Of course, such idealized views did not prevail unopposed through the Christian era. Efforts had to be made constantly to enforce orthodoxy. In the Middle Ages and Renaissance, Christians began slipping into polytheism through the worship of saints and angels. Magic appeared in the worship of relics. Sexuality re-emerged in the person of Mary the Virgin.

The Protestant Reformation was in part a reaction to this slippage. It reasserted the grip of Christendom on idealism by emphasizing sin and guilt and allegorizing those scriptures dealing with the immanent attributes of God. Protestantism is the Christianity of the Enlightenment. It tended to deemphasize the mystical and exalt reason. It was often hard on ritual and exhibited a preference for the humanistic elements of religion: emphasis on the Bible, authentic texts, linguistic scholarship. Even conversion was usually predicated upon literacy and one's ability to rightly understand holy writ. Though early Protestants claimed to reject the pope, they did not reject his claim to temporal authority (which they often claimed for themselves or their political supporters). Rather, they rejected the pope's claim to spiritual and mystical authority and replaced it with the more controllable and reasonable authority of scriptural texts. Still within Protestantism there have always been attempts such as the Protestant charismatic movements, pentecostalism, and fundamentalism to counteract this emphasis on strict rationalism. Of course complete rejection of the rational leads to

extremism, anti-intellectualism, and bigotry. We are not putting forth
the concept of the holy here as a rejection of reason and the intellect,
but as a means of balancing the tendency in our culture to view perfection in static and ideal terms.

Every religion struggles with this tension between the holy and the
ideal. Mormonism was revealed as antidote both to the Greek idealism
embodied in Catholicism and the idealism of the Enlightenment as
preserved in Protestantism. Joseph Smith's teachings on the nature of
God reaffirmed the holiness of God and contradicted God as a philosophical ideal. Although many orthodox Christians deplore this revelation of an anthropomorphic God with gender and sexuality and of a
female divinity in the Godhead, nevertheless, these teachings make possible the concept of the divine marriage, the doctrine of the Eternal
Father and the Eternal Mother, mystically, emotionally, intellectually,
and sexually united as The Eternal One.

This notion is enough to make the most charitable orthodox Christians shudder. The very idea seems to them to be an affront to God.
Others, more deeply offended, damn the notion as heretical and blas-
phemous and feel certain that Mormons are not Christians at all. But
this conclusion is inevitable to those who do not distinguish between
the ideal and the holy and who find unpalatable the notion that the
Most High could possess in perfect form characteristics which in imperfect form have caused mortals so much shame, consternation, and
confusion. Our bodies, our sexuality, our specificity, all lie dangerously
beyond complete understanding and complete control. This God concept, though unacceptable to some, is not unscriptural. Many passages
of the Old Testament are troubling to Christians because they suggest
that God is holy but not ideal. Yahweh walked in Eden with Adam and
Eve. God sat with Abraham in the plains of Mamre and bargained
over the fate of Sodom and Gomorrah. God put Moses in a "clift of a
rock" and then showed him the divine "back parts." God is portrayed
as a deity of anger, jealousy, love, and boundless mercy. God is a war
lord with a remorseless sense of justice, but he is also meek and merciful, willing to mourn freely for the sins of his children. God can be
approached and coaxed to change his mind.

In the New Testament Jesus Christ is presented as the incarnation
of God. In Jesus, the God-Man, we see more clearly how divine holiness contradicts human expectations of the ideal. In Christ we learn
that God is personal, anthropomorphic, approachable, knowable, and

sexual. The incarnation of God in Jesus Christ "points toward the im-manence of the divine in human life, [and] makes little sense if the process of human generation is not sanctified and if purity is associ-ated with abstinence from fleshy passion" (Phipps 1970, 190). It seems impossible to us that the very sexual desires and processes that are in-trinsic to the generation of life should be divorced from the life-affirming mission of Jesus, the well-spring of eternal life. It seems far more prob-able to us that the God who wept for the dead, who gave life to the dead, who gives life to the dead, should be a God of gender, sexuality, and desire.

The sexuality of Jesus is for us confirmed in his marriage. Such an event is not accepted by orthodox Christianity, but as biblical scholar William E. Phipps (1970) points out, good evidence for it exists. In Jesus' day Jews considered marriage a positive good and a requirement for a rabbi. It is unlikely Jesus could have preached publicly without criticism from his detractors had he been unmarried. The New Testa-ment depicts a close relationship between Jesus and Mary Magdalene, the first resurrection witness, as well as between Mary and Martha, whose domestic and household affairs involved Jesus.[1] Also, Jesus as-sumed the appellation "bridegroom," which suggests that he did not exclude himself from marriage.

A married Jesus favors the holy over the ideal. We cannot agree with the suggestion that connecting God with sexuality simply limits and confines him. The orthodox God can be just as limited because of God's exclusion from such realms. Perhaps it is presumptuous to spec-ify what God cannot be and do. Moreover, the orthodox reaction to the God concept in Mormonism tends to ignore the damage caused by the idealized view such as the unhealthy dualism that tends to favor male over female, spirit over matter, and mind over body, and that en-courages a belief in God the Father to the exclusion of God the Mother. Defenders of the ideal view of God argue that an emphasis on God's immanent attributes tends to desacralize rather than make God holy, to trivialize Christ rather than exalt him. We agree. It is unfortunate that modern Mormonism tends to cast him in the role of an earthly rather than a heavenly parent. But Mormon scriptures do not do this.

---

[1] Early Mormon leaders such as Orson Hyde, Jedediah M. Grant, and Brigham Young taught that Jesus was a polygamist (JD 1:345–346; 2:79–83, 210; 4:259–260). Phipps acknowledges but rejects this notion (9–10).

They affirm divine immanence, while simultaneously affirming divine transcendence. In Mormon scripture, God is both our enthroned sovereign and our common bread and cup.

Because Joseph Smith described the Godhead in anthropomorphic, sexual, and personal terms, the way was paved for additional teachings distinguishing Mormon Christianity from orthodox Christianity, such as his teachings on the holiness of human sexuality, of certain forms of magic, and of monolatry, which is a form of polytheism.

Orthodox Christianity has often taught that approaching God requires the repudiation of one's sexuality, especially if one is a woman. Instead Joseph Smith taught that God is approached through marriage and sexuality, an idea perhaps comparable to certain kabbalistic teachings that the longing for God is similar to sexual "desire." Whereas ideal religion denies, represses, or punishes the expressions of sexual desire, religions emphasizing the holy are inclined to accept these desires as godly and to create forms for their full legitimate expression.

Idealized religion also tends to persecute manifestations of magic, while religions emphasizing the holy see certain aspects of magic as part of the religious experience. The scriptures themselves rather unabashedly accept what we would call magic as a peripheral manifestation of both Judaism and Christianity. We read of Moses' staff, Aaron's strange garb, the Urim and Thummim, Joseph's cup of divination, dream interpretation, rhapsodic trances of members of the later prophetic schools, the witch of Endor's conjuring of the spirit of Samuel, the competitive exhibition conducted between Elijah and the priests of Baal, and the strange method Elijah employed to raise from the dead the widow's son. Such examples suggest the close connection between magic and religion.

For many religious people of the past, magic and ritual bore the same relationship to religion as do modern science and technology today. It was perceived as another means of discovering the secrets of the universe and controlling the environment. Magic was also a form of ritual for sacralizing life, for connecting the natural with the supernatural world, for finding God in the ordinary occurrences of life. Ritual was mythology in motion. Of course magic and ritual do have a dark side. But the evangelists testified through their accounts of Jesus the "miracle worker" that there is also a proper place for elements of magic in a Christian context.

We moderns are usually put off by anything contradicting or threatening our comfortably rational categories. For this reason many have been irritated to learn of Joseph Smith's involvement with ritual, myth, and magic. We find it difficult to admit that such teachings may help us to accept the mysterious, to correct our prejudices against the shadowy world of intuition, and to balance our preference for the bright, clear world of rational thought.

The same may be said of Joseph Smith's teaching that humans, if they are faithful to God, will become gods themselves. From this some have concluded that Mormons are polytheistic. This is wrong. What we believe in is monolatry — the worship of one God and the simultaneous acknowledgment of the existence of other gods, whom we do not worship. The perception of God varies among Mormons as it does among other Christians, but it is a rare Mormon indeed who believes we worship many gods. Some historians of religion have argued that the early Hebrews held a similar view: "Israel's earliest beliefs were monolatrous, i.e., other gods were acknowledged to exist but they were all subject to the God of Israel who reigned over them in the divine 'council of the gods. . . . ' This belief was eventually modified into extreme monotheism, or the belief in only one God" (Kirkland, 78–79). Monolatry is not contradicted by the first commandment. The words, "Thou shalt have no other gods before me," allow for the existence of other gods but insist upon the sovereignty of the One. Strict monotheism is not consistently supported by the scriptures, which speak of the Elohim ("the gods") and of angels, spirits, and weak local divinities. The New Testament, of course, presents the concept not of one God but of a godhead — Father, Son, and Holy Ghost — attended by angels, saints, spirits, and other supernatural beings including demons and fallen angels.

The attraction which monotheism holds for ideal religions is its simplicity, its elegance, and its reasonability. Monotheism provides us with a very straightforward model of the cosmos. Unfortunately, it can also lead to the deistic view that God is a solitary, detached, and remote Supreme Being and that we humans live our lives disengaged from the supernatural. How different life is for those who see gods and spirits everywhere, for whom no aspect of life is free from divine intervention, for whom every action is pregnant with mystery and every day is the day of reckoning.

Joseph Smith's monolatrous teachings are paradoxical. For him there was but one God, male and female, in whose image and likeness we were created.[2] But Joseph also taught that in the universe there were many individuals whom God had transformed into gods. Many of these beings have lived on this earth. They bring messages to and watch over the people of the earth. Christ is the tree of life, and these other beings are like birds resting in his branches. We, too, are part of this vision, this paradox of nature and supernature, in which there is no escape from God. Each of us is a child of God. Each of us may become a god. Even now we are either growing closer to or further away from the realization of that potential.

Though these Mormon ideas are repugnant to the staid categories of philosophy and deeply disturbing to those who prize parsimony in their theological speculations, they do have the redeeming virtue of affording us the freshness of holiness while avoiding the drabness of idealism.

In sum, Mormonism is not a smooth religion; it is a rough one. It partakes of the human and the divine. It is full of contradictions and conundrums. But it is also full of beauty and peace. In it one can find substance for ridicule and for admiration. It is at once of the spirit spiritual and of the earth earthy. It is both ironic and sentimental. It comforts and chastises. It is a revelation of power and of weakness. In it the glory of God and the foolishness of humanity walk hand in hand toward a destiny that is as dim to us as it is clear to God. It is not a religion of philosophical fastidiousness, nor does it prize a foolish consistency. Those who desire an exemplary religion must look elsewhere. For in Mormonism the watchword is not idealism for humanity, but holiness to the Lord.

---

[2] Evidence shows that Joseph Smith taught the doctrine of a mother in heaven, although one of his plural wives, Eliza R. Snow, popularized it with her hymn (Wilcox, 65–66).

~ CHAPTER FOUR ~

THE GOD OF
FLESH AND GLORY

Most Mormons if asked what orthodox Christians believe about God would say: Orthodox Christians believe in a God without body, parts, or passions. A God who is absolute, who exists beyond time, space, and matter. A God who is omniscient, omnipresent, omnipotent, and omnibenevolent. A God who is all-understanding but cannot be understood. A cause without a cause. A beginning without an antecedent. An end without a sequel. A being who is beyond imagination, beyond description, and beyond reach.

If asked what Mormons believe, most orthodox Christians would probably say: Mormons believe in a God who is merely a superior man. A being with a body of flesh and bones, who exists in time and space and who is still learning and developing. A being who is finite and law bound. A being who is sovereign but not supreme, superior but not sublime, eternal but not primal. A being too similar to trust and too proximate to worship.

Though in some respects accurate, these descriptions are incomplete. They arise out of misunderstandings and serve more as caricatures than as real portraits of belief. The fact is that neither orthodox Christianity nor Mormonism has taken positions as extreme as these descriptions would suggest.

Orthodox Christian theology has always availed itself of the Bible's language to describe God as capable of love, knowledge, anger, and other human attributes. And there has always been an element of finitism in this language. On a popular level, lay Christians inevitably think and talk about God in a personal way. Even if orthodox Christians believe the theological proposition that God is beyond all categories of thought, it is nevertheless true that those same Christians spend a great deal of time thinking about God anyway. Many orthodox Christian theologians, undoubtedly aware of this fact, have tried to reconcile the God of orthodox theology with the God Christians encounter in their worship. This reconciliation usually involves making a distinction between the two ways in which God relates to creation. Transcendence refers to the concept that God is over, above, beyond, and more than the creation, that the divine power is not exhausted by creation, and that God is the source and "ground of all being." In contrast immanence refers to the nearness of God, to the idea that God dwells in each of us and throughout all creation and that God's presence sustains and preserves all life. Orthodox Christianity has usually claimed that God is both transcendent and immanent. In this way it has sought to avoid the extremes of deism on the one side and pantheism on the other. Deism is a belief system that insists God stands apart or outside creation and does not guide it or interfere. Pantheism equates God with nature.

In spite of this quest for balance, at various times one or the other of these concepts has dominated. Today liberal Protestantism emphasizes the immanence of God and shuns metaphysical speculations. In doing this liberal Protestants emphasize human problems and the ethical nature of the gospel. As a reaction to this view, Protestant neo-orthodox or neo-reformers have emphasized the transcendence and holiness of God, the sinfulness and powerlessness of humanity, and humanity's dependence on the divine. The see-saw effect caused by the failure to balance such concerns has happened in other arenas of the intellectual tradition of the West. The excesses of one age have more than once triggered countervailing excesses in the next age. Thus the formal rigidity of Neoclassicism was followed by the emotionalism of Romanticism, which was in turn followed by the verisimilitude of Realism, which was then followed by the subjectivism of Expressionism.

The question is whether the Mormon view of God represents an extreme or a balance of extremes. Were Joseph Smith's statements on God's finitude meant to be an utter rejection of God's transcendence or merely a corrective to the over-idealization of God common in the nineteenth century?[1]

---

[1] Mormon writers such as Sterling McMurrin, Kent Robson, and Blake Ostler have rightly asserted that the absolute, wholly other deity of orthodox Christianity has not been a part of traditional Mormon discussions. Mormonism has stressed instead the finite characteristics of God: his body of flesh and bones, his existence in time and space, and his progressive and dynamic nature. Moreover, as these writers have also pointed out, the concept of an absolute God was not derived from the Judeo-Christian scriptural texts but rather from the early Church Fathers, who were highly influenced

It may seem contradictory to be obsessed with balance, but we are. We believe it is not only unnecessary but positively harmful to be required to choose between the extremes of a totally finite and a totally infinite God. A balanced perspective more closely fits the descriptions of God in the revelations and sacred texts of our Judeo-Christian tradition. In our view the God of Mormon scripture is personal, embodied, approachable, and knowable but also a God of transcendent glory, wisdom, power, and goodness.

Perhaps Joseph Smith's most startling theological claim was that God is an anthropomorphic being: "The Father has a body of flesh and bones as tangible as man's; the Son also; but the Holy Ghost has not a body of flesh and bones, but is a personage of Spirit" (D&C 130:22). Joseph Smith's tangible God also emerges from descriptions found in other Mormon scripture. In the Book of Abraham we read: "Thus, I, Abraham talked with the Lord, face to face, as one man talketh with another; and he told me of the works which his hands had made" (Abr. 3:11). Similarly Moses relates his theophany: "And he [Moses] saw God face to face and he talked with him, and the glory of God was upon Moses; therefore Moses could endure his presence" (Moses 1:2). In the Book of Mormon, Moroni recounts a similar experience: "And then shall ye know that I have seen Jesus, and that he hath talked with me face to face, and that he told me in plain humility, even as a man telleth another in my own language, concerning these things" (Eth. 12:39).

Examples could be multiplied, but none of these Mormon scriptural assertions is radically different from similar statements found in the Old and New Testaments, where anthropomorphism also abounds. In spite of this most scholars believe that texts attributing human characteristics to God are either remnants of a primitive mind-set or metaphors for the immediacy of the experience of God (*Concise Sacramentum Mundi*, 14).

The incarnation of God in the person of Jesus Christ, however, presents a serious problem to those denying the anthropomorphism of God. Because God appeared as man, we are led to ask: What is the meaning of God's revelation of himself in human form? And what is the meaning of the resurrection of Christ? Are we to take this event literally or figuratively? Such questions are today fiercely debated.

---

by the ancient Greek philosophers and their concept of an ideal God, who is beyond all categories and description.

Though there is a general trend among Christian scholars toward figurative interpretations, the centrality of Jesus as the revelation of God keeps them from entirely rejecting a personal God with human attributes (Richardson). For example, the *Roman Catholic Encyclopedia of Theology* states: "In a fully developed theological anthropology, however, man appears as *the* manifestation and revelation of God — as that which God becomes when he expresses himself in a medium other than himself. . . . The mystery of the incarnation is the supreme justification of anthropomorphism" (13–14).

In spite of statements like this, the concept of a fully anthropomorphic God remains for most Christian thinkers naive, primitive, idolatrous. For this reason Christianity has tended to shun or deny God's humanity, a fact which in itself raises some important questions: What is the point of depicting God as anthropomorphic, if he is not? Is this mere rhetoric to make God seem more accessible, real, and personal? But if God is none of these things, why talk as if he is? Why not say he is beyond us and will ever be beyond us? And why is the idea of an anthropomorphic God inherently inferior to the concept of an abstract God? What is it that makes people reject an embodied God? Are we ashamed of our own bodies? Are we afraid we have made God in our own image, that he is not real?[2] Are we afraid such a God would be limited or powerless?

In contrast, Joseph Smith expressed a view that linked power with embodiment. For Joseph that which has no physical existence has no existence at all (WJS, 60). He further explained that having a body adds happiness and power: "The great principle of happiness consists in having a body. The Devil has no body, and herein is his punishment. He is pleased when he can obtain the tabernacle of men and when cast out by the Savior he asked to go into the herd of swine showing that he would prefer a swines body to having none. All beings who have bodies have power over those who have not" (ibid., 60). On another occasion, Joseph stated: "before foundation of the Earth in the Grand Counsel that the Spirits of all Men ware subject to oppression & the express purpose of God in Giveing it a tabernicle was to arm it against the power of Darkness" (ibid., 62; cf. 2 Ne. 9:8).

---

[2] The Greek philosopher Xenophanes was one of the first to attempt to undermine anthropomorphism by arguing that the Greek gods had been created in the image of humans.

Rather than see an embodied God and a God of great power as contradictions, Joseph Smith taught that a body of flesh and bones extends the power of God. It gives God direct access to and experience with the physical as well as spiritual worlds. For Joseph, both of these realms are equally real.

Joseph Smith's God, however, is not just a human on a slightly higher level of progression or existence. God is also a God of glory. In Mormon scripture "glory" does not refer merely to honor or dignity but to spirit, power, comprehension (D&C 93:36; 84:45–46; 29:31; cf. 1 Pet. 4:1). It is a synonym for the light of Christ (D&C 88:5), the power of the Holy Ghost (Moro. 10:4), the power of the priesthood (D&C 121:36–37), and light and truth (93:36).

The exact metaphysical nature of God's glory is open to debate. But according to Joseph Smith, whatever it is, God's glory is not totally other. Joseph taught: "All spirit is matter, but it is more fine or pure, and can only be discerned by purer eyes; We cannot see it; but when our bodies are purified we shall see that it is all matter" (131:7–8). The glory of God then is something real, tangible, and in part knowable. Section 93 of the Doctrine and Covenants equates glory with God's intelligence (93:36). In the King Follett funeral sermon, Joseph Smith stated that glory is the everlasting burnings of the celestial kingdom (TPJS, 347–48). Joseph Smith taught that glory dwells to some extent throughout the universe (ibid., 353). Section 88 of the Doctrine and Covenants states that the various types of glory can be imparted to us in various degrees or portions: "Ye who are quickened by a portion of the celestial glory shall then [in the resurrection] receive of the same, even a fulness. And they who are quickened by a portion of the terrestrial glory shall then [in the resurrection] receive of the same, even a fulness. And also they who are quickened by a portion of the telestial glory shall then [in the resurrection] receive of the same, even a fulness" (v. 29).

This same revelation also informs us that God's glory is in the sun, the moon, the earth, and the stars. It is the same light that quickens our understandings (D&C 88:7–11). Human perfection consists in obtaining the fullness of celestial glory (50:24–27). If our eye is single to the glory of God, our bodies will be filled with divine light, and there will be no darkness in us. We will comprehend all things (88:67). Benjamin F. Johnson, a Nauvoo contemporary of Joseph Smith, stated that:

[Joseph Smith was] the first to teach in this age "substantialism," the eternity of matter, that no part or particle of the great universe could become annihilated or destroyed; that light and life and spirit were one; that all light and heat are the "glory of God," which is His power, that fills the "immensity of space," and is the life of all things, and permeates with latent life, and heat, every particle of which all worlds are composed; that light or spirit, and gross matter, are the two first great primary principles of the universe, or of being; that they are self-existent, co-existent, indestructible, and eternal, and from these two elements both our spirits and our bodies were formulated (Andrus 1974, 95).

So powerful is this glory that a person cannot look upon God and live unless the person is first transformed by this power. This was Moses' experience as recorded in the Pearl of Great Price. And even after God departed from him, Moses fell and lay upon the earth for several hours before he received "his natural strength" again. Then Moses exclaimed: "Now, for this cause I know that man is nothing, which thing I never had supposed. But now mine own eyes have beheld God; but not my natural, but my spiritual eyes, for my natural eyes could not have beheld; for I should have withered and died in his presence; but his glory was upon me; and I beheld his face, for I was transfigured before him" (Moses 1:10–11).

In Section 88 of the Doctrine and Covenants, the word "glory" is used as a synonym for "truth and light." This revelation states that God in his glory "comprehendeth all things, and all things are before him, and all things are round about him; and he is above all things, and in all things, and is through all things; and all things are by him, and of him, even God, forever and ever"(v. 41).

These verses, because they dwell upon the glorious or transcendent characteristics of deity, accord with descriptions of God favored by orthodox Christianity: God is omniscient, omnipotent, and omnipresent, in and through all things. Both the Book of Mormon and the Doctrine and Covenants contain superlative language to describe God's "infinite goodness" or "infinite mercy" (2 Ne. 1:10; Mos. 5:3, 28:4; He. 12:1; Moro. 8:3) and portray God as having "all power" and "all wisdom" or knowledge (see Jac. 2:5; Mos. 4:9, 29:19; Al. 12:15, 26:35; 44:5; Eth. 3:4; D&C 61:1, 84:28, 88:41, 100:1, 132:20). Section 20 of the Doctrine and Covenants speaks of God as "the glorious Majesty on high" and bears testimony to his greatness: "By these things we know that there is a God in heaven, who is infinite and eternal, from everlasting to everlasting the same unchangeable God, the framer of heaven and earth, and all things which are in them" (vv. 16–17; TPJS, 56).

Another example of usage common to both orthodoxy and Mormonism is found in the Book of Mosiah. There Jesus Christ is referred to as the "Lord Omnipotent," who has all power, knowledge, and goodness. The text admonishes us to "Believe in God; believe that he is, and that he created all things, both in heaven and earth; believe that he has all wisdom, and all power, both in heaven and in earth; believe that man doth not comprehend all things which the Lord can comprehend" (4:9; 3:5, 8, 17, 18, 21; 4:2, 5, 6, 11, 12, 19; 5:2, 3, 15).

We cite these verses to demonstrate that Mormon scriptural texts clearly and often depict God in transcendent terms. Of course an argument could be (and undoubtedly has been) made that none of these scriptures should be used in constructing a Mormon theology of the divine nature. According to this view, such references come from the early 1830s and reflect Joseph Smith's earlier doctrinal views, which were influenced by Protestantism but which he later rejected. Though undoubtedly Joseph's views matured over time, no evidence suggests he rejected God's transcendence in favor of God's immanence. Rather Joseph refined, expanded, and balanced these ideas. Joseph never stopped using exalted language to describe God. For example, in a written prayer dated 23 August 1842, Joseph Smith exclaimed: "O, thou who seeth, and knoweth the hearts of all men; thou eternal, omnipotent, omniscient, and omnipresent Jehovah, God; thou Elohem, that sitteth, as saith the psalmist, enthroned in heaven; look down upon thy servant Joseph, at this time; and let faith in the name of thy Son Jesus Christ, to a greater degree than thy servant ever yet has enjoined, be conferred upon him" (PWJS, 536). Even in the King Follett discourse, Mormonism's primary text for a progressing, finite God, Joseph Smith still spoke of God as "the Almighty" and said that we can know nothing about the character of God without "the inspiration of the Almighty" (WJS, 344, 348–49). He also used the phrase "all things which God of his inf[inite] reason has seen fit to reveal to us in our mortal state" (ibid., 352). In this same discourse Joseph spoke of human progress as going from "grace to grace," "from a small to great capacity," "from exaltation to exaltation," until we are able to "dwell in everlasting burning & everlasting power" as God does (ibid., 341, 344–45, 350, 355, 357).

Though Joseph taught that the "God that sits enthroned is a man like one of yourselves," he also said: "If the veil was rent to day & the great God who holds this world in its sphere or its orbit — the planets — if you were to see him to day, you would see him in all the person image, very form of man, For Adam was created in the very fashion of God. Adam received instruction walked talked as one man with another" (WJS, 357). This controversial statement was not meant to deny the majesty or power of God (for in the very same breath Joseph referred to the "great God who holds this world in its sphere"), but to emphasize that God is an actual person, an embodied being to whom we can relate. An important support for our view is found in Joseph's 9 July 1843 answer to the question "How is it that you Mormons hold that God is an omnipresent being at the same time that he is a personage of tabernacle?" He replied, "What part of God is omnipresent read the 37 chap of Ezekel. It is the Spirit of god which proceeds from him consequently God is in the four winds of Heaven and when man receives inteligence is it not by the spirit of God" (ibid., 230).

Certain Mormon writers have argued that when Joseph Smith used such words as "infinite," "omnipotent," and "omnipresent," he was not employing them in the usual Christian sense and that, therefore, in order to avoid confusion, we Mormons should omit these words from our religious vocabulary. The problem with this view is that it assumes that Mormon theology is totally unique and shares nothing in common with the belief structures of other Christians. It also fails to account for the common scripture, history, and customs which Mormons share with others within the Judeo-Christian tradition.

Though Protestants and Catholics may mean something different than Mormons when they refer, for example, to the "infinite goodness and mercy of God," we think this is an insufficient reason for Mormons to abandon such expressions. If this logic were taken to its extreme, we would be required to abandon every aspect of our religion which we share in common with others: the story of the incarnation, the passion, the resurrection, the New Testament, the messianic prophecies, etc. It seems more sensible to employ these usages because they are found not only in the scriptural texts we share in common with non-Mormons, but in our own uniquely Mormon texts as well.

Besides how helpful is it to emphasize only the ways in which we differ from other groups? If we want to be viewed as Christians, shouldn't we emphasize similarities? For example, when Joseph Smith uses the word "omnipotent" to describe God, he undoubtedly meant to use the word to mean that God has all power that is possible to have. But is this usage really different from that employed among orthodox Christians? For even Thomas Acquinas pointed out that God can do everything only if we mean by "can" that which is genuinely possible. Though there will be arguments as to what is genuinely possible, there is common ground here for beginning a dialogue, for building bridges of love among various religious communities.

Perhaps in this spirit Joseph Smith made the following conciliatory statement toward other religious traditions: " 'Wherein do you differ from other in your religious views?' In reality & essence we do not differ so far in our religious views but that we could all drink into one principle of love One [of] the grand fundamental principles of Mormonism is to receive thruth let it come from where it may. — We believe in the great Eloheim who sits in yonder heavens. so do the presbyterians" (WJS, 229). At other times Joseph was quick to point out the narrowness of the "sectarians" and the differences between his outlook and theirs. On 15 October 1843 he said: "I cannot believe in any of the creeds of the different denominations, because they all have some things in them I cannot subscribe to though all of them have some truth. but I want to come up into the presence of God & learn all things but the creeds set up stakes, & say hitherto shalt thou come, & no further. — which I cannot subscribe to" (ibid., 256).

Both orthodox Christianity and Mormonism have tended to "set up stakes," in other words, to set limits on what God can or cannot be. So orthodox Christians are apt to see God as a being utterly unlike us. And Mormons are just as apt to see God as a being who is just like us. In either case the temptation is to picture God in a comfortable way, whether by putting the divine beyond our reach or totally in our grasp. In our own view, God is best pictured as a being of paradox, a balance of extremes, a being who is immanent to the extent God is with us and like us and transcendent to the extent we are not yet like God. For us, as for many Mormons, God is a paradox of flesh and glory.

Nevertheless, our understanding of the divine reality always remains imperfect. All of our concepts of God are only pictures. And if we insist upon the finality or completeness of any one picture, we "set up stakes" for the Almighty and say "hitherto shalt thou come, & no further." Of course we need pictures in order to relate to God. But how can we ever know which picture of God is right and which is not? How can we avoid idolatry? Here we must trust in the grace of God. Ann Ulanov puts it well: "it is very much a human impulse to try to picture God and God does come to find us in those very pictures as well as in the smashing of them. . . . Our inability to cross over the gap between our pictures and God's reality is met by the unbelievable miracle of God crossing over to us" (1986, 4). Finally the love of God must rescue us from our limited vision, from our failure of imagination, from our inadequate and even dangerous pictures of the divine. For this reason the scriptures promise we shall one day see God in the face but in God's own time, in God's own way, and according to God's own will (D&C 88:68).

~ CHAPTER FIVE ~

THE DIVINE MOTHER

The concept that God is paradoxically transcendent and immanent has important theological implications for the place of the feminine in Christianity. Some feminist theologians such as Rosemary Radford Ruether have correctly observed that classical and early Christian (including neoplatonic and gnostic) dualism has leant support to traditional theological arguments for the inferiority of the feminine. Dualism presents a world divided into pairs — light and darkness, heaven and earth, reason and instinct, culture and nature, spirit and body — and connects the female with what has traditionally been viewed as the less desirable component of a pair: darkness, earth, instinct, nature, and the flesh. Ruether observes that "women are symbolized as analogous to the lower realm of matter or body, to be ruled by or shunned by transcendent mind" (79). Because women in this view are connected with the body, they also symbolize sexuality and carnality, both as objects of sexual desire and as reproducers of children. To quote Ruether again, "Women, as representatives of sexual reproduction and motherhood, are the bearers of death, from which male spirit must flee to 'light and life' " (80). For Ruether the only way to end the subjugation of women is to eliminate the idea of duality itself.

Although we agree with much of this analysis, we disagree with the conclusion for two reasons. First, it may be impossible to rid ourselves of duality since it seems ingrained in our way of perceiving the world. Second, we do not believe it is duality itself which leads to the subjugation of the feminine but rather the failure to see each component of a paired set as equally valuable and the tendency to associate one component exclusively with women and the other exclusively with men.

A theology of a God of flesh and glory provides a model preserving binary opposites but refusing to favor one component over the other or to link the so-called less favorable component with the female. If God is both body and spirit, then we may believe that both are equally necessary and valuable.

For us God is not only flesh and glory but also male and female. We disagree with those who assert that avoiding sexism means picturing God as a being beyond gender and sexuality. A picture of a God beyond all categories and relations encourages the very spirit/matter dichotomy which has denigrated women and sex.[1] In our view the more salutary doctrine is one that sees God as spirit and body, male and female. For this reason we have come to accept both a male God and a female God, each of whom is simultaneously transcendent and immanent. Rather than seeing the male as the God of sky, spirit, day, and reason and the female as the God of the earth, body, night, and intuition, we see each of them as both.[2]

In our view elevating women and ending distrust of the feminine depends not on accepting a deity beyond sexuality but on accepting a powerful Goddess within the Mormon and Judeo-Christian tradition. This need was recognized a century ago by Edward W. Tullidge in his remarkable work, *Women of Mormondom*: "Henceforth shall the mother half of creation be worshipped with that of the God-Father; and in that worship woman, by the very association of ideas, shall be exalted in the coming civilization" (189).[3] Such a Goddess concept is not, as might first be supposed, alien to the West. Though in comparison to our images of the male God, feminine images of the divine are few, still these have been surprisingly irrepressible. No matter how many times she is

---

[1] As Christians we believe that the present world is corrupt and fallen and in need of redemption; however, it is not materiality and sexuality as such that constitute this corruption but the entropic powers of corruption and alienation from the love, truth, and spirit of God.

[2] Here we agree with Reuther that it is a mistake to connect the Goddess only with immanence, nature, and nurture as is done in some modern Goddess worship. Reuther says that the result of this is "the creation of a Goddess religion that is the reverse of a patriarchal religion" (52). In chapter 7 we argue that it is necessary to move beyond the battle over which of these powers (i.e., male or female — transcendence or immanence) is superior and to see the question from a different perspective.

[3] In 1910 Mormon apostle Rudger Clawson recognized that women and men have a need to worship and "yearn to adore" a mother in heaven. He felt that the worship of the "Eternal Mother" did not detract from our worship of the "Eternal Father" (Wilcox, 72).

rejected and even killed, the Goddess always re-emerges in one form or another.

Raphael Patai in *The Hebrew Goddess* notes that "the religion of the Hebrews and the Jews was never without at least a hint of the feminine in its God-concept." And at times the feminine divine expanded in the Jewish religion into a full-fledged Goddess, who on a popular level almost over-shadowed the male deity (1978, 258). In Christianity the female deity has survived as the Virgin Mary, the Mother Church, and even as a feminine Jesus. There seems to be a human need for the mothering and nurturing aspects of divinity that finally brings God the Mother back into all religions from which she has been rejected.

This motherly aspect of deity, so appealing to some, can be offensive to others. A person who has had either an over-bearing or a neglectful mother may have no desire for another mother, even a divine one. The converse is also true. A person whose father was authoritarian, judgmental, and harsh or distant, unfeeling, and cold may project these images onto a heavenly father and reject him. This points to one problem with imaging God only in terms of father or mother. In addition such images tend to contract our view of God and how we should imitate God. Because in Mormonism the female deity has been seen almost exclusively in a mothering role, many have been inclined to restrict women to the sphere of mothering and nurturing. We have taken the model of patriarchal marriage and projected it onto our heavenly parents, thus reinforcing the prevailing view that women should be subordinate and function as homemakers and nothing else.

For these reasons we think it essential to find alternative images for the female divinity as well as the male. This is not to demean the mothering function of the Goddess but to expand our concept of her divine attributes, to see her as a Supreme Being independent from though united with her male counterpart. This is why we refer to the Heavenly Mother by the word "Goddess," a term of power emphasizing her godhood and implying a scope which includes but exceeds mothering.[4]

---

[4] It is, of course, equally important to see the nurturing aspects of the male deity as well. For this reason the notion of Jesus, our mother, is for some very moving. For example, St. Anselm, using the scriptural image of a hen gathering her chicks, said:

In the following paragraphs we will be drawing upon God images from other religious traditions, not to prove or reinforce Mormon concepts of deity but rather to explore and expand the possibilities for imaging God, and especially to provide a picture of the female divinity to which we can relate.

Certain images in the Judeo-Christian tradition depict a powerful and multi-faceted female deity, a being not merely associated with mothering but also with wisdom and sovereignty. In ancient Judaism the divine attribute of Wisdom (*Hokhma* in Hebrew) became almost a separate feminine divinity. This same process occurred in early Christianity, especially in the Gnostic sects, where Wisdom (*Sophia* in Greek) also came to be seen as a goddess. Many feel that these figures were more than personifications; they functioned as divinities in their own right.[5] In Proverbs, which forms part of the wisdom literature of the Old Testament, Wisdom speaks in her own person and says she was with God before the foundations of the world: "The Lord possessed me in the beginning of his way before his works of old. I was set up from everlasting, from the beginning, or ever the earth was. . . . when he appointed the foundations of the earth. . . . Then I was by him, as one brought up with him: and I was daily his delight, rejoicing always before him" (8:22–23, 29–30). Though connected with God the Male, Wisdom has a life of her own apart from him. She herself addresses humanity in the authoritative manner of a divine being and gives commandments to Israel just as the male God does. And like him she addresses Israel as her children: "Now therefore hearken unto me, O ye children: for blessed are they that keep my ways" (v. 32).

The writer of Proverbs pictures Wisdom as having great power and dominion: "By me Kings reign, and princes decree justice. By me princes rule, and nobles, even all the judges of the earth. I love them

---

"Christ, my mother, /you gather your chickens under your wings; /this dead chicken of yours puts himself under those wings." Bernard of Clairveaux in an even more passionate statement said: "Suck not the wounds, but rather the breasts of the crucified. He shall be as a mother to you, and you as a son to him" (Warner, 196–97). Julian of Norwich also referred to Jesus as mother and used the image of Christ's breasts.

[5] Raphael Patai deals at length with the problem in Judaism, a monotheistic religion, of a female deity, which he sees as a departure from the idea of the one God. On the one hand, Patai argues, those in Judaism who made use of female divine images did so as a form of mystical and theosophic speculation about the nature of the one God. On the other hand, the nature and effect of the female images was very similar to that of pagan goddesses.

that love me; and those that seek me early shall find me.... For whoso findeth me findeth life, and shall obtain favor of the Lord. But he that sinneth against me wrongeth his own soul: all they that hate me love death" (vv. 15–17, 35, 36). Wisdom is also described in the same terms used for the male God. She has eternal life, honor, peace, riches, and power. She is a tree of life, an image connecting her with other ancient Near Eastern deities as well: "Length of days is in her right hand and in her left hand riches and honour. Her ways are ways of pleasantness, and all her paths are peace. She is a tree of life to them that lay hold upon her: and happy is everyone that retaineth her" (3:16–18).

Moreover, Wisdom is not presented as an ancient stereotype of acceptable female behavior. Virginia Mollenkott makes the following observation: "Proverbs 1:20–33 depicts Wisdom (*Hokhma*) as crying aloud at street corners, raising her voice in the public squares, offering her saving counsel to anybody who will listen to her. Wisdom's behavior runs directly counter to the socialization of a proper lady, who is taught to be rarely seen and even more rarely heard in the sphere of public activity. Assertive, insistent, and noisy: according to modern definition, Wisdom is a woman, but no lady!" (98).[6]

The medieval Christians were drawn into the embrace of a female divinity in the person of the Virgin Mary. Her attributes and characteristics were many, including wisdom, which was symbolized at times as milk or honey. As one scholar writes, "The complex of symbolism that associated the Virgin with Wisdom and with the Church transformed her into the nursing mother of many penitents, visionaries, and saints" (Warner, 198). In the east Mary's "identification with Wisdom [was] very close: Sophia appears, for instance, in an Armenian gospel miniature of 1323 suckling the apostles Peter and Paul" (ibid.). This image suggests that the wisdom of God is communicated to the saints through the intercession of the Virgin. Thus, the image of motherhood is extended beyond the physical to the spiritual realm, where life and enlightenment are imparted through the nurturing process. At this time the sovereignty of Mary was also emphasized in her title as

---

[6] Philo, a Hellensitic Jewish philosopher of the first century A.D., also saw Wisdom as a feminine aspect of the divine nature and connected her with sovereignty. Moreover, while Philo believed like Jews in general that God was really "one," he felt that the two chief powers of God, "goodness and sovereignty," took a male and female form (Patai, 72). Philo's concept of the male and female aspects of deity were not literal in the way Mormons see them.

"Queen of Heaven," which she acquired upon her assumption. This aspect of her divinity is represented pictorially by her crown and throne. "Seated in majesty on a throne, the Virgin Queen contains a multi-layered message: she belongs to a classical tradition of personifying cities and institutions as goddesses, and as such, in the heart of Rome, she embodies the new Rome, which is the Church" (ibid., 104).[7]

Anciently Wisdom was also connected with God's spirit. The feminine deity was intercessor and comforter. In late Talmudic literature Wisdom's function was taken over by the Shekhina or Holy Spirit. The Hebrew word *shekhina* means "dwelling" or "presence" of God. Eventually the Shekhina came to be thought of as an "independent feminine divine entity prompted by her compassionate nature to argue with God in the defense of man" (Patai 1978, 99). In certain passages of Jewish sacred literature, the Shekhina takes the role of mediator, persuading humans to obey God and God to be merciful to humanity: "The Holy Spirit comes to the defense [of sinful Israel by] saying first to Israel: 'Be not a witness against thy neighbor without a cause,' and thereafter saying to God: 'Say not: I will do to him as he hath done to me' " (ibid., 112). In Catholic theology Mary, the mother of Jesus, plays a similar intercessory role. As a female deity she is " 'the mother of mercy,' the 'life, sweetness, and hope' of the fallen, the advocate who pleads humanity's cause before the judgement seat of God" (Warner, 316). Like Jewish thinkers, Christian Gnostics also saw the Holy Spirit as a feminine deity. In the secret *Gospel of the Hebrews*, Jesus speaks of "my Mother, the Spirit," and in another Gnostic text, *The Gospel of Philip*, the writer refers to the Holy Spirit as the "mother of many." In the *Secret Book of John,* the Spirit is referred to as mother and included in the trin-

---

[7] The image of God, male or female, as imperial majesty no longer has the appeal it once did. Likewise the image of the warrior god or goddess, which role both Mary and the Jewish Matronit have taken (Patai, 169–79), is no longer popular. The acceptance and the rejection of the warrior king/queen images illustrates our tendency to picture God in a way that reinforces or illuminates our own world views. However, these unpopular images are important because they put our own favored images in proper perspective and may present us with truths we are reluctant to accept readily. For example, the war-like goddess is often the same as the fertility goddess. This is true not only in many Near Eastern religions but with Mary and the Matronit. The paradox involves the connecting of love with war and life with death. This tells us something about the interconnectedness of these forces: Every death is a birth of sorts, every birth a death, and the old earth goddess not only gives life to all out of her womb but also receives all back into the tomb.

ity in the place of the Holy Ghost: Father, Mother, and Son (Pagels, 110).

In Jewish Kabbalistic literature, mystical writings dating from the thirteenth century A.D., God is pictured as a divine tetrad: Father, Mother, Son, and Daughter. Some of the names or titles ascribed to the daughter in the Kabbalah suggest other important images or attributes of the female God. These titles include: kingship, Matronit or lady (the equivalent of Lord), pearl or precious stone, discarded cornerstone, the community of Israel, the female, moon, heart, earth, night, garden, well, sea, supernal woman, and light woman (Patai 1978, 143). Mary also has many names. Some of these are taken from scriptural ideas: mother of divine grace, mother of good counsel, virgin most powerful, mirror of justice, seat of wisdom, vessel of honor, mystical rose, tower of David, house of gold, ark of the covenant, gate of heaven, morning star, health of the sick, refuge of sinners, queen of angels, patriarchs, prophets, apostles, martyrs, confessors, virgins, and all saints (Marian Missal, 1407–1408).

The Matronit or Shekhina became associated with Queen Sabbath, the feminine divine presence dwelling in the households of faithful Jews on the Sabbath day. She was also called the bride of God, a title emphasizing her sexual nature and her role as lover of both God and men. In this respect the Matronit, like the love goddesses of the Near East, was both sexual and virginal at the same time. The Shekhina not only coupled with "the divine King who was her lawfully wedded husband" but also with "gods, heroes of Biblical history, and many other men" (Patai 1978, 160–61).

In medieval Christianity Mary too was depicted as both lover and virgin. She is associated with the "bride" in the *Song of Songs* as well as in Revelation (Warner, 124, 128). Sometimes she is depicted as the virgin mother of Christ, at other times as his spouse. In one twelfth century mosaic in Rome, Mary, enthroned at the side of Jesus and embraced by him, is obviously being depicted not as his mother alone but as his bride and queen (ibid., 121). Eventually Mary became the object of passionate devotion and sexual attraction to men like St. Bernard, the founder of the Cistercians, whose "marked love of the Virgin, with its character of personal intensity, was . . . carried all over Europe" (ibid., 131). There adoration of Mary flowered as part of the courtly love tradition.

Of course both the Matronit and Mary are also represented as mother goddesses, but the mother image in the Jewish and Christian traditions differs markedly from the popular Mormon notion of a mother in heaven, who appears to have no other function than producing offspring. The Matronit and Mary as mother goddesses are not pictured as distant, hard-to-reach deities somewhere in the heavens above. Rather each is cast in the image of the Mater Dolorosa, the mourning mother who imposes upon herself a voluntary exile in order to wander with and comfort her children, mourning and grieving in this veil of tears. She is like Rachel weeping for her children. She is Demeter looking for her lost daughter. As the Holy Spirit she is very near and acts as a continual divine presence sustaining us in the lone and dreary world. This is perhaps the most moving image of the Goddess, a divine being who like Jesus suffers with us and understands our pain.

In the Mormon tradition, although the concept of the Goddess or Mother in Heaven emerged during the lifetime of Joseph Smith, little theology has ever been developed about her. Though there have been infrequent references made to the Heavenly Mother in church conferences, the most familiar reference is found in the Mormon hymn, originally entitled "Invocation, Or the Eternal Father and Mother" (Tullidge, 187) but now called ironically *O My Father*:

> In the heavens are parents single?
> No; the thought makes reason stare!
> Truth is reason, truth eternal
> Tells me I've a mother there.
>
> When I leave this frail existence,
> When I lay this mortal by,
> Father, Mother may I meet you
> In your royal courts on high?

In the last century the Mormon Heavenly Mother generally has been described as an ideal woman in a mothering role (Wilcox, 69–70). Usually this description has been advanced to promote a role for women as childbearers and homemakers.

However, a few Mormon prophetic and scriptural statements suggest that Heavenly Mother is a being equal with God in power and glory and a member of the godhead. For example, Section 132 of the Doctrine and Covenants states that those who receive the fullness of the priesthood, which is promised to men and women in the LDS temple ritual, shall become "gods, because they have no end" and because "all things are subject unto them" and "they have all power" (vv. 19–20). A similar point was made by Mormon apostle Erastus Snow in a sermon given on 3 March 1878: "[T]here can be no God except he is composed of the man and woman united, and there is not in all the eternities that exist, nor ever will be a God in any other way. I have another description: There never was a God, and there never will be in all eternities, except they are made of these two component parts; a man and a woman; the male and the female" (JD 19:270). Not only is the female God equal with the male, but neither would be God without the other.

We may well ask why Mormonism has not developed more theology around God the Mother since we Mormons were early to sound the theme. One cause of our failure has been perhaps our certainty about the nature of the godhead. We mistakenly assume we have a complete picture and understand all about their character and their comings and goings. We tend to use Joseph Smith's 1838 account of his first vision as a final statement about the nature of God rather than as a starting point. By refusing to expand our views, we refuse to mature beyond the religious ideas we held as children. Joseph Smith said: "When things that are great are passed over with[ou]t even a tho[ugh]t I want to see [truth] in all its bearings & hug it to my bosom — I bel[ieve] all that God ever rev[eale]d & I never hear[d] of a man being d[amne]d for bel[ievin]g too much but they are d[amne]d for unbel[ief]" (WJS, 381).

This statement suggests another reason why we fail to see the need for the worship of the Goddess or to recognize her influence: fear. We are afraid to deviate from accepted God-concepts. Joseph Smith encouraged us not to be afraid. By knowing the true nature of the Gods, we can come to understand our own nature, our place in the universe, our potential: "If men [and women] do not comprehend the character of God they do not comprehend themselves. what kind of being is God? — Eternal life [is] to know God. — if [a] man [or a woman] does not know God, [then he or she] has not Eternal life. — ... Soon as we begin to understand the character of the Gods [they] begin to unfold the heavens to us. —" (ibid., 340–41). In our view none of us need be afraid or ashamed of our desires to comprehend the gods and specifically to know more about the attributes of God the Mother. We should not feel we are treading on forbidden ground. Yearnings for God the Mother and Daughter are as holy as yearnings for God the Father and Son.

Of course these statements are not meant as invitations to believe anything and everything or to be unconcerned about distinguishing truth from falsehood. But they are calls to open our minds to new

ideas. Many Mormons are afraid to do this because they do not wish to
be wrong. But we are all wrong. Entertaining wrong views is an inevitable part of the process of spiritual and intellectual growth. We are
admonished by the apostle Paul to try new ideas, to discard what we
find inadequate or bad, and to hold to the good (1 Thess. 5:21). Our
pictures of God, male and female, are bound to fall short of the divine
reality. Even our actual spiritual experiences, our contacts with deity,
should not be used dogmatically to declare the final word about what
the godhead is like.

We should remember that many rejected Jesus when he revealed
himself on earth in the flesh. He did not fulfill the prevailing expectations of what a divine being would be like. If this is true of God the
Male, it is undoubtedly true of God the Female. If we focus on our own
narrow picture of her and close off other possibilities, we may not recognize her when she reveals herself to us. A paraphrase of scripture is
to the point: "Beloved, now are we the daughters of God, and it doth
not yet appear what we shall be: but we know that, when she shall appear, we shall be like her; for we shall see her as she is" (cf. 1 John 3:2).

In the beginning woman was made in the image of her heavenly
parent — the divine Mother. And in the spiritual re-creation, women
are spiritually transformed in her image. We may not yet know what
that image is, but we know that women can become like her. For this
reason we believe that more revelation about her is sorely needed. Belief in God the Mother can give women a sense of self-worth and an
elevated sense of destiny.

However, the goddess concept is not without its dangers. There is
a negative side to the worship by females of the female divinity just as
there is a negative side to the worship by males of the male divinity. In
either case complete identification with the deity can lead to idolatry,
to the mistake of confusing God's voice speaking in us with the voice
of our own ego. This occurs in some modern Goddess worship as well
as in the traditional worship of the Father and the Son whenever we see
in God, male or female, merely the projection and personification of
our own values and views. The result of this mistake is self-worship,
the inverse of which is self-hatred. Self-worship and self-hatred seem to
go hand in hand and are perhaps the two greatest temptations of the
twentieth century. Of course self-esteem, rooted in respect for God's
love and respect for both human potential and limitation, is healthy.
But self-worship is unhealthy. It looks not to God but to the human

heart for the power of salvation. And when human salvation fails, very often self-worship turns to self-hatred.

One of the most important benefits of a belief in God or in the supernatural is its power to draw our attention away from the self toward acceptance of an other, of something different from the self. If we can love only what is like us, we will be narcissistic and closed. For this reason the theology of God the Mother is as important for men as the theology of God the Father is for women. We need to worship something different as well as something similar to ourselves.

In Mormonism the doctrine that women and men can become like their heavenly parents can also lead to self-worship if it is not put in a Christian context. Emphasis on our potential to become like our Mother and Father in Heaven can suggest that our own salvation depends merely upon our growth. Because we are the children of God the Mother and God the Father, some believe that we tend naturally to grow to be like them. It is only a matter of time. But this idea runs contrary to Christ's teachings that salvation is not merely a matter of growth but of change. If we are to be like the gods, we must experience a change of heart and nature, a spiritual rebirth. We must be born of the spirit. We must see that though the seed of godhood is in us, it can only develop by receiving the power of God through the atonement.

We feel very strongly that any theology of God the Mother must be established in a Christian context. This does not mean we should not look to other religions or religious traditions for knowledge about the female divinity. We believe that the pagans, for example, had great truths about the Goddess under various names — truths that can open us to further revelations about the nature of God the Mother. But we are Christians and believe that Jesus is savior, the name through which we receive salvation. For us then a theology of God the Female must be compatible with the revelation of God the Male in the person of Jesus of Nazareth.

A story about a friend makes this point. At a difficult time in her life, our friend was full of despair and felt that something was very wrong with her — that her femaleness was in some way insufficient. She had an overwhelming desire to have some contact with Heavenly Mother. Since her usual way of praying seemed to fail her at this time, she decided to use a visualization technique she had recently learned. She pictured herself in a beautiful pastoral setting waiting for an animal to appear to serve as her guide. She had expected a magnificent or elegant animal such as a lion or a gazelle. Instead a badger crawled out of the ground and instructed her to follow him. From this point the vision was out of her control. The badger led her to a divine being she knew to be God, that is Jesus Christ. He was glorious, whole, complete, serene, and totally unperturbed at her disappointment.

"I didn't come to see you," said our friend.

"I know," said Jesus. And then he pointed and said, "There she is."

Our friend then saw another glorious being, who was in some way identical to the first in the quality of her godhood. Both were self-existent beings, complete, containing all that was necessary for perfection. And yet this second being was as distinctly female as the first had been distinctly male.

As our friend gazed on this female deity, the Goddess communicated to her two ideas.

"Can you see that what you are is enough?" she said first. And then she added, "You are me."

When our friend told us this story, she explained she understood this latter statement did not mean that our friend was the same as or equal to the divine being but rather that she was somehow part of the Goddess and could someday be like her.

The unexpected in this vision strikes us as particularly true: the badger as the guide, Jesus Christ as the god who acknowledges the divine equality of the Goddess, and the familiarity and at the same time the unexpectedness of what the Goddess is like.

Frankly our attention in the past has not been focused on the female deity. Our own most intense spiritual experiences have been with Jesus Christ and the power of his redeeming love. Perhaps because we have seen ourselves as sinners and our most dire need has been for a savior, our attention has been drawn to the person of Jesus. And yet something unexpected has happened to us as we have studied Goddess images in both the pagan and the Judeo-Christian traditions. We have begun to experience feelings of love and gratitude for God our Heavenly Mother as we have come to understand more about her nature and her presence among us.

We have concluded that knowing about God the Mother is vital and that she is not far away. Perhaps her presence is always with us, and our Lady and our Lord together sustain us with their love. Perhaps this prayer, adapted by some Jewish women from traditional liturgy (Janowitze, 176), may express something of this feeling:

Blessed is She who spoke and the world became.
Blessed is She.
Blessed is She who in the beginning gave birth.
Blessed is She who says and performs.
Blessed is She who declares and fulfills.
Blessed is She whose womb covers the earth.
Blessed is She whose womb protects all creatures.
Blessed is She who nourished those who are in awe of Her.
Blessed is She who lives forever, and exists eternally.
Blessed is She who redeems and saves.
Blessed is Her Name.

CHAPTER SIX

JESUS CHRIST
AND THE MORMON PANTHEON

In most religions the godhead is the primary mystery. Because of the apparent clarity and certainty of Joseph Smith's eventual awareness of God, Mormonism has been unappreciative of the often inscrutable complexity associated with God concepts in other religious traditions. Ironically, the simple and straightforward concept of deity of popular Mormonism stands in stark contrast to the complex teachings on the godhead found in Mormon scriptures and prophetic statements. This tangle begins with the first vision itself. In 1832 Joseph Smith dictated the earliest known report of the first vision, a theophany which has since been accepted as the genesis of Mormonism. In that account he states that in the spring of 1820 while praying in a grove near his father's upstate New York farm, "the Lord opened the heavens upon me and I saw the Lord and he spake unto me saying Joseph . . . I am the Lord of glory I was crucifyed for the world" (PWJS, 6). Later in an 1835 account of the same vision, Joseph stated: "[A] personage appeard in the midst of this pillar of flame which was spread all around, and yet nothing consumed, another personage soon appeard like unto the first, he said unto me thy sins are forgiven thee, he testifyed unto me that Jesus Christ is the Son of God; and I saw many angels in this vision" (ibid., 75–76). In his 1838 version, which was officially canonized in the Pearl of Great Price, Joseph stated: "When the light rested upon me I saw two Personages, whose brightness and glory defy all description, standing above me in the air. One of them spake unto me, calling me by name and said, pointing to the other — *This is My Beloved Son. Hear Him!*" (Joseph Smith 2:17).

Who did Joseph Smith see in this vision? Was it Jesus alone as suggested in the 1832 version? Was it Jesus and an unidentified personage, an angel perhaps, who testified of the Son of God as suggested by the 1835 version? Or was it the Father and the Son as suggested by the 1838 version? This is not to imply that we think these versions are inaccurate or false. We accept them as statements of truth and believe that the discrepancies in them can be explained or harmonized. But what do they really tell us about the godhead?

Is the godhead a unity made up of a single deity as set forth in the Old Testament? And if so who is this one God? Eloheim? Jehovah? Or is the godhead a duality made up of two beings of equal glory and dignity as implied in the fifth Lecture on Faith? And if so who makes up this godhead? Is it the Father and the Son as the lecture states? Or is it the Heavenly Father and the Heavenly Mother as suggested by other Mormon commentators? Or is the godhead a trinity, as stated in the New Testament and the Doctrine and Covenants (John 14; D&C 20:28)? If so who are its members? The Father, Son, and Holy Ghost? Elohim, Jehovah, and Michael as implied in the Mormon temple endowment? The Father, the Mother, and the Son? Or is the godhead really a council of gods as stated by Joseph Smith and suggested in the Book of Abraham (Abr. 3:22–28)?

And who are the gods behind these titles? Jesus is the Son of God, but who is the Father? And does the Father have a father? And what are we to make of the nineteenth-century Mormon teachings about Adam? Was Adam really Michael as Joseph Smith taught (WJS, 8–13)? Is Michael-Adam also God the Father as suggested by Brigham Young (JD 1:50–51)? If so is Eve the Mother Goddess, the "Mother of All Living," as stated in the temple ceremony and as taught by Brigham Young? And how does Jesus relate to these other deities? Is he their God or are they his? And what of the Holy Ghost? Is she a female personage as suggested by the dove symbol and the nurturing functions? Or is he a male as is usually taught? And Mary the mother of the son of God? Is she a deity too as suggested by her marriage to God the Father? And if so who is her divine consort? What is the nature of these beings? Are they resurrected? If so, who resurrected them? Or are they spirits? And if so, will they enjoy a future resurrection? Are they equal in their godhood? Or are some superior to others? Is one of them supreme? If so which one? And what is the basis of their ranking? Seniority? Sacrificial service? Function? And what of the angels? Are they lesser gods? And what of devils? Are they fallen gods?

The point of these questions is that for Mormonism as well as other religions, the godhead remains the primary mystery. This is not to say that Mormons know nothing about God. Our religious texts have a great deal to say about the being we pray to, trust in, rely upon, and connect with spiritually — the being whom the prophets proclaimed and for whom the martyrs died.

We believe that the clearest revelation of the divine nature was given to us in the person of Jesus. Before Christ, the God of the Hebrews was often perceived as an awesome personage of supreme power, passionate intensity, fierce holiness, and relentless justice. God if not totally other was inaccessible to all but a few of his chosen people. This perception did not so much encourage love as fear. Though fear may prevent humans from doing their worst, it is not likely to encourage their best.

One of the primary purposes of the incarnation of Christ was to proclaim the good news of God's unconditional love for us. Thus we have a basis to love him in return rather than merely fear him: "For God so loved the world that he sent his only begotten Son, that whosoever believeth in him should not perish, but have everlasting life. For God sent not his son into the world to condemn the world, but that the world through him might be saved" (John 3:16–17). Christ's mission was not primarily to reveal the character, nature, and day-to-day lives of the members of the godhead but to establish that the right attitude toward God is not fear but affection. Jesus' messianic mission was to show us that God loves us much more than he hates our sins, that he loves us in our sins, that he willingly takes the burden of our sins upon himself, that he prizes us above his own divinity, and that he loves us no less than he loves holiness and truth. Yes, Christ came to save us from death and hell, but he also came to save us from the fear of God. Whatever else we learn about God as a result of this tremendous act is incidental but not trivial.

In Christ we learn that God is a real individual with body, parts, and passions. Christ was revealed to us in the person of a Jewish carpenter so that we could picture him and relate to him as a commoner, as a young man stripped to the waist perhaps, his muscles working, his brown skin wet in the hot, dry air as he smooths down a wooden surface with a sharp plane. He wants us to approach him, interrupt him, and speak to him. He wants us to know that he will turn from his work, wipe the sweat from his face, and look us in the eye, that he will offer us a drink and sit with us in the shade to hear our complaints, our heartaches, and our disappointments — to weep with us perhaps. He is after all a man of sorrows and acquainted with grief. We know from his story that he pities the blind, the deaf, the halt, and the lame.

Sometimes he heals them. More often he comforts them. And he knows things — about wealth, farming, fishing, law, and medicine, about sheep and goats and sacrifice and worship. He knows what is in the Law and in the Prophets and in our hearts. He knows what is said in this city and in that tribe. He understands foreigners, their languages and customs. He seems to know their gods. He knows about hate and cruelty, about disillusion and despair. He knows about miracles, about birth and life and death and eternal life. Yes he knows many things.

But the longer we are with him, the less we seem to know him. There seems always to be more, some new side to him we had not expected. Who is he, this Jesus? What should we think of him? The New Testament tells us that he is the Son of Man, the son of God, the promised Messiah, and more: "Philip saith unto him, Lord, shew us the Father, and it sufficeth us. Jesus saith unto him, Have I been so long time with you, and yet hast thou not known me, Philip? he that hath seen me hath seen the Father" (John 14:8–9). Could this be? Could Jesus be God? Was he not merely God's son, God's messenger, God's mouthpiece, someone who spoke by divine investiture of authority as if he were God?

According to its title page, the Book of Mormon was brought forth to convince "Jew and Gentile that Jesus is the Christ, the ETERNAL GOD, manifesting himself unto all nations." In this book the prophet Amulek is asked, "Is the Son of God the very Eternal Father?" His answer is, "Yea, he is the very Eternal Father of heaven and of earth, and all things which in them are; he is the beginning and the end, the first and the last; And he shall come into the world to redeem his people; and he shall take upon him the transgressions of those who believe on his name" (Al. 11:38–40). In the Book of Mosiah, where Christ is called "the Lord, who is the very Eternal Father" (16:15), we are presented with the prophet Abinadi, who was slain for teaching that "Christ was the God, the Father of all things, and . . . that he should take upon him the image of man, . . . and take upon him flesh and blood, and go forth upon the face of the earth" (7:27). And that "God himself shall come down among the children of men, and shall redeem his people" (15:1). And that Christ was both the Father and the Son: "The Father, because he was conceived by the power of God; and the Son, because of the flesh, thus becoming the Father and Son — And they are one God, yea, the very Eternal Father of heaven and of earth" (vv. 3–4).

This means that the being worshipped as God the Father condescended to manifest himself in the form of a human being. The Father became a son in order to make himself accessible to us, to suffer with us, and to suffer for us, so the will of God could be accomplished: "And thus the flesh becoming subject to the Spirit, or the Son to the Father, being one God, suffereth temptation, and yieldeth not to the temptation, but suffereth himself to be mocked, and scourged, and cast out, and disowned by his people. And after all this, after working many mighty miracles among the children of men, he shall be led, yea, even as Isaiah said, as a sheep before the shearer is dumb, so he opened not his mouth" (Mos. 15:5–6).

How is this possible? Theologically how can the Son be the Father? Are they not two separate and distinct beings? Did not Christ pray to the Father and proclaim the Father? Was he not proclaimed by the Father at his baptism? The answer to these questions, we believe, is yes. But Christ's God and father is not our God and father except through Christ, our intercessor. The scripture tells us that "we are Christ's and Christ is God's" (1 Cor. 3:23; D&C 76:59). Our God and Father is Jesus: "Behold, I come unto my own . . . to do the will, both of the Father and of the Son — of the Father because of me, and of the Son because of my flesh" (3 Ne. 1:14). In the text of the Book of Ether, Jesus explains: "Behold, I am he who was prepared from before the foundation of the world to redeem my people. Behold, I am Jesus Christ. I am the Father and the Son. In me shall all mankind have life, and that eternally, even they who shall believe on my name; and they shall become my sons and my daughters" (Eth. 3:14). When Jesus appeared to the Nephites as a resurrected being, he identified himself as "Jesus Christ, the Son of God. I created the heavens and the earth, and all things that in them are. I was with the Father from the beginning. I am in the Father, and the Father in me; and in me hath the Father glorified his name. . . . And as many as have received me, to them have I given to become the sons of God [Jesus Christ]" (3 Ne. 9:15, 17).

Perhaps the most radical theological concept of Mormonism is the Book of Mormon assertion that Jesus Christ is the God of the Old Testament, "the God of Israel, and the God of the whole earth" (3 Ne. 11:14): "Behold, I am he that gave the law [of Moses], and I am he who covenanted with my people Israel; therefore, the law in me is fulfilled. . . . Behold, I am the law and the light. Look unto me, and endure to the end, and ye shall live; for unto him that endureth to the end will I give eternal life" (15:5–9). What the Book of Mormon proclaims more clearly than any other book of scripture is that Jesus is our Heavenly Father.

But how could Jesus be the Father if, as Mormons believe, Jesus was but one of many pre-mortal spirits sent to earth to receive a body of flesh and bones? The answer is that he could not have been merely another pre-mortal spirit. He was a deity who had been resurrected, perhaps many times. He like his god and father had power within himself to lay down his life and take it up again. Jesus voluntarily disembodied himself in order to assume a new mortality and bear in his own person the sins of the world. This concept, the mystery of the condescension of God, was revealed by Jesus at the time he appeared to the brother of Jared: "Behold, this body, which ye now behold, is the body of my spirit; and man have I created after the body of my spirit; and even as I appear unto thee to be in the spirit will I appear unto my people in the flesh" (Eth. 3:16). Here, the words "body of my spirit" are nearly always understood by Mormons to mean "spirit body." However, Jesus does not say "spirit body," but rather "body of my spirit," in other words the resurrected body in which his spirit dwelt.

In this theophany the brother of Jared was given to understand that Jesus was a resurrected being before his incarnation, a point underscored in the following verse: "And now, as I, Moroni, said I could not make a full account of these things which are written therefore it sufficeth me to say that Jesus showed himself unto this man [the brother of Jared] in the spirit, even after the manner and in the likeness of the same body even as he showed himself unto the Nephites" (Eth. 3:17). Jesus appeared to the brother of Jared "in the spirit," that is in the brilliance of his glory. But he appeared "in the likeness of the same body even as he showed himself unto the Nephites." In other words, he appeared to him in a resurrected body in the likeness of the resurrected body in which he later appeared to the Nephites. When the brother of Jared understood this, when he saw the body of the Lord, he fell down and worshipped him. And Jesus said to him, "thou shalt not suffer these things which ye have seen and heard to go forth unto the world, until the time cometh that I shall glorify my name in the flesh" (v. 21). The Book of Mormon further explains: "And in the day that they shall exercise faith in me, saith the Lord, even as the brother of Jared did, that they may become sanctified in me, then will I manifest unto them the things which the brother of Jared saw, even to the unfolding unto them all my revelations, saith Jesus Christ, the Son of God, the Father of the heavens and of the earth, and all things that in them are" (4:7).

Though for many, Jesus is the incarnation of God, we believe that he is and has been worshipped in many other names — as Yahweh,

Elohim, Adonai, Allah, Brahma, Shiva, Vishnu, Ouranous, Kronos, Zeus, Jupiter, Jove, Apollo, Dionysos, Hermes, Vulcan, Thor, Odin, Osiris, Horus. He is the Unknown God, the God known by countless names, the God of countless faces. We think that all these names represent but labels for differing clusters of attributes that only approximate the divine attributes of the true God we worship. This means that our own concept of Jesus is only an approximation of the reality. In Jesus, we have a revelation of the divine, but not a complete one. As Christians, then, we may expect in the next world to be as surprised by the nature of the true God as any one else. In this life, however, each of us worships the name we know and the face we see. This does not mean that every idea about God is correct, that no heresies exist, or that every event attributed to God is an act of God. It does mean that those who seek divine love and truth and goodness by any name and in any tradition are worshippers of the true God.

Most Mormons accept from Joseph Smith that God has a body, that God progresses, and that God is not exactly as the Catholics and Protestants have described him in the creeds. But what we fail to see as clearly is that the God referred to by Joseph Smith in his revelations, in his visions, in his sermons, in the King Follett discourse, is Jesus Christ, the resurrection and the life, the Everlasting Father, the Prince of Peace.

Instead most of us think of God the father of Jesus as the person who created a plan for the earth requiring a savior. This concept is derived from a misreading of certain verses in the Pearl of Great Price: "And the Lord said: Whom shall I send? And one answered like unto the Son of Man: Here am I, send me. And another answered and said: Here am I, send me. And the Lord said: I will send the first" (Abr. 3:27). The "Lord" in these verses is thought to be God, the father of Jesus. The "one like unto the Son of Man" is thought to be Jesus. And the third person, the one referred to as "another," is thought to be Lucifer. This interpretation depicts God choosing between two sons volunteering to become the savior. We do not interpret these verses in this way. For us Jesus is the "Lord." Michael, an archangel, is the one "like unto the Son of Man" (in fact in Hebrew the word Michael means "one like unto God"). The third person is the angel Lucifer. What is being depicted here is not a contest over which angel — Christ or Lucifer — would be the savior, but which angel — Michael or Lucifer — would be chosen to become Adam, the first man.

The point is that "all mankind were lost; and behold, they would have been endlessly lost were it not that God redeemed his people from their lost and fallen state" (Mos. 16:4) and that "God himself atoneth for the sins of the world, to bring about the plan of mercy, to appease the demands of justice, that God might be a perfect, just God, and a merciful God also" (Al. 42: 15). For this reason the Book of Mormon seeks to persuade us "that the right way is to believe in Christ, and deny him not; and Christ is the Holy One of Israel; wherefore ye must bow down before him, and worship him with all your might, mind, and strength, and your whole soul; and if ye do this ye shall in nowise be cast out" (2 Ne. 25:29).

God did not send someone else to be crucified to redeem his people. He did not shift the sacrificial burden onto anyone else's shoulders. God bore the cross himself. This is in part what is meant in the Book of Mormon by the condescension of God (1 Ne. 11:13–18). Jesus is the father we always feared or held in awe. Jesus is the son we can love and reach. Jesus is the spirit of truth (John 14:17–18) which lights every one coming into the world and nurtures them (15:5; D&C 93:2). He is the one who calls us home. Jesus is the keeper of the gate, where he employs no servant (2 Ne. 9:41). He, the Son, will reveal himself as the Father and will also show us the Mother, who is his Bride. But in his earthly ministry, Christ did not make all the mysteries of the godhead clear to us. Instead they were to be kept in reserve for a time "in which nothing shall be withheld, whether there be one God or many gods, they shall be manifest" and "all thrones and dominions, principalities and powers, shall be revealed and set forth upon all who have endured valiantly for the gospel of Jesus Christ" (D&C 121:28–29). Until this time comes for making the mysteries clear, we must content ourselves with looking through the dark glass of personal revelation and speculative theology.

We are admonished by the scriptures to seek for the revelation of God's mysteries (1 Ne. 10:19; Al. 12:9–11; D&C 11:7, 42:61, 63:23). This process is by its very nature speculative. This is not bad. Speculative theology can be an antidote for dogmatism. It can break open new categories. Mormonism presents plentiful substance for such speculation, but we shy away from the process largely because of our fear of being deceived, of encountering mysteries that might challenge our faith or lead us into apostasy or unbelief. These are real concerns. But they should not frighten us more than the opposite danger of being deceived by our accepted traditions and unofficial creeds and catechisms. The danger of doctrinal chaos is not greater than the danger of doctrinal stagnation.

The proper purpose of speculative theology is not to create a new gospel or a new church but to move us more deeply into our religion and to help us find hidden treasures of spiritual truth. Seen this way speculative theology is a process of mythmaking or myth interpretation. It is an attempt to harmonize and unify disparate elements in our theological story, to make sense of our religious experience.

Because speculation or mythmaking appears to be the only mechanism available to us for dealing in a non-dogmatic way with the God-concepts of Mormonism, we will use this approach to present our view of Jesus Christ and the Mormon pantheon and their relationship to the story of creation and redemption. This then is our version of the myth:

> In the First Place there was God, male and female. These two beings were mystically united and were the First Parent. With them were many other gods, also male and female, also mystically united. These beings constituted the godhead and were one in glory, power, mind. They were agreed as to their purpose.
>
> These beings did not always exist as members of the godhead nor were they required always to be contained within the godhead. The story of how they came to be one in the godhead can best be understood through the story of how we, their children, may become one with them.
>
> In the beginning the head God, who was the Mother and Father of All Living, took counsel with certain of the gods. These gods were united and had spirit offspring, who desired to be incarnated and become like their parents.
>
> The head God said to the gods that an earth would be created according to the ancient pattern by which many worlds had previously been made. This new world would be peopled with the embodied spirit offspring of these gods. The purpose in doing this was to allow these children to know for themselves good and evil, pleasure and pain, light and darkness, spirit and element. Through these experiences they would obtain knowledge and become one in the godhead.
>
> A time came when the first man, male and female, was to be chosen from among the noble and great ones, that is from among the gods. There was one, male and female, whose name was Michael (which means "in the likeness of God") who said send us. And there was another, Lucifer, who said send us. And God said, we shall send the first. Lucifer was angry at this rejection and left the godhead, and many of their spirit offspring and the offspring of others followed after them. Lucifer, which is Satan the male and female, desired to bring about life without suffering

death and for this reason left the council. When they appear it is often in the sign of God, which is a serpent. For this reason the serpent signifies both light and darkness, both life and death.

After the departure of Lucifer, God sought for a world which the spirits could inhabit. An old world depleted of life forms was found in the darkness of chaos. And God let their glory fall upon the earth. And God created the atmosphere and the sea and the land and the rain and the plants and the animals and planted a garden eastward in Eden for the habitation of man, male and female.

Then God summoned Michael, male and female, and said, here is the earth which we have made. But none of our children inhabit it. We must go down and be fruitful and multiply and replenish the earth. To do this we must break the circle of our perfection and make ourselves low so that our children might be raised up and be like us.

And they went down to the earth. And the head God blessed Michael and divided Michael the male from Michael the female by parting them as it were at the rib. In this way they were no longer mystically one. Then the head God, male and female, condescended to be divided themselves in this same way.

Michael the female was taken up into heaven and became the consort of the Father. In turn the Eternal Mother, the mother of all living, became the helpmeet of Michael the male, called Adam. In this way Michael the male would marry the Eternal Mother. And Michael the female would marry the Eternal Father. This is the pattern of the sacred marriage.

It was the plan of the Gods that the Eternal Mother should condescend to be the helpmeet of Adam. Her name would be Eve. And by her suffering and death, the way would be opened into mortality and temporality for the spirit offspring of the gods. Adam was selected to be her husband, her helpmeet, in bringing time out of eternity. And in the process he would learn to relate to her not as a son but as an equal. Together they would provide bodies for the spirits of the gods of the council.

It was the plan of the gods that in the meridian of time, the Eternal Father would become one of the descendants of Adam and Eve. He would be called Jesus. Through his suffering and death, the way would be opened into immortality and eternal life for all the sons and daughters of Eve and Adam. Michael the female was selected to be the mother of the son of God according to the flesh, the gateway through which eternity would be born out of time. Because it was their plan that the incarnated god be part human and part divine, Michael the male was selected to return to earth as a resurrected being and to beget the body of Christ upon Michael the female, that is, the Virgin Mary, Michael's divine consort.

These strange doings were carried out by the gods as they had planned. Other members of the godhead, the noble and great ones, condescended to suffer death for their children and to be incarnated on this earth to fulfill the purpose of God in the creation and redemption of the world. These incarnations are possible because the gods have the power to play many parts, to lay down their lives and take them up again, and to go from exaltation to exaltation until they acquire the power to resurrect the dead.

The Eternal Father and Mother because of their exalted status were the ones to make the greatest sacrifice. The lesser gods participate and in so doing achieve a more glorious resurrection. If we accept their love and sacrifice, then we shall become like them with power in the fullness of time to participate with them if we desire, to bring to pass the immortality and eternal life of our joint creation.

This is just a myth. It is a synthesis of many ideas. It is asserted to demonstrate the mythmaking process. It is harmless speculation because it is not asserted authoritatively as doctrine or dogmatically as the basis of a claim to a new dispensation. It is not an answer let alone a final answer. The final answers will probably not be relayed to us in words but in experiences, such as the parousia promised by Jesus. Until the day when our eternal parents take us home, we believe we must continue to speculate harmlessly and at the same time to hold fervently to the revelation of the divine in the person of Jesus Christ.

CHAPTER SEVEN

BEYOND MATRIARCHY,
BEYOND PATRIARCHY

In his book, *Jesus Through the Centuries*, Jaroslav Pelikan reminds us that the vitality of Jesus as the central figure in Western religious experience has depended on the flexibility and fullness of his character: "For each age, the life and teachings of Jesus represented an answer (or, more often, *the* answer) to the most fundamental questions of human existence and of human destiny" (2). According to Paul Tillich, the revelation of God in Jesus Christ was final and sufficient in the sense that Christ's nature is expansive enough to include every element necessary for the full revelation of the divine (2:119–20). This is classical Christian theology in both the Catholic and Protestant traditions. Since God revealed himself "once and for all" in his son Jesus, then Jesus becomes the center of human history and society; he becomes the model or norm for human behavior and the focal point for all meaning in existence. Karl Barth states this proposition as follows: "In Him [Jesus Christ] God reveals Himself to man. In Him man sees and knows God. . . . In Him God's plan for man is disclosed, God's judgment on man fulfilled, God's redemption of man accomplished, God's gift to man present in fullness, God's claim and promise to man declared. . . . He is the Word of God in whose truth everything is disclosed and whose truth cannot be over-reached or conditioned by any other word. . . . Except, then, for God Himself, nothing can derive from any other source or look back to any other starting-point" (111).

However, in the past few decades this Christocentric view has been seriously challenged. If Jesus Christ is the complete revelation of the divine, some ask, is the white Western male inherently superior and closer to the image of God than any other race or sex? And if Jesus is the model for human behavior, then how can women, minority races, or Third World peoples fully partake of salvation and participate in the Christian life? (Driver)

These are all good questions, but we will focus on one: Christ's maleness as a revelation of the divine nature. Why did God reveal himself in a male body? Does this affect the status of women? Why didn't a female goddess work the atonement? Or put in another way, "Can a male Savior save women?" (Ruether, 116)

The revelation of God as male has historically been an extremely important buttress of male domination of women. Since the founder of the Christian church was male, only men have been deemed worthy of ecclesiastical and spiritual authority. As recently as 1977 Pope Paul VI justified the banning of women from priesthood ordination on the grounds that since Christ was a male, priests — as his representatives — must also be male (Goldenberg, 5; Ruether, 126).

Because of this attitude many contemporary feminist theologians reject Christ as savior, although not all reject Christianity. At one end of the spectrum, feminist revisionists see much within the Christian church and tradition worth salvaging. In a sense they have turned the question around and have asked, "Can women save a male savior?" Though many of these women cannot accept Christ as the incarnation of God, they do accept him as an important prophetic figure and a savior of sorts, who treated women with great equality for his time and preached a gospel of love, healing, wholeness, and freedom. Feminist revisionists feel that when all the texts are re-examined and separated from their patriarchal overlays, the essence of the gospel emerges as liberation from classism, racism, sexism, and every other -ism (Reuther; Moltmann-Wendell; Fiorenza 1979b, 139–48). This invitation to full humanity is summed up by the apostle Paul: "There is neither Jew nor Greek, there is neither bond nor free, there is neither male nor female: for ye are all one in Christ Jesus" (Gal. 3:28). The revisionists also search canonical and non-canonical texts for feminine images of the divine and historical evidence of women in priestly roles. Among other important finds, Elaine Pagels has discovered evidence of God the Mother in the gnostic tradition, and Elizabeth Schussler Fiorenza has found textual evidence of early Christian women serving as apostles and bishops (1979a).

At the other end of the spectrum are feminists who feel that Christianity is so thoroughly sexist and patriarchal no reform is possible. They ask for nothing less than the death of both God the Father and the Son (Daly 1979; Goldenberg). For such radical feminists, rejecting

Christ as God incarnate is not enough. They also reject him as prophet: "Jesus Christ cannot symbolize the liberation of women. A culture that maintains a masculine image for its highest divinity cannot allow its women to experience themselves as the equals of its men. In order to develop a theology of women's liberation, feminists have to leave Christ and Bible behind them. Women have to stop denying the sexism that lies at the root of the Jewish and Christian religions" (Goldenberg, 22).

In Mormonism feminist issues rarely center on Christ. Instead the battle between patriarchy and matriarchy centers on the relative status of the Heavenly Father and the Heavenly Mother. Is she his subordinate or his equal? Also most feminist research in the Mormon tradition has not been theological but historical. It has focused on nineteenth-century Mormon women in a much-needed attempt both to reclaim a past and to discover possible sources of power for women.

One reason church members rarely ask "Why a male savior?" is that mainstream Mormons seldom think of Jesus Christ as God. He is seen as an elder brother, a mentor, an example of divine love, and a loving savior but rarely as God incarnate possessing the full characteristics of a god before he came to earth. Because Mormons do not usually think of Christ as God, the question of his maleness as a reflection of the divine image does not seem as crucial to us as it does to other Christians. Thus most Mormons would not see the question "Why a male savior?" as concerned with God's nature and personality but rather with the problem of role models. And for many Mormon intellectuals, the whole question seems to be irrelevant. They view the idea that Christ is God as a holdover from Joseph Smith's early trinitarian views, later contradicted by his discussion of a progressing God in the King Follett discourse. Personally we cannot find comfort in either the feminist rejection of Christ as God or in our own church's ambivalence about his status as God and his importance as an object of worship (McConkie 1981).

Feminist theology has served to re-emphasize present human experience as a basis for understanding scripture and tradition. As Rosemary Radford Ruether points out, the experiential basis for theological interpretation has always been recognized; the real contribution of feminism is the explosion of the objective/subjective dichotomy: "What have been called the objective sources of theology, scripture and tradition, are themselves codified collections of human experience. Human experience is the starting point and the ending point of the hermeneutical circle. Codified tradition both reaches back to roots in experience and is constantly renewed or discarded through the test of experience" (Ruether, 12).

The point is that we must rely upon our own experience to understand the meaning of scriptural tradition in our own lives. In a sense we are each like Joseph Smith praying in the grove. He realized he must approach God for himself, since the teachers of religion "understood the same passages of scripture so differently as to destroy all confidence in settling the question by an appeal to the Bible" (Joseph Smith 2:12).

At a time of crisis in our lives, we have each experienced the love and power of Jesus Christ. We are thus unable to reject him as savior or to be ambivalent about his divinity. Still we cannot believe his appearance on earth as a male was meant to reinforce male dominance. Our own experiences with him have been liberating. And yet we have not been able to dismiss Christ's maleness as meaningless or irrelevant. So what does his divine maleness mean? How does it illuminate and relate to the feminine?

Some time ago we began searching for the answers to these questions in the paradoxes of our religion. We live in a world of polar opposites, where everything is a "compound in one" (2 Ne. 2:11). In these unions opposites are not destroyed nor do they lose their individual identities. True union does not remove differences but balances them harmoniously: each opposite is valued and proves a corrective to the excesses of the other. The feminine and masculine are two opposites. Each principle must be valued independently, and yet each must simultaneously be seen in its relationship with the other. In our mortal state this is extremely difficult if not impossible to do. In Jesus' words, "No man can serve two masters" (Matt. 6:24). Perhaps he was suggesting that human finitude, at least in its Western manifestation, may be predisposed toward monotheism. Even in cultures where a pantheon of gods exists, there is often a head god and a rivalry among the lesser gods for supremacy. Many feminist theologians, who reject the worship of the Father God, ignore the option of worshipping a divine couple and advocate the worship of the Mother Goddess of prehistory.

Though we see much value in Goddess worship and feel men and women need access to a feminine deity, most modern Goddess worship is flawed by merely attempting to replace patriarchy with matriarchy, which is in our opinion equally destructive and sexist. Modern Goddess literature sometimes belittles men, who are said to be incapable of equality with the Goddess or with women but can only serve as sons and lovers (Goldenberg, 103).

And just as women in the past have been seen as the source of all evil, symbolized by Eve in Judeo-Christian literature, men have become scapegoats in extreme feminist literature (Daly 1978). The white Anglo-Saxon upper-middle-class man is seen as the source of all evil, even by moderates such as Ruether (179–80). The evil female seducers bow off the theological stage, and the evil male rapists step forward. The devouring vagina and the phallic sword, ancient symbols of the conflict, are by no means obsolete. For example, introducing her essay on the problem of women accepting a male savior, Rita Nakashima Brock recounts her experiences with rape victims and observes: "Essential to that ancient dominant-submissive rape ritual are the rules that give no power and authority to women except through our relationships of submission to men. In Christianity, are women therefore redeemed and legitimated by our reconciliation to the saving efficacy of a male savior?" (56). And in contemporary Mormon leader Hartman Rector's statement to Mormon feminist Sonja Johnson, he uses the image of a black widow spider, evoking the time-honored specter of the devouring female (Gottlieb, 212). So the battle between patriarchy and matriarchy goes on.

How can we get beyond the point where each side thinks of the other as an enemy? For us the answer rests in resolving the tension between our traditional views of the Fall and Redemption and our radical views about the nature of God and the cosmos. Though we believe that Christ was God incarnate and a revelation of the divine, we do not believe that his appearance on earth was a complete, "once and for all" revelation of God and the divine nature. And though we see Christ's sacrificial act on the cross at the center of human existence and history, we also see him encompassed about by the feminine. The feminine marks the boundaries at the far corners of our theological universe. For us the revelation of the Goddess, the consort of Christ who guards the gates at the beginning and the end of time, is inevitable.

To explain what we mean by these abstractions, we will use a model borrowed from Jungian psychology. Jung and his followers, Erich Neumann in particular, describe four stages of human development connected with chronological development, though not every person progresses through these successive stages in the same way and at the same rate. In fact many people may never emerge from the second stage, while others remain fixed in the third stage. And even those who reach the fourth stage are not fully developed individuals, for psychic growth is an ongoing, lifetime process.

The first stage is associated with the pre-natal or infancy period of human development. Here, according to Ann Ulanov, a Jungian analyst and theologian, "The ego exists in an undifferentiated wholeness; there is no distinction between inner and outer worlds, nor between image, object, and affect, nor between subject and object. The ego feels it is magically at one with its environment and with all of reality as a totality." The symbol of this stage is the *uroboros*, the mythical tail-eating serpent representing "circular containment and wholeness" (1971, 67).

In the second stage, called matriarchal by Erich Neumann, who connects this phase with early childhood, the ego sees the mother as the source of all life. Thus the Great Mother prevails as archetype of the unconscious individual (1954, 39). Creation myths, which typically separate the world into opposites, are often interpreted as birth stories of the ego associated with this phase. Though the ego begins to differentiate between itself and the "other" at this stage, it always does so in relation to its mother. Hence males and females learn to relate in fundamentally different ways. The male's primary mode of relationship depends on differentiation and discrimination, since he sees himself as distinct from his mother, as like to unlike. In contrast the female's primary mode of relationship is identification and relatedness, since she sees herself as like to like in her relationship with her mother. Thus, Ulanov extrapolates, the female's "ego development takes place not in opposition to but in relation to her unconscious" (1971, 244).

Neumann labels the third stage patriarchal and connects it with puberty (1954, 408). In ancient or primitive societies, this stage is memorialized by initiation rites in which the boy is separated from the world of women and brought into the ranks of men. The girl also undergoes initiation rites to bring her into the full status of an adult woman. Myth represents this stage by the loss of Eden through the Fall. Eating of the Tree of Knowledge of Good and Evil represents adult consciousness, which distinguishes fully between opposites: inner and outer, subject and object, right and wrong. According to Ulanov: "When the transition to this stage is successfully completed, the archetype of the Great Father becomes the sovereign deity and determines the values and goals of life. Consciousness, rationality, will power, self-discipline, adaption to the demands of external reality, and a sense of individual responsibility become important" (1971, 69). Moreover, in this stage anything feminine is likely to be rejected as inferior: "The values of the masculine are endorsed at the expense of feminine values; the principle of spirit is seen as opposed to earth; order and definition are seen as superior to creative fertility, commandments and obedience are valued over the virtues of acceptance and forgiveness, and becoming is seen as better than 'just being' " (1971, 69).

The final "integrative" stage requires a reconciliation of opposites — both within the self and in the self's relations with the outer world and other people. In particular all elements of the feminine which were rejected and repressed in the patriarchal phase must be reclaimed, both inwardly and outwardly. The integrative stage emphasizes unity and wholeness but not the undifferentiated wholeness of the first and second stages. Rather all parts of the whole are distinguished and recognized but are not perceived as rivals as in the patriarchal stage. Instead the parts are valued for their own unique contribution to the harmonious balance of the whole. It is a circling back to a wholeness lost, but a wholeness with new meaning. In T. S. Eliot's words: "And the end of all our exploring/ Will be to arrive where we started/ And know the place for the first time" (145).

The self, having gained strength through the ego differentiation and self-definition of the preceding stage, must now see the limitations of individual ego and return to the unconscious which it has rejected. As Ulanov puts it: "Whereas in the patriarchal phase the power of being was experienced in terms of the ego's personal goals and meanings, in the integrative phase the power of being is experienced symbolically in the mystery beyond the ego and the ego's powers" (1971, 72). The integrative phase is the most demanding because it cannot be achieved in isolation but must be worked out in relationship to the outer self, the inner self, the outer reality, the inner reality, other people, and God. But paradoxically only in this enmeshed stage does the individual become a separate, individual entity. Here a woman and a man fully represent more than their sexual or social roles; they are distinct individuals "as differentiated from having only collective identity as members of a certain family, or group, or nation" (Ulanov 1971, 71). Jung called this process of integration "individuation," the process by which we become fully our best selves.

In religious terms this process could be compared with sanctification. These four stages of human development can serve as a spiritual model explaining the development of the individual in mortality and also the purification of the individual as she or he makes the cosmic journey of existence from an intelligence to a resurrected and glorified being. In addition it can serve as a model for stages of cultural development.

Adapting this model to an eternal time line, we connect the first or pre-natal stage with our existence as intelligences, the formative period of our development about which we have the least knowledge. Though most Mormon theologians have emphasized the independent nature of intelligence, the actual statements we have on the subject focus on the uncreated nature of intelligence rather than on its complete separateness from God. Joseph Smith's curious statement that our minds or intelligences were "coequal with God himself" (WJS, 359) suggests that as intelligences we may have been connected in some way with our divine parents. This is similar to the undifferentiated wholeness of the Jungian model. Doctrine and Covenants 93:23 states that we "were also in the beginning with the Father; that which is Spirit, even the Spirit of truth." And in the 29 August 1857 edition of *The Mormon,* editor John Taylor suggested that we were once somehow part of the mind of God, "struck from the fire of his eternal blaze, and brought forth in the midst of eternal burnings" (Andrus 1968, 179).

The matriarchal or second stage we connect with the period prior to mortality. Though we have some popular notions of this stage derived from Mormon folklore and speculation, we actually know little about it. For our model the significance of this stage is its domination by the Great Mother figure. In the LDS tradition we most often associate God the Mother with the "pre-existence." In the hymn, "O My Father," Eliza R. Snow implies that her knowledge about the Heavenly Mother is intuited from the forgotten experience of a pre-natal world. Mormon writer Hugh Nibley points out in his discussion of the early Christian poem, "The Pearl," that it is the queen or mother, who is the first and last to embrace the departing hero as he leaves his heavenly home and begins his sojourn in the fallen world (1975, 272).

But is there any corroborative evidence that this stage was connected with a Great Goddess? If so who was she? What was her function and relation to us? And why was she superceded by the Father God? Scholars in the fields of religion, mythology, and archaeology currently debate whether there actually ever was a period of history or pre-history in which the Great Goddess was generally worshipped to the exclusion of a male deity. Some archaeological evidence in the form of cave drawings, goddess figures, and structures built in the shape of the goddess or her life-giving womb seems to support the notion that in prehistoric times a goddess was looked to as the source of all life and the obvious object of worship (Neumann 1955; Stone; Dames; Gimbutas; Thompson 1981). However, lack of written documents renders all such conclusions speculative.

To the archaeological evidence may be added the evidence found in ancient mythologies. Though the mythologies from the Near-Eastern world depict pantheons of gods in which a male deity is almost always supreme, the goddesses are still independent and powerful, often vying with the gods for power. In fact most creation stories from these cultures depict a strong theme of matriarchal-patriarchal struggles. Writes one scholar, "It is as though the writers [of the creation myths] believed that civilization could not begin or be sustained until the Feminine, as a dominant religious power, had been mastered and domesticated" (Phillips, 4). For example, in the Mesopotamian creation story, *Enuma elish*, the warrior-god Marduk first must kill "Tiamat the dragon-mother of all creation," and then "he creates the world by splitting her carcass into earth and sky; she herself becomes the primordial matter of the universe" (ibid., 5). The Greek poet Hesiod records a similar struggle in his version of the creation story, the *Theogony*, which reads almost like an anti-feminist tract. This misogynist view, which continued throughout the Hellenic civilization, profoundly affected the early Christian church and hence views of women throughout the Christian epoch (ibid. 1973, 77–94).

Many scholars feel that the struggle between the male and female deities in the Near Eastern mythologies represents the historical struggle between older civilizations dominated by the worship of the Great Mother and the rising powers which favored male gods. The domination of the male deities over their female counterparts would then symbolize the historical conquest of one culture over another (Thompson 1981; Morford, 41). But if there was a period, pre-mortal or otherwise, where such a goddess was worshipped, who was she?

Although names and places differ, there is continuity among the Goddess's varying images. For example, in Greek mythology Hera, Demeter, Aphrodite, and Artemis all have distinct personalities and functions, but each goddess is also seen at times, both in art and literature, as a mother goddess figure. Recently several scholars have also connected Eve, the only female in the Judeo-Christian creation story, with the Mother Goddess of other ancient religions. The pattern of her story parallels the accounts of other goddesses of the Near East. Also the name Eve (*Hawvah*) means according to Genesis 3:20 "the Mother of All the Living." This is the title most commonly associated with the great Mother Goddess. And Nibley points out that in Egyptian rituals all the goddesses went by this title at one time or another (1975, 166). In Sumerian mythology there is a connection between the title "mother of all living" and the title "lady of the rib" because of a similarity of word sounds. Both of these titles were used to refer to a goddess who healed the rib of the god of wisdom. According to Sumerian scholar Samuel Noah Kramer: "In Sumerian literature, therefore, 'the lady of the rib' came to be identified with 'the lady who makes live' through what may be termed a play of words. It was this, one of the most ancient of literary puns, which was carried over and perpetuated in the Biblical paradise story" (103).

Though Judeo-Christian tradition depicts Eve as merely mortal, Isaac Kikawada believes that "behind the character of Eve was probably hidden the figure of the creatress or mother Goddess" (34). John A. Phillips concurs with this supposition and adds: "The story of Eve is also the story of the displacing of the Goddess whose name is taken from a form of the Hebrew verb 'to be' by the masculine God, Yahweh, whose name has the same derivation. We cannot understand the history of Eve without seeing her as a deposed Creator-Goddess, and indeed, in some sense as creation itself" (3; cf. Millet, 52; Asche, 16–17; Heller, 655; MacDonald).

Despite its elevated associations, many feminists have objected to Eve's name since it was given to her by Adam. They argue that the act of naming gives the namer authority to define and limit the object named (Daly 1973, 8). And in the ancient Hebrew culture as well as in other Near Eastern cultures, people did believe that knowing the name of something gave the knower power over the object named. Jacob wrestling with the angel and Odysseus' conflict with the Cyclops illustrate the importance of this concept. Traditionally scholars have linked Adam's dominion over the animals with his power to give them names. The same interpretation can be ascribed to his naming of Eve and may lie at the root of much of man's domination of women. By keeping the power of words and history in their control, men have been able to define what women are and can be.

Phyllis Trible acknowledges but objects to this argument, since the formula used by Adam to name the animals is different than that which he uses to address Eve: "In calling the animals by name, 'adham establishes supremacy over them and fails to find a fit helper. In calling woman, 'adham does not name her and does find in her a counterpart. Female and male are equal sexes. Neither has authority over the other"

(1979, 77). Moreover, other traditions present alternative descriptions of this event. For example, in the Gnostic text "On the Origin of the World," Adam gives Eve her name not to dominate her but to recognize her superiority: "After the day of rest, Sophia sent Zoe, her daughter, who is called 'Eve (of life)' as an instructor to raise up Adam, in whom there was no soul, so that those whom he would beget might become vessels of the light. [When] Eve saw her co-likeness cast down, she pitied him, and she said, 'Adam, live! Rise up on the earth!' Immediately her word became a deed. For when Adam rose up, immediately he opened his eyes. When he saw her, he said, 'You will be called "the mother of the living" because you are the one who gave me life' " (Bethge, 173).

The naming of Eve is not the only part of the Hebrew creation story troubling to feminists. To them the whole story is merely an etiological myth, a story used to justify men's domination of women. For this reason many feel the story should be rejected along with the concepts of the Father God and Christ (Millett, 51–54). Recognizing the power of symbol and the need for myth in communicating any idea, some women have turned instead to the figure of Lilith (Plaskow, 198–209). According to Jewish legend, Lilith, Adam's first wife, came before Eve. Adam and Lilith had not been together very long before they began arguing — each refusing to take what they regarded as the inferior position in the sex act. When Adam tried to force Lilith beneath him, she uttered the ineffable name of God and disappeared. In order to fill her place, God created Eve (Patai 1980, 407–408).

We find the character of Lilith fascinating, but our sympathies rest with Eve. For us she is the central figure in the Garden of Eden story. Phyllis Trible, who also takes this view, maintains that Eve is not the deceptive temptress of the traditional interpretation but rather an "intelligent, sensitive, and ingenious" woman who weighs carefully the choice before her and then acts out of "a desire for wisdom" (1979, 78–80). Trible's interpretation lacks only a good reason why Eve's choice is commendable rather than disastrous and sinful.

Mormon theology supplies the perspective that the Fall was necessary for the development of pre-existent spirits. Obtaining physical bodies was part of God's plan, a step toward obtaining the power and likeness of God. Many Enlightenment thinkers interpreted the Eden story in this way. For them the Fall was also a *necessarium peccatum* (a necessary sin) and a *felix culpa* (a happy fault). The Fall was a step forward in human progress, since it took humankind "from blissful ignorance to risky but mature human knowledge, from animal instinct to human reason" (Phillips, 78).

Although Mormonism has treated Eve much more positively than has Christianity in general, she is still seen as deserving a position subordinate to Adam. For example, in the *Articles of Faith*, Apostle James E. Talmage, while insisting that we owe gratitude to our first parents for giving us the chance to experience mortality, argues in Pauline fashion that "Adam was not deceived, but the woman being deceived was in the transgression" (65). For BYU religion professor Rodney Turner, the story of the Fall shows why men have a rightful stewardship over women. Before the Fall men and women both had direct access to God; after the Fall men stood between God and women as their head to lead them back to God (52–53). Strangely Turner does not expect the celestial kingdom to rectify this fallen order: "And Woman, although a reigning majesty, will nevertheless continue to acknowledge the Priesthood of her divine companion even as he continues to obey the Gods who made his own exaltation possible" (311). We have heard other Mormons argue that since the Fall itself is not evil, then Eve's servitude is not simply a punishment or result of sin. It reaffirms her eternal subordinate status, which she overstepped when she took the initiative in eating the fruit.

Puzzling questions emerge in the common Mormon argument over whether Adam and Eve's action should be called a "sin" or a "transgression"—a distinction Mormon official Joseph Fielding Smith endorsed to emphasize the necessary nature of the Fall (1954, 1:112). If mortality is good then why do Adam and Eve commit a sin in bringing it about? Why did God forbid them to eat of the Tree of Knowledge of Good and Evil if that was the only way to introduce them into mortality, a necessary step in eternal progression? It seems at first that there is no way out of this dilemma. Either Adam and Eve (and especially Eve) were evil or God was evil.

Orthodox Christianity has chosen to put the blame on Eve and women in general. Other so called "heretical" sects of early Christianity, such as the Gnostics and Manichaeans, chose to see Adam and Eve as Prometheus figures. They dared to defy the jealous Old Testament God, who wished to keep humanity enslaved in ignorance. Mormonism tends to avoid the question by calling the Fall a "transgression" rather than a "sin." We do this perhaps because we are uncomfortable with the idea that we live in a world where choices between good and evil are not clearly defined.

In our view, however, the answer to this dilemma lies in the paradoxical aspects of the creation story itself. In the Garden are two trees: not the Tree of Good and the Tree of Evil but the Tree of Life and the Tree of the Knowledge of Good and Evil. These trees signal that for Adam and Eve — and for us — the choice between the trees is a complex one. Part of that complexity may revolve around the function of Eve as Mother Goddess. As "the Mother of All Living," Eve must be regarded as in some ways Adam's parent as well as his mate.

Mother Eve's virtue and greatness in our view rest in her ability to perceive paradox. The Garden of Eden was not a place of opposites. It was a place of maternal wholeness and protection, where Eve's children and also Adam could have all their needs met. But the child grows into a healthy adult only by becoming independent. If the mother fails to let the child go at the appropriate time, then she becomes a devouring mother instead of a nurturing one. It is really up to the mother to end the matriarchal stage and lead the child into its next phase of development — the patriarchal stage.

If distinguishing opposites is one of the main characteristics of the patriarchal stage, then Eve's choice can be interpreted as noble rather than impulsive. For she as "the Mother of All Living" saw that the life of all her children could come about only through her death. Consequently she put her life on the altar. She put to death her eternal life in the Garden of Eden to bring about their mortal life on earth. She clearly saw that "there was no other way." Nevertheless Eve's action though noble was still a sin because she had disobeyed God's commandment; she ate when she had been forbidden to do so. But what about God's part in this crime? Is he also culpable or at least at fault in some way? Why had he made it a sin to do that which was necessary for the progression of his children? Again the answer is not a simple one. It rests on a statement made by Joseph Smith: "That which is wrong under one circumstance, may be, and often is, right under another. God said 'Thou shalt not kill, at another time He said 'Thou shalt utterly destroy' " (PWJS, 508).

God may indeed have intended for Adam and Eve to eat the fruit to bring about mortality — but at another time or under another circumstance. Perhaps he wanted them to approach him with their dilemma and ask him how they could fulfill all of his commandments without eating the fruit. And perhaps he planned to grant them the fruit as a result of that request. Might the sin in the Garden be not in the fruit but in the failure to seek it from the hand of God? If so this interpretation sheds light on the nature of Satan's crime as well. His sin was to usurp God's prerogative to initiate Adam and Eve into the lone and dreary world. He was playing God. He wanted Adam and Eve and their posterity to worship him. This becomes even clearer in the Mormon temple version of the story, where Satan angry at his punishment asserts in his defense that he had only been doing what had been done in other worlds.

So Eve was deceived. But not by false ideas. Rather she was deceived because she mistook Satan for a messenger of God. The paradox is that though truth may come from many sources, we are required to obey God not another. Eve's choice to eat the fruit of the Tree of Knowledge of Good and Evil must be seen as a conscious and deliberate act of self-sacrifice. For she knew that her choice constituted her acceptance of the law of opposites: pleasure could only be known through pain, health through sickness, and life through death. She indicates this in the temple version of the story. Symbolically her choice was a yielding of matriarchal wholeness to patriarchal differentiation.

Seen in this light Eve's subordination to Adam was not so much a "prescription" of what should be but a "description" of what would be. God's statement is not that the husband ought to rule over his wife but that he *would* rule over her in the patriarchal stage. Phyllis Trible makes the following comment: "The divine speeches to the serpent, the woman, and the man are not commands for structuring life. To the contrary, they show how intolerable existence has become as it stands between creation and redemption.... Yet, according to God, she [Eve] still yearns for the original unity of male and female . . . however, union is no more, one flesh is split. The man will not reciprocate the woman's desire, instead he will rule over her. His supremacy is neither a divine right nor a male prerogative. Her subordination is neither a divine decree nor the female destiny. Both their positions result from shared disobedience. God describes this consequence but does not prescribe it as punishment" (1978, 123, 128).

When Eve decides to bring about mortality, she does so at a greater expense to herself than Adam. In the temple version Adam also sacrifices by willingly following the woman (Turner, 309; Talmage, 69–70). But Eve takes the blame for their action and assumes the subordinate status. Her action can be illumined by comparing it to the ancient ritual called the humiliation of the king, which was part of the rites of the ancient Mesopotamian New Year Festival. In this rite the king was stripped of his kingly vestments and power, beaten, and made to confess his responsibility for the sins of his people and to wander the streets as a beggar. Finally he or a substitute for him was put to death in order to fertilize the earth and renew the life of his kingdom and people (Engnell, 33–35, 66–67). Though this ritual most often involved the death of a king or male god, reversals were also possible. Mary Renault in her novel, *The Bull From The Sea* (1962), interprets the story of Theseus in this way: his wife Hyppolyta dies in the place of her husband as a substitute "king."

Several Near Eastern goddesses enact the pattern of the humiliation of the king or descent of the god. Inanna, an ancient Sumerian goddess who was queen of heaven and also of the City of Uruk, yielded her royal and sovereign power to her husband Dumuzi. She laid aside all her priestly offices and stripped herself of all her vestments of power, so she could penetrate the underworld and learn its mysteries. Once there she was pronounced guilty and struck dead by Ereshkigal, the goddess of the underworld, who hung her corpse "from a hook [or nail] from the wall" (Wolkstein, 60). After hanging there for three days and three nights, Innana was raised to life again by the intercession of the god of wisdom and other deities. She ascended to heaven, her power over life and death acknowledged by the Sumerians, who looked to her as a fertility goddess in control of all life cycles and seasons.

In the well-known Greek myth of Demeter and Persephone, Persephone, another fertility goddess, descended to the underworld. In the *Homeric Hymn to Demeter* (Athanassakis), she functions as a savior goddess. Though her descent to Hades introduced death and the seasons into what had been a state of paradise, her return to life and to her mother Demeter brought renewal. This myth is believed to be the subject of the ancient Eleusinian mysteries, which presumably gave to initiates hope for an idyllic after-life. Isis, an Egyptian goddess, also functioned as a savior goddess, both in myth through her descent to save Osiris and in cult practice through her promise of comfort and immortality to initiates (Bleeker).

Eve's story parallels these goddesses' in important ways. Like Isis, Eve acted as savior to bring life to others. Like Persephone, Eve's descent into mortality brought about the changing cycle of life and death and brought an end to the timeless state of paradisiacal bliss. And like Inanna, Eve made her pilgrimage into the world of darkness to acquire knowledge both of good and of evil. In their quests both Eve and Inanna turn their authority over to their husbands, who then rule over them.

In his *Lectures on Genesis,* Martin Luther talked about the fate of Eve and all womankind, who are "under the power of the husband." He compares their subjugated state to "a nail driven into the wall," fixed, immovable, and hemmed in by the demands of men. Hence their sphere of influence is confined to the home (1:202). Though Luther does not seem to be aware of the power of the symbol he has chosen, we see a connection with the goddess Inanna, whose corpse hung from the nail on the wall. Isaiah 22:23 and Ezra 9:8 represent God's grace, eventually manifest in the person of Jesus Christ, as a "nail in a sure place" on whom hangs "all the glory of his father's house." According to the *Interpreters Bible*, the "nail" was "a wooden peg which was driven into the wall and used for hanging domestic utensils" or keys (5:293). The same Hebrew word can also refer to a tent peg and appears in Isaiah 54:2: "lengthen thy cords and strengthen thy stakes." From this passage Mormons derive their usage of "stake" as a congregation.

Eve can be seen as the counterpart and parallel to Christ. For Eve too is a "nail in a sure place," the glory of her mother's house. Just as Eve sacrificed herself and was humiliated to bring her children into mortal life, so Christ sacrificed his life and was humiliated to bring his children into eternal life. As Eve's death was necessary to bring an end to the matriarchal stage, so Christ's death was necessary to bring an end to the patriarchal stage. Angela West comes to a similar conclusion: "Christ became Son and not Daughter because the symbol of female power, the goddess, had long since been done to death and needed no further humiliation; and because the daughters of Eve are always and everywhere being brought low through childbearing (or barrenness) and subordinated in the name of the patriarchal God. But in the person of Jesus Christ, God denies the godhead as patriarchal power, and reveals Godself in humanity, in the helpless infant, in the helpless crucified human being" (89).

Nineteenth-century Mormon writer Edward Tullidge, who believed Eve to be the Mother Goddess, also compared Eve's sacrifice to Christ's atonement: "Did motherhood refuse the cup for her own sake, or did she, with infinite love, take it and drink for her children's sake? The Mother had plunged down, from the pinnacle of her celestial throne, to earth, to taste of death that her children might have everlasting life. What! should Eve ask Adam to partake of the elements of death first, in such a sacrament! 'Twould have outraged motherhood! Eve partook of that supper of the Lord's death first. She ate of that body and drank of that blood" (198–99).

We have already implied that mortality can be compared to the third or patriarchal stage of the Jungian model. Seen in this larger perspective, patriarchy becomes a little easier to understand and accept, as just one act in a larger drama, a necessary step in the development of the individual personality and of the human race.

However, we do not mean to justify all the abuses of the feminine that have occurred in the previous millennia. Nor are we advocating doing nothing to correct them. Quite the contrary. Any power system not held in check by a loyal opposition tends quickly to become oppressive. However, though abuses are rampant, we should not refuse to see the necessity and good of the patriarchal stage. This necessity is illuminated for us by the incarnation of God in Jesus Christ, who is the revelation of the father figure for us.

Though Christ's mission was parallel to Eve's, it was not identical to it. Where Eve's mission occurred at the end of the matriarchal stage, Christ's mission occurred in the middle of the patriarchal—in the "meridian of time." And although his mission was meant, ultimately, to doom patriarchal authority, Christ did not put an abrupt end to the power systems as many had expected the promised Messiah to do. The reason for this is important. Christ's first coming was to define the true purpose of the patriarchal stage as a probationary state in which we must make distinctions, differentiate between opposites, and use our knowledge of good and evil to choose the way of liberty and life rather than the way of oppression and death (2 Ne. 2:27).

The symbol of Christ's coming into the world is the cross, represented at times by the two-edged sword, which can divide asunder both "joints and marrow" (D&C 6:2). Christ, as the word made flesh, is also the sword of God's justice, which "hangs over us" (3 Ne. 20:20). But the purpose of the sword is paradoxical. For though God's justice was meant for us, Christ was wounded for our sakes. The sword pierced his side. Thus, the sword which guards the Tree of Life becomes the iron rod that leads believers to the fruit of that tree. The sword is two-edged because it can both destroy life to administer death and destroy death to administer life. Those who allow themselves to be pierced by the word of God, which is his sword (Rev. 2:16), will receive new life, but those who harden their hearts against God's word will cut themselves off.

Christ's mission, like the double-edged sword, is paradoxical. For while he came to show that the true importance of the patriarchal function was to make distinctions and choose, the choice he advocated was the denial of goodness strictly in patriarchal terms and the affirmation of goodness as it exists in something other than ourselves.

Angela West comments on the irony of this paradox: "[The story of Christ is] the only scandal that patriarchy couldn't dare to contemplate; the story of God who de-divinised Godself and became a human historical male who turned out to be a complete political failure. It presents God as the ultimate contradiction to the worship of male power, and mocks all gods and goddesses, who are nothing more than this. In order to show men, and men in particular, that God was not made in the image of man, God became a man, and [when] that manhood was crucified, patriarchal pretensions were put to death. . . . Christ died on the cross cursed by the patriarchal law, and the law of patriarchy is thus revealed as curse and cursed" (88–89).

The very act of God's coming to earth as a human being makes a statement about the need we all have to see the good in our opposites. Though Christ was Father of Heaven and Earth, he made of himself a Son to bring about the Father's will. Though Christ was male, he assumed the role of female to give birth to a new creation through the blood he shed in Gethsemane and on the cross. Though Christ was creator, he became part of the creation to show the inseparability of the two. And though Christ was above all things, he descended below all things "that he might be in and through all things, the light of truth" (D&C 88:6).

The patriarchal stage is important. It allows the ego to develop by making it aware of contrasts and choices. But the important choice of the patriarchal stage is to deny the self-sufficiency of the ego and to move out into the integrative phase of wholeness. There all that was lost is reclaimed, particularly the feminine. The ego sees its own limitations, first by recognizing itself as separate from God, the primary "other," and next by recognizing its own insufficiency—recognizing that it is unable to rescue itself from its own egocentricity and its own narrow categories of perception. To be saved and transcend its limitations, the ego must deny its self-sufficiency and accept what is held in trust for it by God. Once this happens the self is prepared to begin the process of individuation.

However, this process is not easy because it requires the individual to risk uncertainty and personal pain. For men the main obstacle is overcoming the fear that this step means regression into the power of the matriarchal and the undifferentiated unconscious. It is difficult for men to give up their status in a patriarchal system providing them personal comfort and power. Women also can be fixed in the patriarchal structure, often because they are prisoners of a world view denying them power to see themselves as anything but subordinates. There is safety in the status quo. And even patriarchal systems have matriarchal substrata, which afford women status and comfort as the "real power behind the throne." A further danger threatens. Fear of freedom may precipitate women into a safe matriarchal structure, which values the feminine at the expense of the masculine (Ulanov 1971, 244–46).

It takes a heroic leap to get beyond matriarchy and beyond patriarchy to a stage of integration and individuation. Many of our fairy tales and hero myths describe the rescue mission involved in this process. Best known are the stories of the prince, who rescues the princess from the dragon or the tower. Equally important are the stories of the maiden, who rescues the prince from the spell of the witch or sorcerer keeping him in bondage. For us these stories show that each must rely on the other for power to develop into full personhood. When women acknowledge the good in men, men can be freed from the fear of the devouring feminine; when men acknowledge the power in women, women can be freed from the patriarchal prison.

The controlling deity for the integrative stage is neither the Great Mother nor the Great Father but the divine couple locked in an erotic embrace. We take this image from ancient myth and art. The *hieros gamos* (sacred marriage) was an important part of Near Eastern culture for at least 2,000 years (Kramer, 49). Behind this ritual was the belief that the sexual union of a god and goddess, sometimes a sky god and an earth goddess, would insure the fertility of land, beasts, and humans and the flourishing of civilization. The love stories of such gods as Isis and Osiris, Inanna and Dumuzi, Ishtar and Tammuz, and Hera and Zeus are no doubt related to this belief. As a variation on the ritual, a god could marry or have intercourse with a mortal woman, usually a queen or priestess, to assure the fecundity of the entire kingdom. In another variation a king and queen or priest and priestess could ritually reenact the marriage rite as representatives of the divine couple. Many lead plaques engraved with couples in sexual poses have been found in Near Eastern temple sites. According to Elizabeth Williams Forte, "Such scenes are considered representations of the cult of the sacred marriage, which took place annually in each Mesopotamian city" (Wolkstein, 187). Though the scenes are erotic, the positioning of the arms and legs and the intertwining of the god and goddess is such that ritual embraces are suggested, which seem to sacralize the sex act (Nibley 1975, 241).

In the Old Testament the Yahwist prophets repeatedly warned the children of Israel to abandon the worship of the goddess Asherah/Astarte and to forsake her high places. However, in this century some scholars suggest there may have been legitimate Hebrew rituals celebrating the marriage of Yahweh and his consort during certain periods of Israel's history (Hooke, 176–91). For example, Savina J. Teubal explores this ritual in some depth in *Sarah the Priestess* (1984), and Raphael Patai's *The Hebrew Goddess* (1978) provides a thorough analysis of the influence on Judaism of the Hebrew goddess's marriage to Yahweh.

Perhaps the most striking image of the union of Israel's God with the feminine is seen in the Holy of Holies itself. Patai asserts that the Ark of the Covenant, the holiest object in the temple and the center for legitimate worship, contained two slabs of stone which represented Yahweh and his consort. "The idea slowly gained ground," explains Patai, "that the one and only God comprised two aspects, a male and a female one, and that the Cherubim in the Holy of Holies of the Second Temple were the symbolic representation of these two divine virtues or powers. This was followed by a new development, in Talmudic times, when the male Cherub was considered as a symbol of God, while the female Cherub, held in embrace by him, stood for the personified Community of Israel" (1978, 97–98).

So we come again to the image of the divine couple in an erotic embrace. The image of the sacred marriage is not only important historically, but can be projected into the future as well, since the image is also used in Judeo-Christian eschatological literature to represent the promised revival of the marriage relationship of Yahweh and the community of Israel and the marriage of Christ to the church. In both instances, the marriage symbolizes the time, after tribulation and judgment, when repentant Israel or the church returns to God, her husband.

Bible scholar Joachim Jeremias points out that in the rabbinic literature the "marriage time" is often associated with the messianic period of peace and feasting (Taylor, 88). No doubt the rabbis took this idea from the prophets, who often use marriage language to describe the relationship between Yahweh and Israel (i.e, Is. 54:5; Jer. 3:14, 31:32; Hos. 2:19–20). Though Israel is often rebuked as an errant wife, in the messianic period she will be pure and magnificent, a bride adorned with jewels (Is. 61:10). And the Lord will no longer look upon her with disfavor, but "as the bridegroom rejoiceth over the bride, so shall thy God rejoice over thee" (62:5).

All four gospel writers as well as the writer of the Book of Revelation use the bridegroom symbol in connection with Christ. Vincent Taylor argues that the use of such imagery shows Christ's "Messianic consciousness, and especially His close relationships with His community" (88). This argument appears warranted by the bridal imagery in the Book of Revelation: "And I John saw the holy city, new Jerusalem, coming down from God out of heaven, prepared as a bride adorned for her husband. And I heard a great voice out of heaven saying, Behold, the tabernacle of God is with men, and he will dwell with them, and they shall be his people, and God himself shall be with them, and be their God" (21:2–3). Patai, although a Jewish scholar, includes this passage in his book *The Messiah Texts*, because the author of Revelation though Christian nevertheless "described the heavenly Jerusalem in Jewish apocalyptic-Aggadic terms" (1979, 200).

In the New Testament as in the Old, the bridal imagery is connected with an eschatological end period. This is especially evident in the two marriage parables found in Matthew 22 and 25. The kingdom of heaven is compared to ten virgins, who are awaiting the arrival of the bridegroom. Only virgins with oil in their lamps may enter the marriage feast when the bridegroom finally arrives. The listener is admonished: "Watch therefore, for you know neither the day nor the hour wherein the Son of man cometh" (Matt. 25:13). Earlier in Matthew 22 guests at the marriage feast of the king's son must have a wedding garment to be included among the participants. Revelation 19 almost seems to be a commentary on the parable, for we are told that the "fine linen is the righteousness of the saints" and "Blessed are they which are called unto the marriage supper of the Lamb" (Rev. 19:8–9). Looking forward to the marriage of the Lamb is, therefore, synonymous with looking forward to the second coming of Christ.

Such imagery can also be found in LDS scripture, in particular the Doctrine and Covenants, where bridal imagery is connected with the purification of Zion and the second coming of Christ. Echoing the language of Revelation, Doctrine and Covenants 88:92 predicts the coming of the bridegroom during a period of tribulation and judgment: "And angels shall fly through the midst of heaven, crying with a loud voice, sounding the trump of God, saying: Prepare ye, prepare ye, O inhabitants of the earth; for the judgment of our God is come. Behold, and lo, the Bridegroom cometh; go ye out to meet him" (cf. D&C 133:10, 19). As in the New Testament, the Doctrine and Covenants bridegroom image is linked to the marriage supper: "Yea, a voice crying — Prepare ye the way of the Lord, prepare ye the supper of the Lamb, make ready for the Bridegroom" (65:3; cf. 58:8–11). The Doctrine and Covenants also employs the ten virgins, who as representatives of the community of Israel are warned to be prepared for the coming of the Bridegroom: "Wherefore, be faithful, praying always, having your lamps trimmed and burning, and oil with you, that you may be ready at the coming of the Bridegroom" (3:17).

Although the bridegroom image is familiar, we seldom focus on what it suggests about the place of the feminine. Viewing the second coming as a marriage means seeing the ushering in of the millennial kingdom as a union of opposites and a re-affirmation of the values of the feminine, for the marriage of the Lamb to the Bride implictly elevates the female to the status of divinity. Some scholars argue the opposite is true: the symbol of Christ's marriage reaffirms patriarchal marriage. The male continues to rule since Christ's bride is his creation, the church, which must always be subordinate to him (Ruether, 141; Eph. 5:22–25).

But other scriptures and traditions do not speak of the messianic marriage time in patriarchal terms. The writer of Revelation describes "the bride, the Lamb's wife," as a beautiful city not of the earth but come down from heaven, "the holy Jerusalem," having "the glory of God [i.e, having glory equal to God's]: and her light was like unto a stone most precious " (Rev. 21:10–11). The Jewish mystical writings of the thirteenth-century Zohar similarly suggest that the Matronit (Lady or Matron) was part of the godhead in the beginning (the divine tetrad: Father, Mother, Son and Daughter). She was the daughter and the queen married to her brother, the son and king (Patai 1978, 126–52). But she went wandering in the earth in search of her lost children. In the messianic period, she is to be restored to her rightful place in full union with the king. She will shake off the dust and ashes of mourning and put on beautiful garments representing the authority and power she possessed in the beginning (Is. 52:1–2; D&C 113): "But the Holy One, blessed be He, will bring back the Matronit to her place as in the beginning. And then what will the rejoicing be? Say, the joy of the King and the joy of the Matronit. The joy of the King over having returned to her and having parted from the Slave-woman [Lilith], as we have said, and the joy of the Matronit over having returned to couple with the King" (Patai 1979, 186–87).

In the Midrashic literature the gathering of Israel during the messianic period will be led by the Shekhina, God's spirit and consort: "The day on which the exiles will be ingathered is as great as the day on which the Tora was given to Israel on Mount Sinai.... The Shekhina will walk at their head ... and the nations of the world after them, and the prophets at their sides, and the Ark and the Tora will be with them. And all Israel will be clothed in splendor and wrapped in great honor, and their radiance will shine from one end of the world to the other" (Patai 1979, 185).

By separating God's consort from her errant offspring, these writers redeem the wife of Yahweh from a fallen and therefore subordinate role. Thus her exile is not for her own sins but a voluntary sojourn as she laments the loss of her children in the manner of Rachel mourning for her children or the goddess Demeter mourning the loss of Persephone. In the following passage from the Zohar, the writer quotes Isaiah to the effect that the Matronit's children are responsible for her exile. And without her the king is left less than complete and unworthy of glory: "It is written, 'Behold, for your iniquities were ye sold, and for your transgressions was your mother put away' (Is. 50:1). The Holy One, blessed be He, said, 'You have brought it about that I and you shall wander in the world. Lo, the Matronit will leave her Hall with you. Lo, the whole Hall, Mine and yours, has been destroyed, for the Hall is not worthy of the King except when He enters it with the Matronit. And the joy of the King is found only in the hour in which He enters the Hall of the Matronit, and her son is found there with her. [Then] all of them rejoice together'" (Patai 1979, 187).

Isaiah also uses the Jerusalem symbol to depict a mother at one time and at other times her children, which has the effect of elevating the mother figure. In the end time the mother, Jerusalem, is no longer desolate but fertile and life-sustaining: "Rejoice ye with Jerusalem, and be glad with her, all ye that love her: rejoice for joy with her, all ye that mourn for her: That ye may suck and be satisfied with the breasts of her consolation; that ye may milk out, and be delighted with the abundance of her glory" (Is. 66:10–11). This is not a description of an ordinary mother nourishing her children, for Jerusalem's milk will flow like a river to her children while she dandles them on her knees (66:12; Rev. 22:1). This portrayal evokes the image of a fertility goddess, who is commonly represented nursing a child or young god and is often a large-breasted or many-breasted figure (see Neumann, 32–46). We see a similar depiction of Jerusalem as mother in Isaiah 66:8, where she is described as a woman who "travailed" and "brought forth her children."

Revelation 12 includes an image of a woman in labor, who delivers a "man child." In his commentary on Revelation, J. Massyngberde Ford notes that the words "woman" or "women" occur so many times "that the woman symbol is almost as important as the Lamb" (38:188). Moreover, the woman or women portrayed are powerful and pure. For example, the woman in Revelation 12 is described as "a great wonder in heaven," a mighty woman who is "clothed with the sun, and the moon under her feet, and upon her head a crown of twelve stars" (Rev. 12:1). She fights with the great dragon, thus reminding us of Eve in the Garden pitted against the serpent. Being clothed with the sun implies equality with a male sky god, while the moon under her feet connects her with the old earth goddess, who often bore that symbol. The crown is a symbol of power and kingship (Is. 62:3–4), while the twelve stars may be connected with the Zodiac, which was often for Jews a symbol of the twelve tribes (Ford, 197).

Moreover, this imagery connects the bride with still another important set of scriptures. Ford indicates that the text nearest to the portrayal of the woman in Revelation 12 is "the description of the bride in Song of Songs, 6:10" (196). The Song of Songs (or Song of Solomon) compares the bride's beauty to the sun and the moon: "Who is she that looketh forth as the morning, fair as the moon, clear [or bright] as the sun, and terrible as an army with banners?" (6:10). The image is of a powerful woman whose majesty surpasses that of a mere mortal. This is one reason some scholars feel that the poem can be traced back "to the ancient myth of the love of a god and a goddess on which the fertility of nature was thought to depend" (May, 815). Others feel that the poem simply represents erotic love (Pope, 192–205). Its sensuous language has caused a debate since ancient times about the suitability of including the Song of Solomon in the canon. By interpreting it allegorically as the love between God and Israel or Christ and the church, rabbis and later the church fathers decided to include it in the canon (ibid., 89–132).

Though official interpretations of these images in the Song of Songs may emphasize the spiritual, we have already seen how the scriptural images of this marriage relationship fit into the pattern of the

Mesopotamian sacred marriage, which was both spiritual and erotic. In a detailed analysis and comparison with Sumerian sacred marriage songs, Samuel Noah Kramer shows how the Song of Songs follows the same pattern in terms of its setting, images, language, complex dramatic structure, stock characters, themes, and motifs (92ff). One example is "the portrayal of the lover as both shepherd and king and of the beloved as both bride and sister" (92). But for us the most important comparison concerns the bride. In the Sumerian marriage songs, the bride is Inanna or her human substitute. In the Song of Songs, the bride appears first as a mortal, and yet the description already quoted from chapter 6 suggests deity. Marvin Pope observes: "The combination of beauty and terror which distinguishes the Lady of the Canticle also characterizes the goddess of Love and War throughout the ancient world, from Mesopotamia to Rome, particularly the goddess Inanna or Ishtar of Mesopotamia, Anat of the Western Semites, Athena and Victoria of the Greeks and Romans, Britannia, and, most striking of all, Kali of India" (562).

Another remarkable aspect of the Canticle is that the song describes not the love of a dominant male and subordinate female but their mutuality in love. The song contains long dialogues between the two lovers. Phyllis Trible says that in the Song of Songs there is "no stereotyping of either sex. . . . The portrayal of the woman defies the connotations of 'second sex.' She works, keeping vineyards and pasturing flocks . . . she is independent, fully the equal of the man" (1978, 161). Trible sees a connection between the Garden of Eden and the garden in the Song of Songs. Eden is the place of lost glory, but the garden of the Canticle represents a place of redeeming grace, where the errors of Eden are blotted out and man and woman are reconciled to God and each other. Whereas in Eden the woman's "desire became his dominion, . . . in the Song, male power vanishes. His desire becomes her delight. . . . Appropriately, the woman sings the lyrics of this grace: 'I am my lover's and for me is his desire' " (1978, 160).

While working on his translation of the Old Testament, Joseph Smith deleted the Song of Songs on the grounds that it was "not inspired writing" (Matthews 1975, 87). We find it ironic that in spite of his rejection, the description of the bride from this text, which is found nowhere else in the Bible, appears in three of Joseph Smith's revelations: Doctrine and Covenants 5:14, 105:31, and 109:73. In each instance the image describes the purified community of Zion or the church. In Section 109 Joseph prays: "That thy church may come forth out of the wilderness of darkness, and shine forth fair as the moon, clear as the sun, and terrible as an army with banners; And be adorned as a bride for that day when thou shalt unveil the heavens" (vv. 73–74).

So who is the bride? Is she a heavenly goddess? Or the earthly community of Israel? Is it possible that the bride is a symbol of both? Could there be a real goddess—Eve, Mary, the Holy Spirit, Zion, or Jerusalem—as well as a spiritual community of the faithful—Israel, the church, or the covenant people of the Lord? And are the faithful on earth to await like ten virgins not only the coming of the bridegroom but the unveiling of the heavenly bride from above? Is there to be a sacred marriage between her and Jesus Christ? And when is this wedding to occur?

Orson Pratt wrote in *The Seer*: "There will be a marriage of the Son of God at the time of His second coming" (170). Of course the purpose of Pratt's discourse was to show the reasonability and importance of plural marriage, for he stated that Christ would have many wives: the queen described by John the Revelator as the "Bride of the Lamb" and others, including the five wise virgins, who would marry him at the "marriage feast of the Lamb."

Is the final sacramental feast of Doctrine and Covenants 27 a wedding supper? How does all this relate to the statement of Joseph Smith that at Adam-ondi-ahman Adam would turn the keys over to Christ? Who are the virgins who will enter the bridal chamber? What do these symbols mean in terms of Christian and Mormon eschatology?

These questions will not likely be answered either through historical analysis or even through the efforts of speculative theologians. However, as we contemplate and analyze the symbols and rituals of our own tradition and compare them with those of others, we may conclude at least that embedded in Mormonism as in Christianity and Judaism are hidden traces of a *hieros gamos*, a sacred marriage. Such a theology with its union of male and female may serve as the foundation for a fuller and more completely integrated spiritual experience for many people. It is more likely to encourage personal individuation and to create an enviornment where men and women might mature with greater facility beyond the limits and tensions of mere matriarchy or mere patriarchy.

And though the emergence of such a theology may be slow, it rustles through the pages of scripture and seems to illuminate the verses of the "new song" revealed in the Doctrine and Covenants 84:100–101, which is to be sung by the faithful in the end time:

> The Lord hath gathered all things in one.
> The Lord hath brought down Zion from above.
> The Lord hath brought up Zion from beneath.
> The earth hath travailed and brought forth her strength;
> And Truth is established in her bowels;
> And the heavens have smiled upon her;
> And she is clothed with the glory of her God.

CHAPTER EIGHT

THE MARRIAGE OF
TIME AND ETERNITY

In the context of Christian orthodoxy, the word "time" refers to anything available to mankind through the senses, anything which can
be imagined by the human mind. "Eternity," on the other hand, refers
to a realm entirely beyond time. Orthodoxy does not see eternity as the
opposite of time, because the orthodox believe that eternity can have
no opposite. It is beyond all such definitions and comparisons. Eternity
is unknowable because it partakes of God's infinite and "totally other"
nature. For centuries orthodoxy has taught that upon death all humans
will enter eternity to experience either the bliss of heaven or the tor-
ments of hell.

In contrast progressive Mormonism (which emphasizes the finite
and immanent over the transcendent characteristics of God) teaches
that eternity partakes of location, duration, and extension. It is a distinct place, where things and people exist and events occur. It is divis-
ible, for it is comprised of the celestial, terrestrial, and telestial kingdoms, the realm of pre- and post-mortal spirits, and the realm of outer
darkness. After the resurrection most humans will dwell in eternity in
a state of harmony and peace, untainted by sorrow, corruption, sin,
and evil.

We think Joseph Smith's revelations contradict elements of both
points of view. Where orthodoxy sees eternity as inherently incompre-
hensible, Joseph Smith taught that its incomprehensibility lies in
our lack of knowledge and experience not in its existence beyond all
categories of thought. The progressive Mormon idea that eternity is
somehow beyond sorrow, corruption, or evil is also contradicted by
Joseph Smith.

A revelation to Joseph dated 5 April 1843 tells us that "angels do
not reside on a planet like this earth" but "in the presence of God on a

globe like a sea of glass and fire" (D&C 130:7). Angels do not exist in some great beyond but on a globe. God too lives on a planet. "The place where God resides is a great Urim and Thummim," and "this earth, in its sanctified and immortal state," will be just such a "Urim and Thummim to the inhabitants who dwell thereon" (vv. 8–9). This earth when glorified will become the dwelling place of Christ (v. 9). The point is that eternity partakes of location.

The Book of Abraham holds that eternity also partakes of extension. Abraham "saw the stars that they were very great, and that one of them, Kolob, was nearest unto the throne of God" (3:2). The text makes it clear that spatial proximity to God is not employed here as a metaphor: "for I am the Lord thy God: I have set [the planet Kolob] . . . to govern all those which belong to the same order as that upon which thou standest" (v. 9). The earth, a temporal sphere, is revealed to be part of a single continuity which includes the eternal place where God in person dwells. This idea contradicts the notion that eternity is time's transcendent other. Instead time and eternity are presented as two perceptions or components of a single, integrated cosmos.

Joseph Smith's revelations also tell us that eternity, like time, partakes of duration. Section 19 of the Doctrine and Covenants censures as false the orthodox view of hell as a state of endless and eternal damnation. The revelation asserts that the words "endless" and "eternal" do not refer to timelessness but are really alternative names for God (vv. 10–12). Thus the phrases "endless punishment" and "eternal punishment" mean only that the source of the punishment is God, whose names are Endless and Eternal, not that the punishment itself lasts forever. This also means that God and angels though they exist in eternity experience duration.

The Abraham text informs us further that the cosmos consists of different fields of time. The closer we approach the planet where God is, the more slowly time advances. Earth, because its time moves at a relatively rapid rate, is a lower order planet. Spheres of a higher order are deemed superior, not because they are larger or even habitable from a human perspective but because they exist in fields where time moves more slowly than it does on earth (3:5–8). On Kolob, we are told, time moves at the same speed it does for the Lord: one Kolob day equals a thousand years on earth (vv. 4–5). These revelations tell us of an eternity of location, extension, and fields of relative duration.

In Joseph Smith's Book of Moses, we are presented with the story of the prophet Enoch, who in vision beholds God weeping: "And Enoch said unto the Lord: How is it that thou canst weep, seeing thou art holy, and from all eternity to all eternity?" (7:32). Enoch is surprised by this vision. Apparently he held the inaccurate view that eternity was proof against sorrow. In response to his question, he is told: "Behold, these thy brethren . . . are the workmanship of mine own hands . . . but behold they are without affection, and they hate their own blood; . . . Satan shall be their father, and misery shall be their doom; . . . wherefore, should not the heavens weep, seeing these shall suffer" (vv. 32–37). In the Book of Abraham text too, we get a discomfiting glimpse into heaven. There Satan, unhappy with God's plan to create the earth, refuses to submit and leads away many after him (3:26). He and his fellow rebels are eventually cast out of heaven into the earth, where they continue their war upon Michael, his angels, and humans (Rev. 12:7). Such tales of discord do not say much for heaven as a place of uninterrupted peace and security. This contradicts the orthodox and popular Mormon view of an eternity devoid of strife. If all of this is so, then the question remains: What distinguishes time from eternity?

The key to the answer is found in a revelation which states: "The same sociality which exists among us here [in time] will exist among us there [in eternity], only it will be coupled with eternal glory, which glory we do not now enjoy" (D&C 130:2). What distinguishes time from eternity then is not location, duration, extension, sorrow, or evil but God's "glory," which arrests the forces of decay, fragmentation, disunity, mortality, change, and exhaustion. Without God's glory, the entropic processes are not stopped and the elements tend toward disorganization. Eternity is eternal because it is dominated by health, integration, unity, immortality, constancy, and energy. A full measure of God's glory creates a condition of duration without decay, of life without death, of motion without exhaustion — fields of celestial eternity. The lack of a fullness of glory creates in the universe fields of terrestrial and telestial eternity and even fields of outright temporality. So long as we are without a fullness of this glory, disintegration is inevitable. But for resurrected beings filled with celestial glory, time is no longer: "Then shall they be gods, because they have no end; . . . they shall be from everlasting to everlasting, because they continue; . . . Then shall they be gods, because they have all power" (132:20). To be glorified means to have the power of creation and recreation, the power over decay and dissolution, the power to comprehend all things.

According to Section 93, glory is composed of "light and truth" (v. 36) and truth is "knowledge of things as they are, as they were, and as they are to come" (v. 24). This means that the glory of God is a reservoir of information. In Moses 7:61 we are told that the sanctified will be blessed with "the record of heaven; the Comforter, the peaceable things of immortal glory; the truth of all things; that which quickeneth all things; which maketh alive all things; that which knoweth all things, and hath all power." The glorified will have a knowledge of things as they are, as they were, and as they are to come.

To understand how it is possible to have such knowledge, particularly of the future without pre-determining what the future will be, it is first necessary to consider that the glory or mind of God is comprised of both light and truth (D&C 93:36). This idea suggests that God's mind or glory is a duality. Our lives, the world, and the universe contain myriad paradoxes because God is a paradox. Not only is the divine nature a duality of flesh and glory, but God's glory is itself a duality of light and truth.

The Book of Mormon asserts that duality lies at the root of being. In a difficult, if frequently quoted passage from the Book of Nephi, we are told: "For it must needs be, that there is an opposition [not "to" all things, but] *in* all things. If not so . . . righteousness could not be brought to pass, neither wickedness, neither holiness nor misery, neither good nor bad. Wherefore, all things *must needs be* a compound in one; wherefore, if it should be one body it must needs remain as dead, having no life neither death, nor corruption nor incorruption, happiness nor misery, neither sense nor insensibility. Wherefore it must needs have been created for a thing of naught . . . for there could have been no creation of things, neither to act nor to be acted upon" (2 Ne. 2:11–13). As a compound in one, God's glory is a single reality arising upon the interaction between "light" and "truth." Light or energy has two forms, a passive one, similar to "rest energy," and an active form, similar to "kinetic energy." Truth also has two forms, a passive one, consisting of a knowledge of things past, and an active form, consisting of the knowledge of the future — or more accurately the knowledge of all the possible futures.

We believe that in God's view there is not just one future but an infinite set of potential futures. God has a knowledge of all these potentialities. Of course not all these potentials will be actualized, so not all the possible futures will become the present and the past. For example, one may exit a building through many doors. All of these possibilities are real until a particular door is chosen and used. Then all the potentials resolve into the chosen possibility. At the moment of moving through the door, one future is actualized as the present and comes to rest as a historical event, a fixture of the past. This concept is complicated by the suggestion that every actualization creates a new infinite set of possibilities taking into account the new actualized reality. Thus in every moment both the potential and the actual universes are renewing themselves. This is why from God's perspective everything is always new.

The transformation of potential to actual is not the creation of something from nothing. Reality is transformed from one mode of being (a potential) to another (an actual). Thus for God everything is not only new, it is also everlasting. Through such transformation, the futures become the present and the past. If there were only one future, God would need only have a knowledge of it, for it would be the same as the present and the past. But the scripture does not say that the past, the present, and the futures are the same. It says they are "continually before" God. Although God knows all possible futures, we think God does not know with absolute certainty which of the futures will be actualized by the free choices of others. But God knows all the futures that may be actualized by such choices. This is how God can know the futures without determining which of them will become the present and the past.

In addition to knowing the potential futures, God also observes the actualization of the one chosen future as it is transformed from potentiality into actuality. This moment is the present.

God also has a knowledge of the past, which is different from a knowledge of the potential futures or of the moment of actualization. Since the potential futures are constantly recreating themselves every time one of them is actualized and since the present is in a constant state of flux, a knowledge of the past is a knowledge of all of the presents that have ever been. God not only sees us as we are from moment to moment but also remembers us as we were at every moment of our lives. When this earth passes away, as it eventually must, it will no longer exist in the present or the futures. And at that time, a knowledge of the present and the future will provide no knowledge of this earth. But because God has a knowledge of the past, the earth will continue to exist in God's mind as a planet that was. In fact every moment of the history of the earth and the lives of each of its inhabitants will continue to be known by God.

Reality, in our view, consists of an ethereal potentiality becoming a liquid actuality becoming the solid fixture we call the past. But we must remember that every time a potential future becomes an actual present, the infinite set of potentials is rearranged to create new potential futures. For example, if we at this moment were to call our daughters into our study, that actuality would set up a new set of potentials which would likely result in our not finishing this paragraph. If we do not call them, a different set of potentialities would obtain. So reality is not only potentiality becoming actuality but also actuality creating new potentialities.

Like potentials, actuals are also composed of dualities. The actualized universe is composed of spirit (energy) and element (matter). The interaction of these two creates events. With every event the set of potentials fluctuates and realigns itself but remains constant at infinity, while the set of actualities increases in number. Because we live in the illusion that actualities are real but potentials are not, it is hard to imagine how reality can exist in God as a numberless set of possibilities waiting to emerge as actual reality.

The revelations suggest that what we have here been referring to as a knowledge-of-the-possible-futures or truth-in-its-active-mode is in fact apparent to our senses in an unexpected form. Section 88 of the Doctrine and Covenants reads as follows: "And there are many kingdoms: for there is no space in the which there is no kingdom; and there is no kingdom in which there is no space, either a greater or a lesser kingdom." At first blush this verse seems to say only that there are kingdoms everywhere in the universe. But what are we to make of the phrase, "for there is no space in the which there is no kingdom?" What kingdom exists in the space between the earth and the moon? Or in the space between the nucleus and the electron of a hydrogen atom? And what about the rest of the verse? Why go to the trouble to reveal that every kingdom has space in it?

This verse suggests that space itself is part of the "truth" component of God's glory or mind. Space, perhaps, constitutes the reservoir of infinite potentialities, which may be transformed into the finite actualities we experience as matter and energy. We are not here reasserting the orthodox notion of *creatio ex nihilo*. Rather we are implying that the finite universe was created from the infinite potentials we experience as space.

We speculate that space is the Divine Something out of which everything, spiritual and elemental, was precipitated. Space is not perceived as such because, to use the words of the revelation, it is "too fine or pure" (D&C 131:7), the pure "truth" so to speak. What could be purer than space, the invisible linkage, the consciousness of God, the naked, divine psyche, the matrix of universal reality. Thus there may exist latent at every point of space, no matter how small, an infinite set of possibilities capable of developing into actuality by means of a "quantum leap." This potential dimension of God's glory injects into the finite universe the element of infinitude. Because God is a being of matter and energy, God is finite, but because God has access to unlimited potentiality, God possesses an infinite capability.

Of course, these are but tenuous speculations that may or may not be useful. What the revelations of Joseph Smith teach is that time and eternity are permanent fixtures of the cosmos. They exist side by side, perhaps even intruding into one another. A pocket of time may become an eternity, which may eventually spawn new pockets of time, that themselves may be transformed into new eternities. And those who have eternal life are those with access to a fullness of God's glory or power that allows them to continue from time to eternity and from eternity to time, again and again (D&C 29:30–33). This metaphysics, as we shall explore further, forms the backbone of some of Joseph Smith's most important contributions to Christian doctrine: his teachings on the nature of God and humanity, good and evil, and Christian redemption.

Joseph Smith declared the paradox of time and eternity. Orthodoxy and, to some extent, traditional Mormonism have attempted to deny or ignore one or the other element of this paradox. But we cannot do this without denying a part of ourselves. Jesus could not do this. Eve could not do this. They could not deny time, or flesh, or the potential for evil. Instead, they reaffirmed these realities by showing us that the divine kingdom is a realm of spirit and element, flesh and glory, light and darkness, good and evil, pleasure and pain, life and death. It is a kingdom in which time and eternity are espoused. And for the preservation of this kingdom, these deities laid aside their glory and godhood; each journeyed into an appointed garden, unprotected, to wrestle with pain, humiliation, and death. Eve went to Eden and her tree like a bride to the bridegroom. Christ went to Gethsemane and his cross like a bridegroom to the bride. And in them, the intersection of the cosmos, the source and repose of paradox, the marriage of time and eternity was consummated.

PART III

Redemption

~ CHAPTER NINE ~

DIVINITY AND HUMANITY

Orthodox Christianity teaches that each individual was created from nothing, probably at conception or birth. There was no pre-mortal existence for us. Because God creates us *ex nihilo*, we are entirely contingent upon God. Popular Mormonism teaches that we are co-eternal with God. The word "co-eternal" comes from B. H. Roberts's interpretative footnote to the King Follett discourse (TPJS, 353), considered to contain Joseph Smith's most powerful discussion of the doctrine of human self-existence. This discourse was transcribed by a number of individuals as it was spoken. In none of these variant transcriptions does the word "co-eternal" appear. What Joseph Smith said was that spirits were "co-equal" with God, that is equal in age or extent (ibid., 353; WJS, 341, 346, 352). Roberts preferred the word "co-eternal" because it avoided the connotation that humans were co-extensive with or part of God.

Traditional or progressive Mormonism has by and large accepted Roberts's view that the irreducible seed of each individual's personality always existed independent of and side by side with God. Thus progressive Mormonism has taught that we are not dependent upon God for our being. Ultimately God cannot be blamed for our failings; nor can God take the credit for our goodness. In Mormonism human self-existence is seen as the foundation of free agency. Self-existence is what keeps us from the grip of the divine determinism that would be inevitable had God created us to be what we are. For to have been created out of nothing would be for God to have encoded into us from the start all that we could ever be. And we could never escape that encoding no matter what we did. In addition, traditional Mormonism insists that people are not only self-existent, but innately good. Evil exists as a cosmetic affair, resulting from ignorance, fear, and desperation. Remove these by education, kindness, and prosperity, and the deep down forever goodness in people will emerge.

In our view, the revelations of Joseph Smith contradict the orthodox view of *ex nihilo* creation. But they also contradict the traditional Mormon view that humans existed independently of God and that they are innately good. Our view, we think, is supported by the following statement on the nature of God and humanity: "Man was also in the beginning with God. Intelligence, or the light of truth, was not created or made, neither indeed can be.... All truth is independent in that sphere in which God has placed it, to act for itself, as all intelligence also; otherwise there is no existence" (D&C 93:29, 30). This means that until we were made independent, our self-existence or intelligence was merged with God's self-existence. At some point God put our intelligence in a separate state where it could act for itself. Without such a sphere we could have no self-awareness and no existence except as part of God. The revelation goes on to say: "Man is spirit. The elements are eternal, and spirit and element, inseparably connected, receive a fullness of joy." This suggests that the independent sphere in which God placed us was the sphere of our spirit bodies and later our fleshy bodies. Our bodies function as veils obscuring the essential connectedness of the universe. This is what God intended for us. God gave us our bodies so we would become independent from God. Our bodies allow us to have our own awareness and consciousness independent of God's. As mortals we lack the fullness of divine glory, intelligence, or divine consciousness, so the universe appears to us to be discontinuous. We are trapped temporarily in the illusion that we exist as entities entirely separate from all other living things including God. But when our spirit and fleshy bodies are inseparably joined and we receive a fullness of God's glory, we shall perceive that though we are independent of God, we are one in glory. This complicated situation is the essential paradox of being: to be and not to be a part of God simultaneously. This paradoxical state is possible because our bodies make us independent and God's glory makes us one.

Section 93 further states that "The elements are the tabernacle of God; yea, man is the tabernacle of God." We are part of a universe saturated with God's mind or intelligence. Thus the whole of creation, including mankind, is an extension of the person and being of God. This is how Christ can be all knowing and all powerful in his kingdom. But his kingdom (at least the actualized portion) is not infinite. Though it is large beyond human comprehension, it has its limits. It is contained within the larger kingdom of that God who is the father and mother of Jesus Christ. The text of the Book of Abraham states: "If two things exist, and there be one above the other, there shall be greater things above them" (3:16).

The revelations of Joseph Smith present God's body and God's glory as equally essential to divinity. God's body constitutes an independent sphere allowing God to have self-awareness and self-existence independent of any superior God. The body of God provides the focal point of all the levels of the divine consciousness and intelligence. God's body is where his/her glory is centered. It proceeds forth from them to the uttermost verges of their creation. God as the union of actual and potential, of time and eternity, of flesh and glory, does not stand outside the creation but is a part of it. God not only observes the cosmos but participates in it. The furthest reaches of the cosmos are as much a part of God as his and her fingers and toes. Thus in relating to mankind or to nature, God is self-relating. For God the universe is continuous, organic, and conscious. The "continuation of the seeds," we are told, is synonymous with God's "eternal lives" (D&C 132:19). This means that God lives our lives. God not only lives an independent life, but being present in us in spirit, the divine mind also simultaneously lives in each of us.

In other words God is pregnant with unborn kingdoms. We are part of those kingdoms. There is locked in God the Father and God the Mother something not quite their own, something yearning for birth, maturation, and equality. We are part of that something. In a parallel way, there is locked within each of us some part of a potential kingdom, something not quite part of us, something which can through a divine union be born, mature, and become our equal. Just as the intelligence of God includes our intelligences, so our intelligence includes the intelligences of others. These intelligences are not created. They exist as infinite potentials which can be liberated or actualized. As celestial beings we may participate with others in unleashing these intelligences into their own independent spheres of existence.

In light of these ideas, it is possible to say that without God we could not exist and that without us God could not exist as God. We are both necessary. And we are both contingent on each other, like mother and fetus: the fetus depends on the mother for life, and the mother depends on the fetus for her identity as mother. Because we always existed in God as an independent potential we always had an independent will; therefore, God did not create our freedom from nothing.

Though we always existed in God, this freedom was always ours. But until we were given an independent sphere of action, our freedom existed only in a latent or potential modality. The work of our divine parents is to free us by giving us our bodies and to make us equal to them by filling us with their glory. From this perspective the traditional Mormon notion of eternal progression gives way to the more complex concept of eternal egression: an eternal unfolding from infinite potentiality to finite actuality in which kingdom emerges from kingdom and universe grows out of universe.

Just as time and eternity are intertwined, so God and humanity are interdependent. The scripture teaches that the work and glory of God is "to bring to pass the immortality and eternal life of man" (Moses 1:39). In our view, God grows in light and truth because God is involved in the dynamic process of bringing individuals to physical, intellectual, and spiritual maturation. Thus, God's existence and growth depends on our existence and growth. This means that neither we nor God is self-sufficient. We need each other. We are bound together with hoops of steel. We are part of God's body as much as God is a part of ours. The ultimate divine purpose is to unite us all without obliterating our individuality.

CHAPTER TEN

BRINGING GOOD
OUT OF EVIL

Orthodoxy, neo-orthodoxy, and progressive Mormonism all see good and evil as static, polar opposites. All suggest that goodness is a state of purity, evil a state of corruption, and never the twain shall meet; that evil should be shunned and good embraced, that no evil can come from God, and that the origins of evil are disobedient humans or rebellious angels.

We have a different view. Within the metaphysical model we have been exploring in this book, we define evil as that which denies, mitigates, or wars against God's glory, intelligence, and power of life. This evil is referred to in the scripture as the "blasphemy against the Holy Ghost" (D&C 132:27). In contrast good seeks, accepts, or affirms the powers of heaven.

In our view evil and good exist in the universe both as potentialities and actualities. As humans we actualize both good and evil. Devils seek to actualize only evil. And God actualizes only good. For this reason we say that God is good and there is no darkness in God. But in our view the potential for good and evil exists not only in humans and devils but in God as well. The potential for evil in God is unavoidable because God is a free and intelligent being. According to the Book of Mormon prophet Lehi, the potential for evil in God means the God could "cease to be God" (2 Ne. 2:11). As humans we have the potential to do both good and evil and are able to actualize both because we inherit this potential or freedom from God. Therefore God as the source of our freedom is the ultimate source of the good and evil actualized in the world. Like everything else in the universe, good and evil are projections of the kingdom emerging from God.

If we are right, if the cosmos is truly the mind of God and if we are even now part of the divine, cosmic tabernacle, then the evil in the universe done by devils and humans is an unavoidable part of God. The evil happening on earth is not only our responsibility but God's. Because good and evil are inextricably linked, none of us can live utterly uncontaminated by evil. Every good can go bad. An angel can become a devil. And by the same token every evil can generate a good. The personal sin of David and Bathsheba gave rise to the lineage of Jesus Christ. But if good and evil are inextricably interlinked, how can anyone be good? More importantly how can God be good?

In our view God is good not because God is utterly disassociated from evil but because, as a being of glory, God can recognize evil, circumscribe it, and primarily through personal sacrifice God can bring good out of evil, light out of darkness, fullness out of emptiness, health out of sickness, and perfection out of imperfection. God is good because God wills not to actualize evil. Instead God uses the divine power in love to transcend evil. This is the meaning of the phrase in the Lord's prayer, "lead us not into temptation, but deliver us from evil." In other words, let us not be led into trials unless, Lord, you bring good out of the evil. In this prayer Jesus acknowledges the potential for evil in the universe. He does not ask God to eliminate evil. He asks only that God bring good out of evil. This means that Jesus accepts evil, potential and actual, and uses the power of heaven to transform it. This process lies at the heart of Christ's gospel: the justification of the unjust, the sanctification of the unholy, and the glorification of the powerless.

Because we believe that potential evil lurks in each of us, the first step toward actualizing evil is to deny the truth of its existence. On the other hand, the first step toward bringing good out of evil is to accept it. This does not mean to give evil scope, or repress it, or be paralyzed by guilt about it. It means to discern it, admit its existence, its power, its full dimensions, and to do what is necessary to grow spiritually and to cooperate with God in bringing light out of darkness.

In our view then Adam and Eve were not put in the Garden to avoid the Fall but to experience it and its consequences and to participate with God in bringing about the redemption of the world. Eve recognized the secret darkness that crept like a serpent into Eden, and she sacrificed her eternal life to bring good out of evil and time out of eternity. Christ recognized the evil in the world and sacrificed his eternal life to bring good out of evil, to bring eternity out of time. Similarly we are not sent to earth in order to see if we can maintain our innocence. We are not here to avoid pain and impurity but to bring good out of evil while immersed in all the manifold convolutions of a temporal world.

To do this we must stop telling ourselves and our children that marriage, family, church, and work should always be heaven on earth. We must admit that for most of us marriage is a crucible, family an ordeal, church a cross, and work a bore. If not there is plenty else in the world which will try us. The purpose of life is not to reject everything different and everything risky but to accept the world with love and face the good and evil of it. As interconnected parts of God's cosmic tabernacle, we cannot escape the evil of others nor can they escape ours. Evil in one or done to one is evil in all and done to all. If we deny this, the evil will worsen and inevitably surface elsewhere.

Moreover, we must recognize that our judgment and condemnation of each other based on rigid moral codes and a fetish for purity are irrelevant to the central purpose of our lives and the central teaching of our religion. We must come to accept that the worthiest of us are not those who have sought to deny the darkness within or to avoid the darkness in the world, but those who have seen it, acknowledged it, accepted it, and then have transcended it by seeking God's light shining in the darkness.

If we can accept the idea that goodness in the cosmic and ultimate sense is a matter of spirituality rather than legality, it may, perhaps, be easier to accept the fact that, as mortals, we are all sinners because none of us is glorified as Christ is glorified and, therefore, we all fall short of the glory of God.

One of the principle problems of the modern world and the modern church is that we tend to deny or downplay our own evil and limitations. Virtually everybody recognizes that the world has problems. We would be hard pressed to deny the existence of error, corruption, temptation, and even malice. This is our universal human plight. But our denials often begin with our attempts to answer the questions: Why is there evil in the world? And what can we do about it?

The first question is the most important, and two very different answers can be proposed. Some say evil exists because we humans are spiritually flawed, that is, we cannot consistently avoid evil and do good. This is not to say that humans are inherently evil. They have the capacity for both good and evil. But in a world of entropy without the fullness of God's glory, we are all subject to evil, just as we are subject to the law of gravity. Others say that though we are spiritually sound, evil exists because we lack knowledge or proper guidance. Each of these answers leads to a different remedy for the problem of evil. If we are spiritually flawed, then the cure is spiritual healing and empowerment. If we are spiritually sound, then the treatment is proper laws, guidance, and education.

We take the view that humans are spiritually deficient and that the remedy for evil is spiritual transformation. Redemption then is a matter of receiving God's spirit not a matter of legislation, moral exhortations, proper examples, rules, regulations, and good education. Though some of these techniques may help deal with evil on a temporary basis, they cannot serve as a lasting solution because they cannot heal the spiritual wound causing our plight. Besides these methods require imperfect people to be in charge of making themselves and others perfect. The blind lead the blind. This situation may have some good effects, but it cannot bring about divine goodness. And often such efforts only end up burdening people with more rules and giving rule makers more power, which in turn feeds the rulers' pride and ambition and creates a syndrome of arrogance and despair in the ruled: those who feel they are perfecting themselves will tend to feel arrogant, while those who are unable to comply or who realize that compliance is not holiness will find themselves carrying a heavier and heavier burden of despair-promoting guilt.

This syndrome can be avoided if we accept that mankind is spiritually flawed and our plight is beyond human remedy. Although this view seems uncompromising and harsh, it is in fact quite gentle. For if we believe that our human limitations are the source of our problems, then each person at heart is no more or less a sinner than anyone else. We are all equally plighted. True the sins of one person may be more serious than those of another, but because we are all flawed, we are all capable under the right (or wrong) circumstances of committing sin. This is why Jesus could say, "let him who is without sin cast the first stone." We all have the same potential for sin. What must be removed is not the freedom to sin but rather our inability to distinguish clearly right from wrong and our powerlessness consistently to actualize the good.

Rules and regulations cannot empower us. The potential for sin can be clarified by the law, but not eliminated by it. That is why the law can only be a schoolmaster to teach us of our plight and to encourage us to look for a cure. The cure is not the law. The cure is Jesus. Because God has set in place the mechanism of our salvation (and we shall discuss this more fully in a later chapter), we can all receive from Christ a spiritual healing and the power to bring good out of evil. This power is made available to us not merely by human effort, but mainly by divine effort. Christian salvation does not depend on what we humans can achieve through our own efforts, but on what we receive from God.

If this sounds too easy, it is because it was meant to sound easy. The gospel of Jesus Christ was meant to be accessible to everybody. But it is not so easy in practice. To submit to an invisible God, to rely and follow such a being, to set aside the vanities and achievements of the world, to be forever in conflict with one's culture, these things are not easy. It takes much less effort to be active, to be in control, to imagine oneself as the architect of one's destiny. A sense of progress, even a false one, is often more appealing than lying still under the divine surgeon's knife — especially if there is no anesthetic and if the pain itself is often the therapy. This is not to say we do nothing to further our redemption. Seeking the spirit, accepting it, remaining sensitive to it, following it, becoming God's instruments, forgiving, repenting, loving, and enduring in the business of bringing good out of evil requires effort. But our work is principally to accept the work of God in us.

The New Testament contains stories of Jesus' miracles: his incarnation and escape into Egypt; his changing of water into wine; his multiplying the loaves; his replenishing the nets; his healing the sick, giving sight to the blind, and raising the dead; and his own passion, crucifixion, resurrection, and ascension into heaven. These miracles are variations of but one miracle, the miracle of bringing good out of evil, of making the unholy holy, the profane sacred, the sinful righteous, the dead alive, the human divine, and the divine accessible. It is the miracle of the work and glory of God to bring to pass both immortality and eternal life.

CHAPTER ELEVEN

THE CASE FOR GRACE

The picture of the universe set forth in the previous chapters is, we believe, entirely consistent with the doctrine of salvation by the grace of Christ. The marriage of time and eternity, the interconnectedness of humanity and God, and the inextricability of good and evil are all compatible with the teaching that God laid aside his glory, assumed a mortal body, suffered and died to make atonement, and then rose again from the dead.

In our view, Christ sacrificed his life for us for three principle reasons.

First, his divine sense of justice, fairness, and equanimity required him to take responsibility for his part in projecting evil into the universe. This is the meaning of his justice: he recognizes the shadow in himself as well as in us. He accepts this shadow of evil, takes responsibility for his part in it and ours, and brings good out of it.

Second, his attribute of divine love or mercy caused him to reach out to us in our state of powerlessness. Although we are connected to God, we are not his equals in glory or goodness. Because he loves us he desires to make us equal with him, to fill us with the same joy he experiences. Though he takes responsibility for our sins, we cannot realize the benefits of this act until we freely accept his spirit in an act of free will. With the spirit we can begin to love God and our fellow human beings. This is the purpose of the gospel: to allow us to receive the glory of God which will make us into godly individuals.

Third, Christ's divine death is essential to his own eternal growth and development. God is a progressing deity. But he progresses by breaking the circle of his perfection and assuming a greater perfection. God possesses all the glory his resurrected body can endure. But this glory though incomprehensibly great to us is not infinite in amount. If

God wishes to grow in glory, to expand his kingdom, to bring about greater good, he must die. He must willingly set aside his body of flesh and bones, his spirit body, and his glory in order to obtain a new and more glorious resurrection. He must "descend below all things . . . that he might be in and through all things" (D&C 88:6). We believe it is through such a process of repeated resurrections that God grows in glory, power, and dominion. This, we believe, is one of the meanings of Jesus' saying: "Except a corn of wheat fall into the ground and die, it abideth alone: but if it die, it bringeth forth much fruit" (John 12:24). For this reason God himself laid aside his glory and eternal life and entered fully into the shadow of time, assuming the mortal aspect of his children, taking upon himself their sickness and their sin. He did not avoid contamination. He descended below it all so that his light and our light could grow brighter. He made himself equal to us so that we could in due time be made equal to him. He died so that he could rise again and bring the whole of time up with him into eternity. He died to teach us that God is not beyond location, extension, duration, or freedom. He died to show us that God is good because he takes responsibility for evil, because he accepts our imperfections, because he loves us more than he hates sin.

Jesus' atonement is the center of our religion. His gift to us of eternal spirit, eternal element, and celestial glory; of spirit birth, mortal birth, and the resurrection; of justification, sanctification, and glorification is the greatest of all the gifts: the gift of eternal life. Giving us this gift constitutes his grace and his gospel. Such ideas are rarely the focus of popular Mormonism, and for this reason a discussion of the Mormon theology of grace requires careful groundwork.

Orthodox Christianity and Mormonism both maintain that God originally made Adam and Eve in his perfect image, but they fell from this perfect state. In order to close the resulting breach between God and humanity, they and their posterity needed to be reclaimed or saved. Christians seem always to have found in both the Old and New Testaments this message that something must be done to bring about the salvation of humanity. Since the fall of humanity resulted from a particular act, it seems only consistent and reasonable that its redemption requires a particular act as well.

But what act? What must be done? Possible answers range across a spectrum from those minimizing human involvement and maximizing the role of the divine to others suggesting the reverse. Since the fall of humanity was brought about by the free act of the first perfect beings, Adam and Eve, some Christians believe that salvation from the Fall can result only from the free act of yet another perfect being, Jesus Christ. Under this theory the involvement of ordinary humans — the posterity of Adam and Eve — is minimal. Humans are presented as cosmically powerless with little input into either the negative dynamic bringing about the Fall or the positive dynamic bringing about the Redemption. On the opposite end of the spectrum, other Christians believe that Adam and Eve are only representatives of all males and females. Each is created "good" rather than "evil" and is free to err (sin) and to change for the better (repent) and thus is primarily responsible for learning what pleases God and for doing it. Under such a theory the involvement of God in salvation is minimized, human involvement maximized. Between these extremes are theories variously balancing the influence of the human and the divine in the salvation process. What we are describing here, of course, is a spectrum bounded by the most extreme formulations of salvation by divine grace and of salvation by human works.

The conflict between grace and works has traditionally plagued Catholicism and Protestantism and to a lesser extent Mormonism. To many moderns these disputes seem silly, like arguing about how many angels can dance on the head of a pin. Why, we ask, would people be willing to fight each other over grace and works? It strikes us as more sensible to worry about more concrete problems. How many inchoate liens can dance on the head of an interest in realty? Shall we have capitalism or communism? Individual freedom or social justice? Big government or small? Regulation or de-regulation? Tax breaks for individuals or corporations? It is our belief, however, that the most basic human concerns change very little over time. At bottom our modern controversies over power and money are merely reassertions of the issues involved in the venerable old grace/works controversy: Is a person's salvation an individual matter, as taught by Martin Luther? Or is it principally the concern of the priesthood and the church, as taught by the papacy?

These religious questions are very like their secular counterparts: Is a person more likely to find happiness on earth in a society that values individual initiative in a free market system? Or in a society that values the needs and wants of the community as distilled by experts in a system that is heavily or even totally regulated? Moreover, secular people go about seeking their answers to these questions in much the same way that religious people do: by appeals to authority. In a religious context, people resort to the scripture or the priesthood, while in a political context, they resort to constitutions, statues, or legal precedent. Also, in the secular context, there are strict constructionists of law as well as true believers in the reliability of science and the knowledge of professionals just as, in a religious context, there are those who believe in the inerrancy of scripture or the infallibility of the priesthood. In a secular context, there are those who reject strict constructionism and believe that constitutions, statues, and other such writings are subject to reinterpretation in light of new conditions and unforeseen circumstances and that the opinion of experts must be tempered by the concerns of lay persons just as, in a religious context, there are those who see scripture and religious leadership as but one source of truth — a source that must be balanced against such others as tradition, revelation, and experience. Our point is that the issues at the heart of the grace/works controversy, far from being irrelevant and immaterial, touch the very quick of our lives.

The stand any of us takes on these issues affects how we define justice, mercy, power, and happiness — the basic foundations of our social structures. This is so whether we think of salvation in spiritual terms as eternal happiness in another world or whether we think of it in secular terms as happiness here and now. If, for example, we believe that salvation, either temporal or eternal, depends on human works, then we are likely to reject divine or governmental intervention on grounds that each promotes complacency, postpones maturation, and encourages dependence and timidity in the weak and self-indulgence and tyranny in the strong. But if we believe in salvation by grace, we may object to ecclesiastical or political systems fostering competition, rewarding the rich and disadvantaging the poor, encouraging corporatism and legalistic observance of rules and regulations, or favoring the strong and arrogant over the weak and humble.

In Mormonism the conflict between grace and works has two primary manifestations. The first arises solely within Mormonism. The second arises between Mormonism and fundamental Christianity. The controversy within Mormonism focuses on a conflict between the salvation doctrine in Mormon scripture and the doctrine promoted by the Mormon ecclesiastical institution. Mormon scripture teaches salvation by grace, while the ecclesiastical institution throws its weight behind self-reliance, self-help, self-atonement, and self-salvation. This ecclesiastical commitment can be seen in requirements for church attendance, family home evenings, genealogical research, temple attendance, tithing, and conformity to the sex and leadership role models defined by the church.

The second Mormon manifestation of the grace/works conflict arises between Mormonism and fundamentalist Christian groups. These groups insist that because the Mormon church ignores or denigrates grace, Mormons are not Christians. In response to these attacks, some Mormons counter-attack with the argument that salvation by grace is simply a Christian heresy (McConkie 1984; Ensley). Others argue that Mormons believe people are saved by grace but only after they have done all that they can do. Yet other Mormons, ourselves included, argue that Mormonism is founded on the doctrine of salvation by grace and that the present works-oriented posture of the ecclesiastical institution is simply mistaken.

That Mormon scriptures teach the doctrine of salvation by grace has been amply demonstrated by a number of Mormon writers. In her article, "Toward a Mormon Concept of Original Sin," Janice Allred argues that Mormonism does *not* reject the doctrine of original sin, although it differs with the traditional interpretation of the Fall. She further shows that Mormonism gives three answers to the question, "Why is sin inevitable?" First, conflicts arise among the commandments making it impossible to obey some without disobeying others. A classic example arises when one's personal beliefs appear to conflict with what priesthood authorities are commanding. The church requires service in the armed forces, but an individual may be a conscientious objector; the church encourages marriage, but an individual may not be so inclined.

The second reason why sin is inevitable, according to Allred, follows from human finitude, egocentricity, and ignorance, which impair our ability to see choices clearly or foresee their consequences. A priesthood leader excommunicates an unrepentant sinner only to discover that the excommunication alienates from the church the sinner's religiously faithful wife and children. This leader's finitude keeps him from foreseeing the evil consequences of what he considers a priesthood duty.

The third reason for the inevitability of sin is the solidarity or interrelatedness of all humanity, which makes it impossible to put the blame for a particular wrong exclusively on one individual. As Allred points out, "no one is ever totally responsible for what he does in the sense that his decision or action is the only causative factor in his choice.

There are always many reasons for a choice and many of these may be beyond the control of the principal agent" (Allred, 14–17). Thus Allred concludes that not only does Mormonism accept a concept of original sin, it also admits that sin is statistically and theoretically inevitable due to the essential lack of perfection in the human condition.

In another article, "Understanding the Scope of the Grace of Christ," Donald Olsen demonstrates that Mormon scripture not only accepts the doctrine of humanity's fallen condition but also teaches that "no law, not even the law of Moses, provides a way to remove the effects of sin" (cf. 2 Ne. 2:5). This does not mean the law is useless. The law, says Olsen, "brings an awareness of and responsibility for our sins and errors," and the law of Moses additionally provided "a foreshadowing of Christ," who was to "redeem man from sin" (cf. Mos. 16:14–15).

Of course, as Olsen states, a "misplaced devotion to the law" and works can "sever us from the grace of Christ." He adds, "The scriptures seem to categorically exclude works as a means of obtaining forgiveness and reconciliation." This point is made by Paul in Romans (4:2–8), where he also argues that we cannot both be saved by works and by grace (11:6). Good works are valuable within the human context, but they cannot be used or relied upon to "actuate a relationship with God." Olsen provides a lucid discussion of the concept of justification, a word translated from the Greek *dikaiosis*, referring to the imputation or "attribution of Christ's righteousness to the undeserving sinner so that he appears righteous to God" (cf. 4:6, 22–25). In other words, because "Christ has fully paid for past sins . . . the justified sinner is not accountable for them" if that sinner has faith in Christ, repents, is baptized, and receives the gift of the Holy Ghost. However, the ordinances are not in themselves "good works." They are the means by which we ritually reenact Christ's saving work while rejecting the salvific efficacy of all human works. And as Olsen states, "baptism cannot be done by oneself. The candidate must receive this ordinance from God's priesthood holder," another symbolic repudiation of the efficacy of self-atonement.

Olsen also discusses the meaning of sanctification, which refers to "a state of holiness or righteousness in behavior and thought." He shows that this state is "attained through the grace of Christ." Olsen further shows that salvation by grace refers not only to the gift of the resurrection from the dead but also to the gift of the redemption from sin. The famous Book of Mormon phrase that "it is by grace we are saved, after all we can do" (2 Ne. 25:23) does not mean we are saved after we have met all the requirements. It means we are saved in spite of ourselves, and our own best efforts. Works are the product of grace; they are a spiritual gift. They do not serve as prerequisites to grace or salvation (Olsen, 20–24).

Such arguments demonstrate that in Mormon scripture the doctrine of grace corresponds to traditional Protestant salvation theory. However, some Mormon writers go further and show that Joseph Smith expanded this traditional grace concept. In "I Am Not Under the Law," J. Frederic Voros, Jr., demonstrates that Joseph Smith in his revision of the Book of Romans did not reject Paul's view of grace but boldly amplified it. Among his examples Voros cites the King James translation of the scripture: "Therefore being justified *freely* by his grace through the redemption that is in Christ Jesus." Voros shows how this verse is changed in Joseph Smith's revision: "Therefore being justified *only* by his grace through the redemption that is in Christ Jesus." Thus "justified *freely*" becomes for Joseph Smith "justified *only*." As Voros observes: "if *'freely'* shuts the door on the role for works, *'only'* locks it."

In "Beyond Orthodoxy: Joseph Smith's Amplified Doctrine of Grace," Daniel Rector argues that Joseph Smith expanded the scope of Christ's grace by revealing the following doctrines: (1) mortality as a probationary state is a gift given out of Christ's grace; (2) we demonstrate our willingness to please God not by human works but by ritual ordinances revealed by his grace; (3) mortals who reject Christ will not go to hell but to lesser glories, which exist because of the grace of Christ; (4) young children are not accountable for their sins because of the grace of Christ; (5) those who die in ignorance of the gospel or without a knowledge of the law or of their sins are spared the demands of justice because of the grace of Christ; and (6) exaltation in the highest kingdom does not depend upon works but upon one's growth from "grace to grace" until one attains the fullness of the measure of the stature of Christ.

In spite of these scriptural and critical evidences, those in the Mormon ecclesiastical structure, influenced by the teachings of progressive Mormons, tend to ignore the doctrine of salvation by grace. The progressive school has for many years asserted that Mormonism is an antidote to such orthodox Christian concepts as God's transcendence, human depravity, and salvation by grace. Adherents to the progressive school have been powerful voices in the Mormon intellectual community. And although a number have been criticized by Mormon leaders for their liberalism, they have nevertheless been effective in re-defining

Mormon theology in favor of salvation by works. In doing this they assert that Joseph Smith's major contribution to Christianity was his teaching that humans and God are of the same race and that humanity principally by its obedience to the commandments or by its achievements can become godlike.

These ideas seem to echo and reinforce popular twentieth-century notions that people are innately good, that the doctrines of original sin and the fallen nature of humanity are leftover bits of fallacy from the dark ages, and that in truth we humans have all the authorization and power we need to improve ourselves and the world through our own unaided efforts. Thus Mormon progressives have successfully re-interpreted Joseph Smith's complex teachings in humanistic terms and have made of him an early exponent of self-atonement, self-reliance, self-improvement, and social progress. Progressive Mormons dismiss Joseph Smith's grace-affirming views in the Book of Mormon and the inspired version of Romans as examples of his early religious notions, which he later rejected for the more mature, progressive, and humanistic views of his Nauvoo period.

Going further progressive Mormonism has argued that the doctrine of salvation by grace is false because it contradicts the idea of free agency. If we are saved by God's divine act of grace, then all human decisions and actions would necessarily be unimportant, and we would have no control over our destiny. This idea, progressives assert, contradicts Joseph Smith's teaching that humans are not created out of nothing but are eternal beings just as God is. They are not dependent upon God for their existence or their salvation, because they are beings of free will, who were created "good" and who have the innate power to make themselves perfect.

We have several objections to this humanistic re-interpretation.

First, although Mormonism makes it clear that we have always existed as beings co-eternal with God, we find nothing in the teachings of Joseph Smith or Mormon scripture establishing that humans as eternal beings have been eternally self-aware or aware of moral choices. As we have already shown, certain scriptures suggest that as pre-mortal intelligences, we were once part of God, who liberated us from this state and gave us a sphere in which to actualize our free choices.

But even if this were not true, even if we were always self-aware, free, and morally responsible beings, there is nothing in the scripture or the teachings of Joseph Smith establishing that we were initially perfect or "good" or even inclined to do "good" or that we always possessed the innate power to perfect ourselves. Joseph Smith in his King Follett discourse did indeed advance the concept of human eternality but only to discredit the orthodox Christian teaching that we were created out of nothing. He never discredited the concepts of human sinfulness, human dependence on God for salvation, or salvation by grace. And even if Joseph Smith believed that humans are essentially "good," he never denied the fall of humanity with all of its dire consequences. In fact a revelation containing one of the earliest renditions of the theme of human eternality also reaffirms the doctrine of salvation by grace: "And God, having redeemed man from the fall, men became again, in their infant state, innocent before God" (D&C 93:38). We believe Joseph Smith did oppose the concepts of predestination and the irresistibility of grace, arguing that humans must choose God before they can receive his saving grace, but such opposition does not argue against grace itself, only against determinism.

This leads to our second point. Exponents of progressive Mormonism argue that the doctrine of grace contradicts Joseph Smith's teachings on free agency and human responsibility and inevitably supports predestination. This argument is unpersuasive because determinism is not tied exclusively to the idea of grace. It fits into the idea of works too. Similarly free will can be espoused by grace advocates or works advocates. Works advocates can argue that because we are free and responsible for choosing and doing good rather than evil, the burden is on us to be obedient and freely achieve the righteousness which will please God and earn us exaltation in his kingdom. But grace advocates can argue that freedom itself is a gift of God, a manifestation of his grace. We were made free so that we could voluntarily accept God's gift of salvation by grace.

The converse is also true. Works advocates can reasonably argue that we are determined and that our works, good or evil, are not in our control but are products of environment and heredity. Similarly grace advocates can argue (and historically have argued) that God predestined some for salvation and others for damnation and that his grace is prevenient, irresistible, and unshakable. Thus a doctrine of grace does not favor determinism any more than does a doctrine of works.

Our third point relates to our second. Though works advocates see themselves as champions of human freedom, in practice their views tend to promote religious intolerance and rigidity. For those who believe in salvation by works, the question of which works to do and which to avoid becomes critically important. This concern leads naturally to the promulgation of rules and regulations, punishments and rewards defining which works to do and which to shun. When these laws become calcified in a religious institution, the result is not freedom as one might suppose but a rigid religious legalism, a modern Pharisaism, a holier than thou, my-works-are-better-than-thine attitude. An emphasis on human achievement also leads to an elitism of achievers, which rivals the elitism of the elect.

Our fourth point concerns the institutional church. Although the church has demonstrated considerable resistance to intellectual trends of all kinds, it has fallen prey to progressive Mormonism's salvation-by-works position at least in part because this doctrine tends to lend power and importance to the ecclesiastical structure. It reinforces the church's role as definer of good and bad attitude and behavior in every department of life from sex to parenting, diet, doctrine, economics, politics, and social attitudes. In short salvation by works feeds the church machine, empowering it to reward the "faithful" and disenfranchise the "rebellious." And this results in the syndrome of arrogance and despair we have mentioned before. This is one of the reasons why the grace/works controversy persists. When people despair of their futile efforts to perfect themselves through works, they become disenchanted with legalistic Mormonism and its institutional rigidity. They hunger for inner spiritual life, which cannot be satisfied by an ecclesiastical structure dedicated to making its members conform rather than allowing them to experience contact with God. In such a pressure cooker, some turn away somewhat from the institution and begin to privatize their religion, seeking comfort in scripture, family, and networks of like-minded friends. Ironically, the emphasis of the institution on the institution inevitably leads some individuals to reject the institution, just as the emphasis on works inevitably leads either to arrogance or to the despair that sometimes brings people finally to believe in the grace of God.

Our fifth point concerns the claim that Joseph Smith is the source of progressive Mormonism. The argument has been made that Joseph Smith espoused grace in his early years but later, especially in Nauvoo, gave it up in favor of a more "positive" view of humanity. Superficially this position seems credible, but on investigation it proves illusory. This was demonstrated by J. Frederic Voros in his article, "Was the Book of Mormon Buried With King Follett." There Voros provides strong evidence that Joseph Smith in his later years never abandoned his concept of salvation by grace alone. As Voros observes, if Joseph Smith had believed that salvation depended upon human works, he would likely have encouraged people to do good works in traditional terms (Voros 1987b). But since Joseph Smith believed that he was not under the law but under grace and that what was wrong under the law was no longer wrong under grace, he was free to advance ideas about sex and marriage which contradicted traditional moral concepts. No one who thinks of Joseph Smith as the author of progressive Mormonism has yet explained how or why Joseph Smith could or would have been promulgating humanist views at the same time he was immersed in a magic-religious world view (Quinn 1987), when he was in the throws of developing the mystical temple ritual, and when he was privately teaching and practicing celestial marriage.

Our sixth point is that the doctrine of grace is not as some have argued opposed to good works. Paul, considered the most ardent ancient advocate for this teaching, exhorts his readers to pray (Rom. 15:30), to succor the needy (16:1–2), to avoid fornication (1 Cor. 5:1), to avoid covetousness, extortion, and idolatry (v. 10), to avoid fraud (7:5), to have faith, hope, and charity (13), to be of one mind and live in peace (2 Cor. 13:11), to avoid the works of the flesh, such as witchcraft, hatred, variance, emulations, wrath, strife, seditions, heresies, envyings, murders, drunkenness, and revellings (Gal. 5:20–21), and to cultivate the works of the Spirit such as love, joy, peace, longsuffering, gentleness, goodness, faith, meekness, temperance, and to live and walk by the spirit of God (vv. 22–25).

The works condemned by Paul and other grace advocates are works people claim can earn God's favor and secure to them discharge of their guilt and sin. What is rejected is the theory that humans can self-atone, self-justify, and self-sanctify. Within the world view of grace, good works are the effect of God's salvation not the cause of it. Salvation cannot be earned. It is free. This does not mean that it can be attained without effort but rather that no human can pay God anything equivalent to the gift of salvation.

But what of the teaching that we shall be judged by our works? This teaching has unfortunately been misunderstood. Scripture warns that if we do not accept the grace of Christ, we will be judged by our works. Our choice is simple: to be judged by our works and merits or to be judged by the works and merits of Jesus Christ. This is the burden of Alma's discourse to his son Corianton in the Book of Mormon. "It is requisite with the justice of God that men should be judged according to their works," says Alma (Al. 41:3). Under aegis of divine justice "all men that are in a state of nature . . . in a carnal state, are in the gall of bitterness and in the bonds of iniquity" (v. 11). And because of divine justice, "there is a law given, and a punishment affixed" (42:22). This punishment will be meted out to all those whose works fall short of the perfection of Christ. But, says Alma, though "justice exerciseth all his demands," there is something else: "mercy claimeth all which is her own" (v. 24). Then Alma makes his point: "thus none but the penitent are saved" (ibid.). And who are the penitent? Alma explains: "those who partake of the waters of life freely" (v. 27). The "waters of life" are his symbol for "the plan of mercy," which "could not be brought about except an atonement should be made" in which "God himself atoneth for the sins of the world ... to appease the demands of justice" (v. 15). Hence for Alma all of our works good and bad condemn us before divine justice. The choice then is between our works and God's works, between our human righteousness and God's divine righteousness. It is only if we reject Christ's grace that we will be judged for our works.

But if good works cannot qualify people for salvation, what can? The answer was given by Jesus. At that time people believed pleasing God meant conforming to the whole of the law of Moses with its specific ethical, spiritual, ritual, and dietary requirements. Jesus' answer contravened this teaching. Jesus brought to closure salvation by law and initiated salvation by love. We believe the Gospel of John, although compiled late in the first century, contains the most mature expression of Christ's teachings on this point. Christ introduces this change in soteriologies with the phrase "A new commandment I give to you." This commandment would not only replace the previous commandments. It was meant to circumscribe them, absorb them, and supersede them. Christ stated: "A new commandment I give to you, that you love one another; even as I have loved you, that you also love one another. By this all men will know that you are my disciples, if you have love for one another" (John 14:34–35, *New Annotated Oxford Bible*).

Then Christ explains, "if you love me, you will keep my commandments" (v. 15). This statement has been misinterpreted, especially among Mormons, to mean that if we love Christ we will show it by strictly adhering to all the scriptural and church rules and regulations. But in context this admonition means something quite different: the very act and attitude of loving Christ constitutes keeping his commandments. The same point was made by Jesus when he affirmed that the greatest commandment was to love God and the next to love one's neighbor unconditionally. Upon these commandments hung all the law and the prophets. In other words his requirement to love God and humanity embraced and superseded all the other commandments, which are derived from this admonition about love. Christ clarifies this teaching in John: "If a man loves me, he will keep my word" (v. 23). In other words if we love Christ unconditionally, we shall by this act of love be keeping Christ's new commandment. Then he says, "he who does not love me, does not keep my words" (v. 24). In other words no matter what good works we do, we will not be keeping Christ's commandments if we do not love him. Salvation is not predicated on the commandments to do works but on the commandments to be full of divine love. "As the Father hath loved me, so have I loved you; abide in my love" (John 15:9). And again, "this is my commandment that you love one another as I have loved you" (v. 11). "You are my friends if you do what I command you" (v. 14). "This I command you, to love one another" (v. 17).

But how can mortals love as God loves? Jesus answers, "I am the true vine. . . . you are the branches. He who abides in me, and I in him, he it is that bears much fruit, for apart from me you can do nothing" (John 15:1–5). His apostles then ask, How do we abide in you and you in us? Jesus replies that he will soon depart from them (John 16), but he prays that they may be one in his Spirit (John 17). He promises to leave them his Spirit, which will fill them with divine love. Again it is not good works but the divine love of God which is the prime requisite for salvation. This love is not a product of human effort or emotion; it is a gift of the spirit. Paul explains that *karitas* or charity is the greatest of all the gifts (1 Cor. 13:13). The Book of Mormon similarly admonishes: "Wherefore . . . pray unto the Father with all the energy of heart, that you may be filled with this love, which he hath bestowed upon all who are true followers of his Son, Jesus Christ, that ye may become the [children] of God, that when he shall appear we shall be like him" (Moro. 7:48).

Our seventh and final point is that the salvation by works view misperceives what God requires of us. At the heart of Judeo-Christianity, in our view, is the concept that human beings were made in God's image, but after the fall, this was no longer completely true. In Jesus' time people believed that to correct this distorted image individuals had to conform to God's law. They emphasized outward cleanliness and appearance rather than inward holiness. Christ reversed this emphasis. He taught that God is a being of divine, unconditional love and that in order to be recreated in God's divine image, people must have planted in them the same divine unconditional love God has for humanity.

Thus, matching God's divine image is not a matter of outward appearance, but of inward light and love and holiness. This is why the gospel teaches that, to be conformed to God's image, people must be born of the spirit, be recreated from above, so they may receive the spiritual gift of divine love so that they may love others as he loved them first. For this reason Joseph Smith taught that "until we have perfect love we are liable to fall" (TPJS, 9). And as late as 1843, Joseph Smith stated that at the time of the Fall, each human being did not completely lose the image of God "but his character still retaining the image of his maker Christ who is the image of man [and] is also the express image of his Fathers person. . . . And through the atonement of Christ and the resurrection and obedience in the Gospel we shall again be conformed to the image of his Son Jesus Christ, then we shall have attained to the image glory and character of God" (WJS, 231).

Mormonism teaches not a different gospel but a restored gospel. In Mormonism salvation is by grace alone. It is brought about by Christ's free, sacrificial act through which he assumed our sins and imperfections and imputed to us his own righteousness. The heart of the gospel is Christ in our hearts. To be saved means to accept the crucifixion in ourselves of all our wasted expectations of human perfection and to be filled with the Holy Ghost, to be freed from the fetish of justice, to be imbued with mercy, to have power to love and to embrace the world and its people in their imperfections even as Christ did, and, by that act, to be sanctified beyond the evil of the world and be remade in a new likeness and a new aspect, the matchless image of the Most High.

CHAPTER TWELVE

METAPHORS OF SALVATION

If a Sunday school class of average adult Mormons were asked to define "the gospel," they would undoubtedly generate on the blackboard a long and familiar list of everything from prayer to Sunday school parties. Unfortunately most of us have come to see the gospel as either a catalogue of commandments or as an inventory of "all truth." But is Jesus' gospel merely an index? Can it be summed up glibly as a list of do's and don'ts? Must we keep *all* the commandments and believe in all the right doctrines before we can be said to truly be living the gospel? The Book of Mormon, we are told, contains "the fullness of the gospel." Yet the Book of Mormon contains very few commandments and does not begin to deal with "all truth." What then precisely is "the fullness of the gospel?"

In our view the gospel of Jesus Christ is a small, distinct body of teachings and rituals enabling us to receive the power of God and be transformed into creatures of light who will eventually mature into beings like God. The gospel then is not all truth but the pathway to all truth. It is not a list of commandments but the power to keep the commandments. The gospel of Jesus is the spirit which helps us overcome our mortal plight. It is the formula for grace, the way to regain the lost glory of Eden.

We have an old friend who is fond of saying, "The gospel is one of the best kept secrets in the church." His point is that many Mormons, though active and devout, have only a vague notion of what the gospel really is. The religion of Jesus has been expounded in many languages, in many cultures, by many teachers, and in many ways. Some teachers describe the gospel as a series of steps. Others explain it in terms of covenants or of being born or planting a seed. Still others describe it in the legal sense of being acquitted of an offense against the law. Embedded in these views are various symbols or figures, which often conflict and obscure rather than clarify understanding.

Perhaps the simplest, most straight-forward approach to the gospel is the step-by-step method which focuses on its first principles and ordinances:

> First, faith in Jesus Christ as Redeemer and Savior of humanity (not just as creator, elder brother, or co-pilot), obtained by hearing or reading the word of God and being convinced of its truth by the power of the spirit.

> Second, repentance, by which we mean not a change in behavior or mood, but a change of heart, in which we reject all lesser gods and trust in and rely upon Jesus with a willingness to endure whatsoever he sees fit to inflict upon us.

> Third, baptism by immersion for the remission of sins, by which we ritually reenact the condescension, incarnation, the death, resurrection, and glorification of Jesus as the only enduring and effective means of salvation; in this way, we impute our sins and weaknesses to him, and he imputes his spiritual power and righteousness to us.

> Fourth, the reception of the gift of the Holy Ghost by the laying on of hands, by which Christ imparts to us the gift of the constant companionship of his spirit — the divine transforming power whose indwelling in us in fullness is the end purpose of the gospel.

This check-list approach to explaining the plan of salvation has the advantage of providing a simple outline of what we must do to subscribe to Christ's atonement. It also demonstrates that gospel responsibilities extend beyond mere declaration of belief in and reliance on Jesus. However, this method tends to reinforce the false view that salvation depends mostly on our efforts. This can be corrected by presenting the gospel as a set of principles or doctrines. In 3 Nephi 27:1-22 in the Book of Mormon Jesus makes a speech which yields the following list of gospel principles:

> (1) The Incarnation: Jesus Christ is God and was begotten from above, born of the Virgin Mary, and lived as a mortal on earth.

> (2) The Messianic Mission: Jesus Christ entered into his creation with the power and authority necessary to redeem us from our state of helplessness and powerlessness.

> (3) The Atonement: Jesus Christ suffered in Gethsemane and died on the cross to take responsibility for the sins of the world, to show forth his unconditional love, and to grant to us immortality and eternal life.

(4) The Redemption: because of Christ's sacrifice all people who have faith in him and repent and forgive and accept his power are redeemed from the plight of mortality and are saved from spiritual death.

(5) The Universal Resurrection: because of Christ's sacrifice physical death will not have an enduring hold upon us.

(6) The Judgment: Jesus Christ assumed upon his own person the judgment decreed upon us for our sins; we who accept his salvific work will be judged as if we were Christ just as Christ was judged as if he were each of us; but those of us who reject his work will be judged by our own meager works.

(7) The Justice of God: we cannot be trusted with the powers of heaven unless we are made pure even as Christ is pure.

(8) The Mercy of God: God willingly accepts responsibility for having allowed our imperfections and sins and takes upon himself punishment for them; if we repent, God justifies and purifies us by the power of his spirit.

(9) The Priesthood: Christ has offered to all who come to him the opportunity to mature in the powers and gifts and callings of the spirit, to become like him and to hold his authority to bestow these spiritual powers on others; this is the priesthood, a necessary component of spiritual growth, maturation, and sanctification.

(10) Continuing Revelation: Christ will continue to pour light and knowledge on those who seek him; thus they may be led into all truth.

This doctrinal approach works quite well, but it implies that the gospel is essentially an intellectual affair — a plan of study rather than a plan of rescue worked out by God at great sacrifice to himself. Summarizing the responsibilities which devolve upon Christ and upon us within the gospel plan helps correct this emphasis on intellect.

Christ's responsibilities include: creating the earth as a place of probation for mortals; setting aside his glory and transcendent nature, entering into mortality, assuming the aspect of his children, taking responsibility for the sins of the world, suffering for those sins, dying on the cross, and rising from the dead; dealing with humans out of divine love rather than divine condemnation; accepting all those who love him as members of the body of Christ, pouring out his spirit and striving with them for the sake of their redemption.

Our responsibilities are: faith, repentance, baptism, receiving the Holy Spirit, enduring in the spirit, and forgiving and repenting unto death.

This approach also has its limitations. It gives the impression that salvation is a tit for tat proposition, a kind of penny-in-the-slot theory with Christ's efforts matched by our own. This error can be corrected by another metaphor. The gospel is an exchange. We give to God our corruption, and he gives us his incorruption. We give him our weaknesses, and he gives us his glory. We impute to him our sins, and he imputes to us his righteousness. We place upon him the heavy burden of achievement and self-atonement, and he gives us the bright and buoyant yoke of his affectionate grace. This is what the Book of Mormon means when it says we are saved by the merits of Christ (2 Ne. 2:8, 31:19; Al. 24:10; He. 4:13; Mor. 6:4). In this way we become "new creatures," members of the family of Christ, whose sins have been acquitted and who are justified by the reception of the spirit. With the spirit our imperfections fade as we grow toward spiritual maturity and there flowers in us the fruits and gifts of the spirit: love, forgiveness, peace, gentleness, meekness, mercy, justice, courage, and strength. And if we seek them, we are also promised revelations, visions, and powerful spiritual insights. We are promised the words of eternal life in this world and eternal life in the world to come.

Possibly the best metaphor of salvation is the comparison between salvation and birth. Mormon scriptural texts refer to four ways we can be born: of the flesh, of the word, of water, and of the spirit (sometimes referred to as born of fire and the Holy Ghost). These births are followed by a period of spiritual maturation, which includes receiving priesthood in the temple in preparation for union with God.

We are born of the flesh when we come into the world as infants and receive physical bodies. Physical birth and development involves conception and fetal maturation, birth out of the amniotic waters of the womb, a washing and cleansing of the newborn, the rubbing down of the newborn's skin with oil or salt, the wrapping of the infant in swaddling clothes, and the naming of the child. Then the child is nurtured. Eventually, it grows to adulthood and acquires the powers of sexuality and procreation. We mention these stages because in Mormonism they are ritually reenacted as ordinances of spiritual rebirth and growth.

Mormon doctrine teaches that before our sojourn on earth, we existed first as primary intelligences and then as beings with spirit bodies who lived in the presence of God. We came to earth as a matter of choice to receive bodies of flesh and blood to begin the process of maturing spiritually in order to be reunited with God in a more profound way. Paradoxically then, our physical birth into mortality is an indispensable step of our spiritual birth.

Once born of the flesh we must be reborn of the spirit. Jesus told

Nicodemus: "Verily, verily, I say unto thee, except [one] be born again, [one] cannot see the kingdom of God" (John 3:3). Joseph Smith taught that being born to see the kingdom is different from being born to enter (TPJS, 328). Being born to see refers to the process by which a person hears or reads the word of God and, touched by the spirit, is able to see and understand the things of God and to know that they are true. This event in our spiritual life is similar to physical conception. We and God connect, as do the egg and sperm, to create a new spiritual life.

Spiritual conception is followed by a period similar to fetal maturation. During this time we are nurtured within the protecting womb of God's grace. This period may take a few hours or many years. During this time we sort out the meaning of God's call to us, change our hearts and minds, and repent, giving up our idols and accepting the will of Christ as our will.

Eventually this period leads us to the first outward ordinances of the gospel. Jesus said to Nicodemus: "Verily, verily I say unto thee, except [one] be born of water and the Spirit, [one] cannot enter into the kingdom of God" (John 3:5). Though faith in Christ brings life, to endure we must be born out of the protective waters and become spiritually independent. In baptism we reenact Christ's death and resurrection and also our own awakening from the deadness of human limitation into a newness of spiritual life. In baptism our sins are remitted, and we are acquitted of guilt. We are born. In this new birth Christ's blood rather than our own covers us. We are, as the scriptures state, "washed clean through the blood of the Lamb." Baptism is our entrance into the straight and narrow way. These are all metaphors for God's act of justification or spiritual renewal.

Baptism is followed by the ordinance of confirmation, a ritual which memorializes the imputation to us of God's spirit, power, and righteousness. Once empowered with this spirit, we are capable of genuine spiritual growth, of being transformed into the image and likeness of God. Throughout this period of growth, we abide in the grace of God and have the inspiration of the spirit to guide and comfort us. Confirmation is comparable to the moment a newborn takes its first breath. From this moment we begin to enjoy the powers of the spirit independent of those individuals who spiritually nourished us.

In Mormonism the process of sanctification or spiritual purification and growth entails the reception of other ordinances, including the initiatory ordinances of the temple, the endowment, the marriage sealing, and the final ordinances of the temple. The temple rituals extend the rebirth metaphor — washing away the blood of birth, anointing with oil, clothing in new garments, and acquiring a new name. All these ordinances are ritual symbols of the journey of Christ, the journey of Adam and Eve, and our journey back toward union with the godhead.

Within the context of the gospel metaphors we have been presenting, faith and repentance taken together are referred to as "being born of the word." This concept is the same as "being born to see" (John 3:3). Baptism is "being born of water," and the laying on of hands for the gift of the Holy Ghost is "being born of the spirit" or "being born of fire and the Holy Ghost." (Sometimes the endowment as an extension of confirmation is referred to as "being born of fire": D&C 95:8–10; Lk. 24:49; He. 2:1–4; TPJS, 274).

The metaphor of birth has been linked to the agricultural metaphor of planting the seed, which is used in the Book of Mormon in Alma 32. There the "seed" is God's word or spirit, and faith is referred to as the planting of the seed. The nourishing of the seed involves repentance (breaking the ground) and baptism (watering) and the laying on of hands for the gift of the Holy Ghost (sunlight).

Another gospel metaphor is drawn from the world of business, money, and trade. In this context Christ is said to have paid the "debt" of justice. If we accept his "offer" of salvation, we are "ransomed" or "redeemed" from the just penalty, which condemns us to the debtors' prison of death and hell.

When the gospel is set forth in legal metaphors, faith is equated with obtaining a "witness" or "testimony." Repentance is associated with "confessing" our sinful state to God. Baptism is linked with making a "covenant" with God and with being "acquitted" from sin or having our sins "remitted" and being "adopted" into the family of Christ. The laying on of hands is called "confirmation" — a "ratification" or "seal" placed upon the "deed."

The "covenant" metaphor has had both good and bad effects. On the positive side it suggests that our arrangements with God are based on freedom, on our willingness to follow the voice of God based on our own free will and choice. On the negative side, however, the "covenant" metaphor has led some people to misperceive salvation as a contractual affair in which we pay for redemption with our good works. But the covenant we make with Christ is to put off our human nature and take upon ourselves the divine nature, to trade our powerlessness for the gift of his glory. The word "covenant" refers not to a bargained-for exchange but to a gift. We give Christ nothing but our sins. We unload upon him our chains, and he gives us the freedom of eternal life. This is not a bargain. We do not earn it. What we can earn, we don't want: "The wages of sin is death." Salvation is a bequest: "The gift of God is eternal life" (Rom. 6:23).

All these metaphors refer to the mechanism of salvation, Christ's outline for receiving God's spirit. The condition of those who accept the gospel is also described with various metaphors. In the context of the birth metaphor, this state of grace is referred to as "being alive in Christ" or having been "born again" or having "the image of Christ in your countenance." In the context of the legal metaphor, the resulting state is referred to as "justification" or "adoption into the family of Christ." Employing the agricultural metaphor, the state of grace is compared to the "fruits and gifts of the spirit."

This state, however it is described, is not a state of perfection or rest. In God's grace we suffer ups and downs and even slips from virtue, but we continue to be connected to God through the spirit. Grace does not eliminate the need for forgiveness and repentance. However, the repentance required to enter the state of grace refers to accepting Christ and his spirit, while the repentance required to abide in a state of grace refers to living by the whisperings of his spirit as it leads us to perfection and truth.

As Mormons we do not usually think of repentance in either of these ways. We usually think of the list of rules and regulations we mentioned at the beginning of this chapter. We tend to lose sight of the fact that Jesus came to earth to introduce his gospel for the express purpose of freeing us from the obligation to obey legalistic prescriptions. Through his life, death, and resurrection, Jesus freed us from the strictness of the law, but he gave us the new responsibility of living by his spirit. This is what grace is all about.

Many Mormons object to this view of Jesus' gospel, often for the reason that it sounds too Protestant. As Mormons we tend to reject any religious teaching not uniquely Mormon. We like to think of ourselves as the elect, the chosen. We forget that before the gospel was restored through Joseph Smith, people had faith in Christ, repented of their sins, and trusted in him. This is true today. Throughout the world people claim to be the "people of the Lord." Most believe their faith in Christ, their repentance, and their attempts to live by the spirit and love of God are sufficient to save them. Because we Mormons emphasize the importance of the ordinances of salvation administered by "proper authority," we tend to forget that faith and repentance are gospel principles with power to transform lives without priesthood intervention.

It is, we believe, narcissistic and egocentric to think that such individuals are without the gospel. Joseph Smith did not tell the converts of his day that their former faith and repentance were vain. True, one revelation (D&C 22) chastises some early Mormon converts who wished to rely on their old baptisms rather than to be rebaptized. But the point of this revelation is that for those who accept the new and everlasting covenant within the context of Mormonism, all the former ordinances become obsolete. This is not to say, however, that the ordinances of other religions are dead to those who accept them in faith, sincerity, and love. People who have faith in Christ and repent accept the gospel. This is not the fullness of the gospel, but it is the gospel. Mormonism teaches that faith and repentance constitute the heart of the gospel and are necessary before the ordinances administered through the priesthood can have effect.

In our view God calls different people by different rituals and metaphors to different religious traditions. These differences are not mistakes. They are inspired by God to teach the hard lesson that no religion, no matter how favored or wise, is all-sufficient. In spite of its divine origins, Mormonism can be instructed by the traditions, myths, and rituals of others. This, we think, is one of the meanings of the parable of the olive tree in the Book of Jacob. The Lord has planted many trees in his vineyard. He uses the graft from one to strengthen the weakness in another.

Often when we Mormons are exposed to the powerful religious views and sincere devotion of others, we are shaken. We ask ourselves, "If our church is 'true,' how can the spirit be so palpable among this other, alien people?" This same question is asked by others when they feel the spirit working among us. We forget that Jesus is not merely a Mormon. He is a Jew and a Catholic and a Protestant and a Muslim and a pagan. We are all his people. He does not love us more than he loves them. He has died for all, not for a chosen few. His elect are all who elect him by whatever name and in whatever inherited tradition. This is not to say that all religious traditions are equally true, equally approved, or equally holy. But God does not distance himself because

of religious affiliation or doctrine or ritual. He accepts all who seek
him, yearn for him, love him, and desire him. Jesus accepts the worship of all people as true worship of himself if it is rendered sincerely
and not obviously directed toward the powers of darkness. Our callings to a religious tradition should not promote pride or elitism or
narcissism but rather humility, love, and acceptance of God's work
among all people everywhere.

We are here again called to a paradox. We are required to be true
to a specific tradition with specific promises and specific blessings.
And at the same time we are expected to accept God's work and spirit
among other religious traditions and respect them as we do our own.
We concur with the observation that "Although all roads can lead to
Rome . . . , we can travel but one at a time. When our own chosen
method, whatever it turns out to be, is entered in depth and with commitment, then all the others can be seen to lead in the same direction,
however divergent and 'absurd' their outer symbolism may appear"
(Blair, 250). For this reason, we believe that our message to the faithful
in other religious traditions should be:

> Friends, we know you are not novices in faith. You have loved God.
> We rejoice when you accept our way. But whether or not you do, please
> help us bear our burdens and we will help bear yours. Comfort us and we
> will comfort you. Mourn with us and we will mourn with you. Let us for-
> give one another. Let us bear witness of God and of the marvelous work
> he does in the world. Pray for us, and we will pray for you. And let us
> keep our hearts open to the Spirit and to the many things which God will
> yet reveal to us in ways we cannot know. If we cannot be one in doctrine,
> ritual, and authority, if we cannot share in the rituals of salvation, let us,
> while being true to our various faiths, be one in love with all who have
> longed for God, until all things are made clear and we inherit the peace
> that passes understanding.

Some are bound to object to this view because the scriptures seem
to confirm the idea that the world is divided into US and THEM. After
all is not God a God of judgment? Don't the prophets, Isaiah, Jeremiah,
Ezekiel, Nephi, John the Revelator, and Jesus, speak of judgments to
be visited upon the wicked, the non-believers, the errant? How do such
promised judgments square with the view that God works in all religions?

We have mentioned elsewhere that nearly every aspect of the Judeo-
Christian tradition can be viewed either from the perspective of the
"letter of the law" or of the "spirit of grace." This is true of the divine

judgments too. From the letter-of-the-law position, these judgments represent God's punishment for sin and disobedience. But the scriptures do not present judgment in this light. The scriptures almost always portray the judgments as an extension of God's mercy. Whom the Lord chastens, the Lord loves (D&C 95:1). Christ's love is without conditions. He pours out his spirit without measure upon every individual, every family, every race and nation, every culture and religion. He lets the rain fall on the just and the unjust (Matt. 5:45). Not all perceive it. Not all receive it. Not all employ it. Some reject it. Some despise it. Nevertheless Christ's grace is unshakable.

But God does not always approve of what we think and say and do. We are given wide latitude for growth. God lets us take risks, but if we begin to settle into patterns of evil such as self-deception, narcissism, elitism, authoritarianism, jealousy, envy, spite or if we deny our sins or project them on self-made scapegoats, then God, who is loving, merciful, and caring, is bound to reprove us — sometimes with sharpness. The judgments of God are reproofs not punishments. They are administered not to condemn us but to redeem us. This is why in the scripture the threat of divine judgment is so often attended by the assertion of God's undying love (think of Isaiah and Jeremiah). Thus the bonds of divine love "are stronger than the cords of death" (D&C 121:44).

Of course not every natural disaster and social upheaval should be attributed to God. Most of the problems we suffer in mortality have nothing to do with judgment. They follow from the temporal nature of life. Certainly some people view every calamity as divine retribution on some other person or group — usually an unpopular, powerless, envied, or despised group. But this view of judgment forms no part of our thinking. Rather than blame others for wars, diseases, and droughts, we should examine ourselves. This is one of the themes of the story of Oedipus, the king of Thebes. When his country was cursed with a plague, he sought to placate the gods by finding the murderer of the former king, Laius. In the end Oedipus discovered that he was the murderer. The judgments of God should not serve as a basis for condemning others but for searching our own souls and purifying our own hearts.

We do not believe God concocts catastrophes and inflicts them on various segments of the human race. In our view judgments occur because God withdraws the Holy Spirit. God thus demonstrates that unless God is ever present, we will be overwhelmed by the consequences of our accumulated errors, shortcomings, and sins. The judgments of God then do not take the form God creates for them but the form we create for them.

It is important to remember too that God can revoke judgment. We learn this from the story of Jonah and from other revelations (D&C 56:4–6). Perhaps some of the predicted judgments may no longer obtain. But if they do come, we must not think that God stands apart from them. God suffers with those judged. We are all part of the divine, cosmic tabernacle. A judgment rendered upon God is a judgment rendered upon us. This is what makes possible the condescension of God on our behalf. By the same token any judgment rendered upon us is also rendered upon God. The Divine Parents not only rejoice with us when we are blessed, they suffer with us when we are chastened. The tension between God's mercy and judgment is but another of the paradoxes of Christianity, which can be resolved only if we change our frame of reference. When we see judgment not as punishment but as God working to redeem us (even when we have rejected God's mercy), the tensions of the paradox begin to relax.

The judgments of God predicted in scripture constitute another symbol of God's love for us, another metaphor of the divine passion for our salvation. These metaphors are as diverse as God's dealings with us are various and mysterious. We believe all people have received dispensations of truth from God. No one has all the truth. And more truth will be revealed. When it comes, not only will others be required to change, but so will we. For us there is but one true way to God, but there are many roads leading to the point of departure.

PART IV

Priesthood

CHAPTER THIRTEEN

THE NATURE AND
PURPOSE OF PRIESTHOOD

In Mormonism priesthood is central. Recently, however, priesthood has become a source of concern for some Mormons. This is due in part to the tension created by competing church traditions. On the one hand the revelation of priesthood is seen as the central pillar of ecclesiastical hierarchical governance. On the other hand the Mormon doctrine of free agency reenforces the desire that many Latter-day Saints feel for equality, individual liberty, personal empowerment, and consensus government, all of which seem at odds with priesthood hierarchical rule. This tension is complicated because both sets of ideas can be derived from the scriptures and the teachings and revelations of Joseph Smith.

These opposing aspirations press us to question and reevaluate our assumptions about priesthood. What exactly is the priesthood? How is it related to the gospel? To faith? To spirituality and spiritual gifts? What can be done with priesthood that cannot be done without it? Does the popular concept of priesthood encourage unrighteous dominion, elitism, and hierarchy? Why are only males ordained? How is priesthood related to fatherhood? To motherhood? Are women entitled to priesthood? If so is there any difference in the manifestation and function of the priesthood in females? If women were ordained, would the priesthood be diminished? Would women be corrupted or male-identified by holding it? Would they dominate men? Would men lose interest in church service? Would important distinctions between male and female be lost? Should women hold priesthood but not function as church officers? If everyone holds the priesthood, does it become meaningless or trivial? Should priesthood be dispensed with entirely in order to avoid problems and inequities? Is priesthood essential to the gospel, to godhood, to the godhead? And if so how?

The answers any of us give to these questions will depend upon our understanding of the nature and purpose of priesthood and its relationship to the gospel of Jesus Christ. In reexamining our priesthood doctrines, we wish first to reconsider some of the priesthood statements of Joseph Smith. Although Joseph is identified as the source of most priesthood teachings in the modern church, there is some discrepancy between what he taught and what most Mormons now believe about priesthood.

For Joseph priesthood was not simply a status. It was an ordinance of salvation. This contradicts the view that sees priesthood principally in corporate terms as the authority to act for God, to organize and manage the church, to keep it running smoothly and efficiently, to correlate and control its operations, and to insure a homogeneous and cost-effective organization. Joseph Smith taught that the primary purpose of priesthood is spiritual. For Joseph priesthood was raw spiritual power inextricably tied to the holy spirit, to the glory of God. This power centers in the person of Jesus Christ and emanates from his presence to fill the universe. It is the divine will, a supernatural light giving life and order to all of God's creation (D&C 88:5–11). It is the law by which all things are governed. It is a "perfect law of theocracy" (TPJS, 322; WJS, 244).

The essence of priesthood, then, is the power of the spirit. Any person who receives a degree of the spirit through faith, or repentance, or baptism and confirmation receives some portion of the priesthood. This is why Joseph Smith could say that the "testimony of Jesus is the spirit of prophecy" (TPJS, 119), that the "rights of the priesthood are inseparably connected with the powers of heaven" (D&C 121:36), and that women have the right to heal and bless by virtue of the "ordination" they receive at the time they obtain the gift of the Holy Ghost (WJS, 115). In these teachings, Joseph reflected to a certain extent Martin Luther's notion of a priesthood of all believers.

However, there is more to the priesthood than the spirit. The power of the priesthood must be held together with the rights of the priesthood, which consist of the agency to act for Christ and the keys or authority to perform certain functions in Christ's name. The rights of the priesthood are transmitted in two ways: by the laying on of hands and by the temple endowment.

By the laying on of hands, males are constituted agents of Christ when they are provisionally inducted into the Aaronic or the Melchizedek priesthood orders by the ordinance called "priesthood conferral." As a member of the Aaronic order a man becomes a limited agent of Christ, entitled to be ordained only to one of the offices of the Aaronic priesthood — deacon, teacher, priest, or (if a lineal descendent of Aaron) bishop — offices that carry with them the restricted duties and responsibilities to administer the ordinances of justification and care for the temporal needs of the church. As a member of the Melchizedek order a man becomes an agent of Christ with greater authority and is entitled to be ordained to one of the offices of the Melchizedek priesthood — elder, high priest, patriarch, seventy, or apostle — offices that carry with them the duties and responsibilities to administer some of the ordinances of sanctification and to care for the spiritual needs and the governance of the church. In the church today the conferral upon men of the Aaronic and Melchizedek priesthoods and their ordination to the priesthood offices of bishop and apostle is seen technically to convey to them priesthood keys, that is, the authority to perform gospel ordinances or to authoritatively discharge functions of church governance and service. However, these keys are said to remain inoperative until the ordained individual is "set apart" by the laying on of hands to a church office, at which time the dormant keys become functional. It is important to note that, by the act of setting apart, keys may also be temporarily transmitted to and exercised by others, including women.

The other mechanism for the transmittal of the rights of the priesthood in the modern church is the temple endowment, which personally and nonprovisionally vests in both men and women the fullness of the keys of the priesthood while simultaneously inducting them into the Aaronic and Melchizedek priesthood orders as full-fledged members. This happens as they receive the lesser and greater ordinances of the priesthood. Once endowed, men and women may be sealed in the new and everlasting covenant of marriage in preparation for jointly receiving the last anointing, by which they are inducted into the most comprehensive of the priestly orders — the Holy Order of God. As members of this order men hold the office of priest and king and women, the office of queen and priestess. Membership in this order must be held jointly by the husband and the wife, symbolizing that the male and female are equally necessary to reflect the true image of God. Those of the Holy Order have general authority to perform any ordinance of the gospel and to assume any responsibility and perform any function in the church and kingdom of God.

In our view, then, both the power and the rights of the priesthood are equally necessary. The keys of the priesthood were first revealed to Joseph Smith and Oliver Cowdery so that they could administer to each other the ordinances of baptism and confirmation, by which they in turn, could receive power in the priesthood to carry on the work of the restoration. Later the endowment ordinances comprising the fullness of the gospel were revealed to provide additional power as well as the full complement of priesthood keys. From this perspective, Joseph Smith could say "that the rights of the priesthood are inseparably connected with the powers of heaven, and that the powers of heaven cannot be controlled nor handled only upon the principles of righteousness," that is, upon the principles of the gospel by which righteousness is imputed to us by Christ. "That they may be conferred upon us, it is true; but when we undertake to cover our sins, or to gratify our pride, our vain ambition, or to exercise control or dominion or compulsion upon the souls of the children of men, in any degree of unrighteousness, behold, the heavens withdraw themselves; the Spirit of the Lord is grieved; and when it is withdrawn, Amen to the priesthood or the authority of that man" (D&C 121:36–37). Hence, failure to live the gospel and retain the spirit separates the rights of the priesthood from the powers of heaven so that the priesthood no longer has any spiritual authority. For without the power of the priesthood—the Holy Ghost—there is no revelation, or vision, no speaking in or interpreting tongues, no discernment of spirits, no comprehension of mysteries, no union with God.

The priesthood serves a further gospel purpose not only because it administers the ordinances and powers of the gospel, but because, by receiving and exercising the priesthood, a person follows in Christ's footsteps. This connection between the gospel and the priesthood is suggested by the name of the priesthood: The Holy Priesthood after the Order of the Son of God (D&C 107:2–5), signifying that to receive the priesthood is to share with Christ his power, profession, and spiritual mission, to receive the image of Christ in our countenances. Our spiritual journey was not meant to end with rebirth and justification. We are to be made holy, to be sanctified, as well. Ordination to the priesthood is part of this process because it enables us to act in Christ's name, to be remade in his image by drawing closer to him and our fellow beings through spiritual and priestly service. To reach "the measure of the stature of the fulness of Christ" (Eph. 4:13), we must accept the same priesthood rights and powers bestowed upon him and then freely extend ourselves beyond our own ego-centricity to care about the spiritual welfare of others as much as we care about our own.

This work is represented in the scriptural image of cultivation and nurture. The faithful are like seedlings sprouting in fertile ground. If nurtured and cared for, they will become trees "springing up unto everlasting life." In other words we will become like Christ, the tree of life. But the symbol is more complex than this; for we are also similar to the laborers who cultivate the trees. "I have planted," said Paul. "Apollos watered, but God gave the increase" (1 Cor. 3:6–9). This is another way of representing the work of the priesthood: participating with God to bring about spiritual rebirth, nurture, and perfection in ourselves and in others. Through the priesthood we share in God's work and glory "to bring to pass the immortality and eternal life of man[kind]" (Moses 1:39).

It is important to see that both the giving and receiving of spiritual blessings is essential to the process of sanctification and to the magnification of priesthood. Maturation is a matter of give and take. The cliche tells us that "it is better to give than to receive." But is this so? Giving puts us in the dominant position, and this is flattering to the ego. Receiving takes humility, because it requires us to acknowledge our reliance on others for help. Giving and receiving are equally necessary to spiritual growth. Like breathing out and breathing in, they are part of a single process.

This process points us to what is perhaps the central purpose of the priesthood: the unification of polarities. The highest objective of the Holy Priesthood after the Order of the Son of God seems to be atonement or bringing into unity and harmony all the fragmented elements lying broken and scattered in ourselves and others—in our families, in our communities, and in the cosmos. The priesthood is the power to reconcile the contraries of the universe into a living whole and to heal and perfect them. The work of the priesthood is to seal or bind together not only the families of the earth but also spirit and body, male and female, heaven and earth, humanity and divinity. Because priesthood makes atonement, it lies at the heart of the gospel. In this sense Christ himself is the priesthood, and we grow in priesthood power only as we become like him.

The questions about priesthood initiating this chapter arise upon the tension between polarities. We fail to see clearly how the priesthood encompasses and reconciles male and female, inner and outer, public and private, equality and hierarchy, individual and community. In future chapters we will explore how priesthood harmonizes such opposites in the context of the gospel. Here we will focus on the inner and outer aspects of priesthood, often seen at odds with one another.

A person can have inward priesthood power or an outward ordination or both. The individual with both is not problematical. However, a person with only an outward ordination and few spiritual gifts can be spiritually unedifying, a quite common circumstance which does not usually trouble us because we do not often think of priesthood in terms of inward spirituality. Less common in Mormonism and more perplexing to us is the person with only the inward power. Such an individual worries us because he or she suggests that the need for priesthood ordination is contradicted. But neither of these conclusions is true. Let us illustrate this by comparing priesthood to baptism.

Baptism is an outward sign of an inward spiritual change occurring through faith in Jesus Christ and repentance. A person can be spiritually reborn long before she/he is authoritatively baptized. When this happens the person is still justified and accepted by God as being in a state of grace. The inward change is efficacious. This has led some Protestants to conclude that baptism is not absolutely necessary since it is only a sign of the more important inward change. This view is a reaction to Catholicism, which holds that the sacraments are the primary means of salvation. One of Joseph Smith's most important contributions to Christianity, in our view, was the integration of these views. Joseph said that we might as well baptize a "bag of sand" as a person who has not repented and had faith (WJS, 230). But he also said that through the ordinances "the power of godliness is manifest" (D&C 84:20–22). A person who experiences inner transformation without baptism later may need to be baptized or accept a vicariously performed baptism, while a person who is not spiritually reborn at the time of his or her baptism may nevertheless be encouraged by such ordinances toward a genuine spiritual transformation.

Like baptism, ordination to priesthood is an outward sign of an inward spiritual state, which can lead to spiritually-motivated acts. As with baptism a person can receive the outward ordination without receiving the inward power which should accompany it. But here again the ordinance may facilitate genuine spiritual development. And a person's priesthood will have legal efficacy even if it is not accompanied by inward spiritual power. But there is also validity in many of the words and works of a person with only the inward power of the priesthood. Jesus and Joseph Smith both tested a person in this latter situation by asking whether the person's spiritual acts resulted in good fruit, assuming that good fruit points to God's inspiration.

This is sometimes hard for Mormons to accept. We want to believe that only those duly ordained to the Mormon priesthood can have genuine contact with the divine. We cannot accept the power of God when it manifests itself in a non-traditional way or in other religious traditions. Because we are members of the "only true and living church" (D&C 1:30), we often believe there is no truth or spirituality or salvation outside the church. We confuse our claim of divine institutional authorization with the claim that no priesthood or spiritual power functions outside the church. We forget that the priesthood was restored before the church was organized and can exist and operate independent of a church structure or formal ordination.

But it is clear from the religious experience of many Mormons and of millions of religious people throughout the world that, though Christ is Mormonism's Great High Priest, he is not our God alone. He has planted on the earth at different times many true churches and many authorities. He has, as the Book of Mormon tells us, many trees in his vineyard. There are many promised lands, many chosen people, many lost tribes, many records of his doings yet to emerge. To say that we have the fullness of the priesthood is not to say that others are without spirituality, vitality, or priestly callings. We have said before that the religious traditions of others are valid to those who sincerely accept them. This same concept applies to the priesthood. We must recognize legitimate spiritual power and a form of priesthood among Hindus, Buddhists, Catholics, Protestants, Jews, and pagans. We must see that God bestows gifts and callings upon all cultures and all people. If we have the true priesthood in its fullness, this is no cause for arrogance or complacency. We ought to be compassionate and humble enough to admit that God will not require others to accept the truth he has given to us without requiring us to accept the truth he has given to them. We cannot simply export our religion but must also import from others.

Within our own tradition, however, the inner and outer aspects of priesthood are reflected in both public and private ways. Each member of the priesthood order stands as his or her own priest or priestess before God working out his or her own salvation in personal and individual terms. In D&C 1:20 we are admonished that the gospel was restored so that every person might "speak in the name of God, the Lord, even the Savior of the world." This teaching reinforces the dignity and

worth of each individual. But each person is also part of and responsible to a community or priesthood order. The apostle Paul invokes
the image of Christ's body. Members are not like machine parts, inter-
changeable and expendable, but like body parts, precious and irreplace-
able. One part cannot say to another, "I have no need of thee." Each
member is unique and necessary but also part of the church.

This interconnection points to another paradox: the balance between the power of the individual and of the community. On a practical level this means that though decisions and revelations in the church
can come from the head, we must not prohibit the participation of the
members in the governance of the church. Already we have nearly lost
the concept of common consent. The voting procedure in our general
conferences is all that remains of the general assemblies which sometimes met in Joseph Smith's time to direct church affairs. These assemblies appointed priesthood committees to arrange and publish doctrines and revelations, excommunicated presidencies (David Whitmer,
John Whitmer, William W. Phelps, Martin Harris), and even recommended the excommunication of Assistant President of the Church
Oliver Cowdery.

It can be argued that the church membership constitutes a general
assembly, whose authority equals the First Presidency of the church
(D&C 107: 19–32; Smith 1950, 184–86, 206–206; HC 3:16–19).
We are to be a kingdom of priests and priestesses. "Would that all God's
people were prophets," said Moses, not at all jealous of the spiritual
gifts and powers of others but rather desirous to bring all his people to
the mountain to talk face to face with God. We can never have true
community in the church nor can we ever realize a Zion society until
we understand that the governing principle of the celestial kingdom is
unity and equality in things temporal and spiritual. We must hold all
things in common, without strife, without contention, without jealousy,
and without fear.

The individual and community dimensions of priesthood are mir-
rored in the very word "priesthood." The term "priest," derived from
the Greek word *presbyter* meaning elder, suggests an individual wise in
the counsels of God. The suffix *-hood* probably derives from the word
hat and refers to a covering for the head. People did and sometimes do
wear a hood or hat as part of a uniform to show membership in a community or profession. In such garb an individual becomes a new person and attains a new status as a member of a distinct order. The au-

thor of the Epistle to the Hebrews speaks of Jesus as the "Apostle and High Priest of our profession" (Heb. 3:1).

The essential unity of the inner and outer, the individual and community aspects of priesthood, demonstrate that any division of priesthood by levels or degrees is only cosmetic. The priesthood has a single underlying nature. Joseph Smith recognized this when he taught: "All priesthood is Melchizedek; but there are different portions or degrees of it. That portion which brought Moses to speak with God face to face was taken away; but that which brought the ministry of angels remained" (WJS, 59). In the Mormon tradition the Aaronic and Melchizedek priesthoods exist to administer the ordinances of rebirth and the higher ordinances which enable us like Moses to speak face to face with God. Joseph Smith described "three grand principles or orders of priesthood":

> 1st Levitical which was never able to administer a Blessing but only to bind heavy burdens which neither they nor their father[s were] able to bear
>
> 2 Abrahams Patriarchal power which is the greatest yet experienced in this church [27 August 1843]
>
> 3d That of Melchisedec who had still greater power even power of an endless life of which was our Lord Jesus Christ which also Abraham obtained by the offering of his son Isaac which was not the power of a Prophet nor apostle nor Patriarch only but of King & Priest to God to open the windows of Heaven and pour out the peace & Law of endless Life to man & no man can attain to the Joint heirship with Jesus Christ without being administered to by one having the same power & Authority of Melchisedec. . . . (ibid., 245)

In another discourse, Joseph Smith explained that there were three spirits or powers connected with the priesthood: "[T]he spirit of Elias is first Elijah second, and Masiah last. Elias is a fore runner to prepare the way, & the spirit & power of Elijah is to come after holding the keys of power building the Temple to the Capstone, placing the seals of the Melchezedek priesthood up on the house of Israel & making all things ready then Mesiah comes to his Temple which is last of all. Mesiah is above the spirit & power of Elijah, for he made the world & was the spiritual rock unto Moses in the wilderness" (ibid., 331–32).

From these statements we conclude not only that all priesthood is one but that all priesthood is Messianic or Christological. To receive the full blessings and powers of the priesthood is to become a Savior on Mount Zion, a joint-heir with Jesus Christ in all the Father has. The

Holy Priesthood after the Order of the Son of God, was linked by Joseph Smith to the "Spirit of Messiah," who has "all power in Heaven and in Earth [for he is] Enthroned in the Heavens as King of Kings and Lord of Lords" (WJS, 336).[1]

That Christ is designated as the head of the priestly order has been used by some, particularly Catholics, to support the view that only males should hold priesthood. Mormons too have denied priesthood to women mainly because the scriptures present us only with male priesthood figures and male members of the godhead. In our view, however, the doctrine of God the Mother calls us to accept the legitimacy of priesthood for women. Because godhood is the highest and final dimension of priesthood and because godhood is male and female, it follows that priesthood must be male and female as well. This fact is recognized in Mormon scripture dealing with the fullness of the priesthood (D&C 132:19) and in the practice of anointing to the fullness of the priesthood in Mormon temples men and women jointly.

In defining the scope and privileges of priesthood, Joseph Smith stated: "Now for Elijah, the spirit power & calling of Elijah is that ye have power to hold the keys of the revelations ordinances, oricles powers & endowments of the fullness of the Melchezedek Priesthood & of the Kingdom of God on Earth & to receive, obtain & perform all the ordinances belonging to the Kingdom of God even unto the sealing of the hearts of the fathers unto the children & the hearts of the children unto the fathers even those who are in heaven" (WJS, 329). According to Joseph the "fullness of the Melchizedek Priesthood" opens the "windows of Heaven" out of which are poured the "peace & Law of endless Life" (245). Joseph also taught that receiving this fullness guaranteed one's calling and election "for while the spirit of Elias is a forerunner the power of Elijah is sufficient to make our calling & Election sure. . . . we must have revelations then & we can see that the doctrin of revela-

---

[1] The various degrees or portions of the priesthood have been named after noted priests of God's order. The Aaronic priesthood is named for Aaron and associated with John the Baptist, both of whom functioned in the spirit and calling of Elias, the forerunner, to gather the House of Israel. We associate the patriarchal (and matriarchal) priesthood with Abraham and Sarah, Isaac and Rebecca, and Jacob and Rachel. And we associate the fullness of the priesthood with Melchizedek, Elijah, and Elisha, all of whom wielded supernatural powers and were types and shadows of Jesus Christ. Yet though these individuals are associated with one or more degrees of priesthood connected with their primary missions, we believe that they possessed the fullness of the powers of the Messianic or Melchizedek priesthood.

tion as far transcends the doctrin of no revelation as knowledge is above ignorance for one truth revealed from heaven is worth all the sectarian notions in exhistance" (330). Among the keys embraced by the fullness of the priesthood is the key to commune with God: "thus we behold the Keys of this priesthood consisted in obtaining the voice of Jehovah" (42). Joseph Smith further stated: "This is why Abraham blessed his posterity: He wanted to bring them into the presence of God. They looked for a city, &c — Moses sought to bring the children of Israel into the presence of God, through the power of the Priesthood, but he could not" (9).

This statement suggests that the fullness of the priesthood and the gospel are connected and share the same nature and purpose. Both were given to bring about spiritual renewal and oneness with God. In this vein Joseph Smith said: "Here then is eternal life — to know the only wise and true God [Goddess] and you have got to learn how to be Gods yourselves, and to be kings and priests [and queens and priestesses] to God, the same as all Gods have done before you, namely, by going from one small degree to another, and from a small capacity to a great one; from grace to grace, from exaltation to exaltation, until you attain to the resurrection of the dead, and are able to dwell in everlasting burnings, and to sit in glory, as do those who sit enthroned in everlasting power" (TPJS, 346–47; WJS, 350).

The calling of king and priest and queen and priestess embraces the fullness of this priesthood's keys over temporal and spiritual matters. Those who possess these keys hold authority to unify the spiritual and temporal, the transcendent and the immanent, the earthly and the heavenly. Thus men and women may have a fullness of joy. This priesthood exists to bestow life not merely to impose order. It transforms not merely reforms. It is given to those who accept rather than control, love rather than judge, and bless rather than dictate.

For us the fullness of the priesthood is not merely an esoteric, historical tidbit to be whispered in the corridors of our chapels. Like the doctrines of the Creation, the Fall, the Atonement, and the universal judgment, the doctrine of the fullness of the priesthood is at once a cornerstone of the gospel, a pillar of the temple, and the capstone of Mormonism. Receiving the fullness of the priesthood means being called to the "measure of the stature of the fullness of Christ" (Eph. 4:13), to the image of the divine, male and female, to the work of reconciliation, to the community of the pure in heart, to fellow citizenship with the saints in the household of God.

CHAPTER FOURTEEN

PRIESTHOOD IN
THE BOOK OF MORMON

The Book of Mormon is the earliest Mormon scriptural text discussing both the structure and the nature of priesthood. Printed between August 1829 and March 1830, it is the first published scripture of Mormonism although it was preceded by seventeen then unpublished revelations, many eventually appearing in the 1833 Book of Commandments and in the 1835 Doctrine and Covenants. Prior to publication most or all of these revelations existed in handwritten form and undoubtedly had limited circulation. The content of many of these early revelations (now D&C 2–18) indicates priesthood was being discussed in the early church.

However, when the church was organized on 6 April 1830, the only available Mormon scripture discussing priesthood concepts was the Book of Mormon. Alma 13 contains an extraordinary doctrinal treatise on the nature of priesthood, its source and its scope. This treatise suggests priesthood authority is transmitted or conferred first by means of a "holy calling" (Al. 13:3) and then by an ordination "with a holy ordinance" (v. 8) "given after this manner, that thereby the people might look forward on the Son of God" (v. 16). According to Alma, it is the Lord God rather than humans who creates priests (v. 1). This process begins when one is "called and prepared from the foundation of the world according to the foreknowledge of God on account of . . . exceeding faith and good works." God's call, we are told, is not based on God's whim but upon his knowledge of the faithfulness of the candidates, who were "in the first place, left to choose good or evil; therefore, they having chosen good, and exercising exceeding great faith are called with a holy calling" (v. 3). Though it is possible to interpret the phrase "in the first place" as a reference to a time prior to mortality, this is not essential. The point of the verse is that God's holy calling is predicated on faithfulness, not predestination.

The "holy calling" to priesthood referred to by the Book of Mormon appears to be unmediated; it comes directly from God without the intercession of any human agency. This concept is strongly urged in several places in the treatise by Alma. The text states: "the Lord God ordained priests after his holy order" (Al. 13:1). It is the "Spirit of God" (v. 4) not any human being that extends the "holy calling"; and by implication it is by rejecting this Spirit that one rejects the calling itself (ibid.). This also suggests the calling comes directly through the spirit, not through human mediation.

The Book of Mormon tells of priesthood figures called to preach repentance and the gospel by God without ordination: Lehi (1 Ne. 1:18–20), Nephi (17:48–54), Alma the Elder (Mos. 18:13), Abinadi (11:20; 12:1–2), and Samuel the Lamanite (He. 13:5, 7). Nephi and Alma the Elder not only received unmediated callings but relied on these callings to perform gospel ordinances, including ordaining others to the priesthood (2 Ne. 5:26; Al. 18:18). Similar examples can be found in the Old Testament. Moses, Aaron (Ex. 3, 4), and the prophet Samuel (1 Sam. 3) all received unmediated callings that served as sources of the priestly and kingly authority of others (10:1; 16:1, 13). In the New Testament Paul receives an unmediated calling to the apostleship when Jesus Christ appears to him on the road to Damascus (Gal. 1:1; Acts 26:14–18).

The conversion of Alma the Younger is the most detailed Book of Mormon story about an individual receiving an unmediated calling to preach. Alma, like Paul a former persecutor of Christians, is rebuked by an angel, falls into a trance, awakens, announces to his astonished listeners that he has been born of the Spirit, declares that his soul was snatched from out of eternal torment, and confesses Christ as his redeemer. Then "Alma began from this time forward to teach the people, and those who were with Alma at the time the angel appeared unto them, traveling round about through all the land, publishing to all the people the things which they had heard and seen, and preaching the word of God in much tribulation, being greatly persecuted by those who were unbelievers, being smitten by many of them" (Mos. 27:32).

Alma does not wait to be ordained by human authority: "from this time forward [Alma began] to teach the people." "This time forward" refers to Alma's supernatural experience, his trance and vision of

Christ, who called him to publish the good news of redemption. That Alma rests his authority to preach and teach upon this unmediated calling is clear: "For I am called to speak after this manner according to the holy order of God, which is in Christ Jesus; yea, I am commanded to stand and testify unto this people the things which have been spoken by our fathers concerning the things which are to come" (Al. 5:44). Alma rests his authority to preach the gospel upon his vision. The text mentions nothing about an ordination. This formula is repeated in Alma 5:49: "And now I say unto you that this is the order after which I am called, yea, to preach unto my beloved brethren, yea, and every one that dwelleth in the land; yea, to preach unto all, both old and young, both bond and free; yea, I say unto you the aged, and also the middle aged, and the rising generation; yea, to cry unto them that they must repent and be born again." And in Alma 5:51, we find this statement: "And also the Spirit saith unto me, yea, crieth unto me with a mighty voice, saying: Go forth and say unto this people — Repent, for except ye repent ye can in nowise inherit the kingdom of heaven."

It is by the unmediated act of God through the Holy Spirit that Alma the Younger is called to preach, not by any human being or acknowledged priesthood figure. However, it is not clear whether this holy calling alone was sufficient to empower Alma with the authority to baptize and ordain others. In any case the "holy calling" is presented as only one of two components of priesthood transmittal. The second, according to Alma 13, is the "holy ordinance." By this calling and ordinance, we are told, an individual becomes a high priest "forever, after the order of the Son, the Only Begotten of the Father" (v. 8).

The "holy ordinance" involves at least a designation or appointment through the mediation of a human intercessor and perhaps the laying on of hands. For example, Alma the Younger is called by God but then ordained by his father: "I, Alma, having been consecrated by my father, Alma, to be a high priest over the church of God, he having power and authority from God to do these things" (Al. 5:3). The text presents the holy calling as coming before the ordination: "Thus, being called by this holy calling, and ordained unto the high priesthood of the holy order of God" (v. 6). Alma the Younger relies upon his holy calling to preach and upon his father's act of consecration to preside.

Alma's ancestor Jacob, Nephi's brother and successor, also rests his authority to preach and teach upon an unmediated calling: "Wherefore I, Jacob, gave unto them these words as I taught them in the temple, having first obtained mine errand from the Lord" (Jac. 1:17). Later there appears a clarification: "Thus came the word unto me saying: Jacob, get thou up into the temple on the morrow, and declare the word which I shall give thee unto this people" (2:11). Although this verse refers to a calling to preach a specific sermon on a given occasion, it is significant that Jacob does not mention his ordination or consecration as a "priest" or "teacher." This suggests the unmediated calling of God was more important or fundamental than the ordination. Like Alma the Younger, Jacob is presented as the recipient of both a holy calling and an ordination or "consecration."

Mosiah 18 presents us with the example of Alma the Elder. Without any mention of an ordination, and apparently without benefit of a predecessor, he not only preaches but also baptizes others: "O Lord pour out thy Spirit upon thy servant, that he may do this work with holiness of heart. And when he had said these words, the Spirit of the Lord was upon him, and he said: Helam, I baptize thee, having authority from the Almighty God.... And after Alma had said these words, both Alma and Helam were buried in the water; and they arose and came forth out of the water rejoicing, being filled with the Spirit" (Mos. 18:12–14). On the basis of this calling, Alma the Elder later organizes a church. When his followers join the community of King Mosiah in Zarahemla, Alma seeks an appointment of the king to settle the church in that place and obtains from the king permission to ordain priests and teachers within the church structure (25:19).

Of course it is possible to argue that Alma the Elder had been a priest of King Noah and was relying upon his ordination to that priesthood to baptize, ordain, and organize the church. But for this argument to succeed, we must assume the priests of King Noah were true priests, which contradicts the text (Mos. 11:5). Or else we must assume that the unmediated calling of God is sufficient to transform a false priesthood into a true one. This is virtually the same as arguing that a person with no ordination can by an unmediated calling from God be authorized to baptize.

In our view the Book of Mormon posits two components of priesthood transmittal: the "holy calling" and the "holy ordinance." The calling, coming from God without mediation, establishes the relationship between the called individual and God, and for this reason we believe this calling is the most important feature of priesthood conferral. Apparently if this calling comes to those living within an already existing, divinely authorized church structure, the calling empowers individuals only to preach repentance and teach the gospel. If the calling comes to one living outside such a church structure, it seems to carry as well authority to baptize, to ordain, and even to organize a church. If an acknowledged church structure exists, the "holy ordinance" appears to establish the relationship of the "called" individual to other "called" individuals within the church. Taken together the "holy calling" and the "holy ordinance" establish the recipients' obligations to God and to the community of believers and the order of priests. Thus through the "holy calling" one is committed to the love and service of God. Through the "holy ordinance" one is committed to the love and service of humanity.

The Alma 13 priesthood treatise also suggests another point: the "holy ordinance" does not appear to be accomplished simply by means of the laying on of hands. This is suggested by a verbal formula invoked twice, once in verse 2 and once in verse 16. These passages suggest that when high priests were ordained, the manner of the ordination communicated something about the coming of the Messiah and his redemption (v. 2). We are told that the ordination was done in a way "that the people might look forward on the Son of God, it being a type of his order" (v. 16). The reference to "type" suggests the use of typology, a symbol foreshadowing how Christ would work out the redemption. By 1842 Joseph Smith was teaching that the fullness of the priesthood, which he often called the "holy order," was communicated by the endowment rituals, which are replete with crucifixion symbols and other Christian typology. Whether these or similar gestures, postures, or rituals might be what is hinted at in Alma is impossible to say.

The Book of Mormon view of priesthood might thus be summarized: God calls his own priests directly. But those called must also be ordained by a holy ordinance, which involves a symbolic ritual typifying the salvific work of Christ. By this holy ordinance the ones called are authorized by the divinely acknowledged priestly order to act within the church structure. However, on occasion certain individuals with unmediated callings are presented as not waiting for ordination before embarking upon their ministries. Ordination, therefore, is not presented as necessary for creating a church or priesthood structure where none existed or preaching repentance or teaching the gospel or castigating an existing ecclesiastical or political structure which has become rigid or corrupt (Mos. 11–17; Al. 31–35; He. 13–15).

These Book of Mormon teachings on priesthood have significant implications for the modern church. First, it seems to us that the Book of Mormon advances two types of priesthood authority. The most familiar one is ecclesiastical, the authority to preside in a church office. The other is charismatic or spiritual authority. "Charismatic" comes from the Greek word *kharis* meaning "favor" or "spiritual gift." Christ relied heavily upon this authority when he preached on earth. He spoke from outside contemporary structures or organizations, relying on his "holy calling" rather than on an ordination to ecclesiastical office.

These two authorities have different purposes. Charismatic authority (or inward priesthood, as we have called it previously) comes by the "holy calling" and is the heart of the priesthood. It exists to connect the sacred and the profane, to reconcile the fallen world with God, to make people aware of the numinous, and to bring them into the presence of the Most High. This authority is attended to by prophecy, healings, tongues, and other charismatic gifts. Ecclesiastical authority (or outward priesthood) comes by a holy ordinance and exists to develop, maintain, and protect the church, to promote the teachings of Christ, to perform the ordinances of the gospel, and to provide a refuge for those seeking to flee from the world into the community of Saints. The Book of Mormon teaches that these two authorities comprise the priesthood of God and that they should operate together: the ecclesiastical to care for the structure of the church and the charismatic to keep the Spirit burning brightly there.

Ideally these authorities should exist in each priest, as they did in Book of Mormon personages Nephi, Jacob, Alma the Elder, and Alma the Younger. Often they do not, because they descend to us in different ways. The ecclesiastical authority is conferred by humans through ordination. The charismatic authority comes only from God and is received only if the recipient has faith — "exceeding great faith" (Al. 13:3). As we have said, people without either authority are not a puzzle; neither are those who obviously have both. Problems are created by individuals who have only one or the other. The charismatic is endowed with spiritual gifts: insight, knowledge, truth, the power to teach and convince. The ecclesiastic is endowed with the resources and corporate power of the church and the responsibility to watch over the community. Unless theology harmonizes these separate functions, the balance will usually swing in favor of one and then the other. Mormonism began with a short charismatic period — marked by institutional chaos and doctrinal ferment. Since then ecclesiastical authority has predominated with its concern for institutional order, fiscal stability, doctrinal simplicity and consistency, categorical morality, and public image. Alma

13 with its insistence on both the "holy calling" and the "holy ordinance" suggests there should be a balance between the two dimensions of priesthood; the merits and weaknesses of each are recognized and acknowledged in one system of authority referred to by Alma as the high priesthood of the holy order.

The existence of a charismatic priesthood authority transmitted directly to individuals by supernatural means has important implications for women, who traditionally have been excluded from ordination into priestly orders. It may be argued that their exclusion is merely traditional or cultural and that a woman is just as entitled to a "holy calling" from God as is a man. In fact God's dealings with such women as Eve, Esther, Ruth, Mary the mother of Christ, Mary Magdalene, and Emma Smith may be interpreted as just such non-ecclesiastical "holy callings."

But it is not women alone who suffer disenfranchisement. Men too, if they do not submit to ecclesiastical traditions, conventions, and expectations, may be excluded from ordination. D&C 77:11 speaks of the ordination of high priests of "the holy order of God" as being brought about in "every nation, kindred, tongue, and people, by the angels to whom is given power over the nations of the earth, to bring as many as will come to the church of the Firstborn." But in spite of such texts, the church rejects the concept that priesthood authority may now be conferred without mediation. In the prevailing view such an idea would undermine priesthood control of the church and spiritual security of its members. In the wake of such a doctrine, couldn't anyone make a false claim to priesthood authority? How would the good people of the church know the true charismatic authorities from the false?

The phrasing of such questions assumes that tight control of the ordination process coupled with the power to excommunicate or disfellowship rebels and apostates is sufficient to protect the church from false claims to authority. But how is the church protected from lack of spirituality among its leaders from top to bottom? The apostles at Jerusalem were unwilling to spread the gospel among the Gentiles. This would have permanently crippled the church had it not been for Paul's unmediated calling. In the Book of Mormon, we are presented with corruption at the court of King Noah. The old priests had died or had been replaced with "such as were lifted up in the pride of their hearts" (Mos. 11:5). With corruption at the highest levels, what hope was there for the people of King Noah had it not been for the unmediated calling of Abinadi? Similarly it appears that the church of the

Nephites just prior to the coming of Christ would have remained spiritually comatose had it not been for the unmediated calling of Samuel the Lamanite.

In each of these situations it could be asked: How did the people realize their religious institutions had degenerated and the time to repent had come? How for that matter did the people of the Old Testament know if prophets such as Lehi were true or false? How did the people know that John had authority to baptize or that Jesus was Lord? This very question was put to Christ: "By what authority doest thou these things? and who gave thee this authority to do these things? And Jesus answered and said unto them, I will also ask of you one question, and answer me, and I will tell you by what authority I do these things. The baptism of John, was it from heaven, or of men? answer me. And they reasoned with themselves, saying, If we shall say, From heaven; he will say, Why then did you not believe him? But if we shall say, Of men, they feared the people: for all men counted John, that he was a prophet indeed. And they answered and said unto Jesus, we cannot tell. And Jesus answering saith unto them, Neither do I tell you by what authority I do these things" (Mk. 11:28–33). Though no answer appears to be given, the answer is there: "We cannot tell," said the Jewish leaders. And Jesus replied, "Neither do I tell you."

In our view, this dialogue means that there is no way to validate institutionally the authority of those called directly by God. It is by their fruits that they are known. This was so in the case of Paul and Barnabas (Acts 13:2). Their missionary efforts, at least up to the time of the council at Jerusalem, were carried out on the basis of Paul's unmediated calling from Christ. It was only later that Paul's work was acknowledged and ratified by the leaders of the Christian movement. Joseph Smith provides an additional example. The validity and truth of his ministry is still a matter of debate in the Christian world and may be validated only by the fruits of his work.

The church addresses such uncertainty by insisting that an individual be duly ordained. But the Book of Mormon teaches us that being ordained is not the same as being called — a point that is unsettling to many who demand certainty in matters of authority and are quick to reject any charismatic individual without ecclesiastical authority, but who are strangely willing to accept any ecclesiastical officer, because they assume that proper ordination always includes or presupposes a divine calling. This assumption is made in spite of the teaching of the Doctrine and Covenants that the rights of priesthood and the power of priesthood are very different, although in practice they ought to be indivisible (D&C 121:36). The Book of Mormon teaches that becoming a full priest means obtaining the powers of heaven by a holy calling and also the rights of the priesthood by a holy ordinance. Both components of transmittal are necessary.

The difference between the Book of Mormon notion of the priesthood and our own contemporary Mormon view is focused in the distinction between priesthood offices and ecclesiastical offices. Most Mormons are aware that the priesthood offices of deacon, teacher, priest, bishop, elder, high priest, patriarch, seventy, and apostle are somehow different from the ecclesiastical offices of quorum president, counselor, ward bishop, high counselor, and stake president. The difference is that priesthood offices attach to the person, while ecclesiastical offices vest in the church structure and are not permanent. In the Book of Mormon, the priesthood offices are the most important: God's power is presented as operating through individuals. The church is not depicted as the source of God's power, but as its beneficiary. No reference is made to church offices, with the possible exception of the high priest over the church. In the modern church, however, the ecclesiastical offices are all important. No individual is empowered to act by virtue of his priesthood conferral and ordination alone. He must hold a recognized church office before he can legitimately act in God's name. A man may be ordained to the priestly office of bishop, but he may not function in the church, even to pass the sacrament, unless he is assigned to do so by a presiding church officer or unless he has been set apart to preside as ward bishop. A father, though a high priest, may not baptize, confirm, endow, or perform a marriage even for his own children without express permission from someone in the chain of command.

Thus in the modern church, both "holy calling" and "holy ordinance" have become subordinate to an additional condition: one's setting apart in the church structure. To receive the priesthood in the modern church is not to be empowered in any real sense. It signifies only that one has been deemed qualified to serve if and when he is set apart to a church office. What this means is that the authority to act for God is never vested in individuals. It is always retained by the institutional structure. Thus institutional perceptions rather than personal spiritual gifts drive the church.

One might argue in response that this system has developed by inspiration to insure the worthiness of priesthood bearers to perform ordinances and to meet the record-keeping requirements of the church.

But ordinances are sometimes performed by the unworthy, and it could be argued that worthiness is therefore not essential. If, for example, a person is baptized by an unworthy priesthood bearer, the baptism is still effectual and need not be done again. And the records of the church could be kept just as easily if the authority to act for God was vested in individuals, who were then required as part of their ministries to report all ordinance work performed. The church instead has required setting apart to a church office as prerequisite for full participation in church governance. As a result it has retained the form and name of a lay priesthood while effectively denying the power thereof.

This view of unmediated priesthood conferral is complex and undoubtedly disturbing to those who regard church ordination as insurance against false priesthood claims, but it does provide a theological basis for correcting the ecclesiastical structure if and when it becomes complacent or intransigent. When such problems arise, solutions rarely come from within the hierarchy. The Book of Mormon clearly leaves open the possibility that individuals called of God but not necessarily ordained or acknowledged by the institution might arise and reprove the wayward organization.

A second implication for the modern church may be derived from the fact that the Book of Mormon does not distinguish among Levitical, Aaronic, Patriarchal, or Melchizedek priesthoods. This fact, we think, is important. The earliest converts to Mormonism believed priesthood authority was conferred upon Joseph Smith as a result of his contact with angelic visitants. In other words the first Mormon converts thought of priesthood as undifferentiated in nature and unmediated in origin.

Initially priesthood was almost exclusively connected with the right to preach and teach the restored gospel as opposed to the right to manage and oversee the church. The earliest revelations in the Doctrine and Covenants connect priesthood with crying repentance or going forth to preach or being called to the work or having authority to proclaim the restoration (D&C 1, 4, 11, 15, 16). Apostles were originally seen as missionaries rather than as a board of directors. In short the charismatic rather than the ecclesiastical authority of the priesthood seemed more important in the first few years of the restoration, when Mormons had no reason to be impressed yet with the corporate dimensions of the church. As the church developed emphasis shifted to mediation, ordination, and gradations of priestly authority.

After the church was established and individuals were ordained to various church or priesthood offices, the concept of grades or degrees of priesthood became clear.

The third implication relates to the concept of equality presented in the Book of Mormon. This is not an equality of personal gifts or temperament. The Book of Mormon does not condemn differences in spiritual, physical, or psychological make-up or attitude. It does not seek to eliminate variety in the human personality. Nor is there any suggestion in the Book of Mormon that excellence is to be shunned or leveled or that equality is to be imposed by force of law. This is true even in the economic sphere. The rich repeatedly are castigated for not giving freely to the poor, but no one suggests that wealth be redistributed by coercive means of any kind. The equality of the Book of Mormon is personal and voluntary. People are admonished to esteem others as themselves, to freely give as they would freely receive, to relate to others as loved ones.

This type of equality — equality of status and of treatment — does not mean there is no hierarchy of responsibility or no degrees in intellectual or physical capacity. One individual will be a judge, another a dancer, another a grocer, and another a priest. Some will excel, others will not. These are differences of function, intellect, or talent. They are part of reality. But what the Book of Mormon stresses is that such distinctions should not serve as a basis upon which anyone may claim greater entitlements to love, life, liberty, happiness, privacy, respect, or to equal protection and treatment under the law. In fact because each person is equally God's child, no classes or status distinctions should exist in the church at all. Any form of elitism is anathema, for the teachings of Christ require each person to esteem every other person exactly as if that person were as valuable as Christ himself.

We are told, particularly and emphatically, that those who are called with a "holy calling" and "ordained with a holy ordinance" may not assert these gifts as a basis for privileged treatment. The gift itself is gift enough. The receiver of the gift is admonished to remember the giver and to hold his or her gift in trust for others and exercise it on their behalf. It is in matters of status that the Book of Mormon admonishes us to be equal. And this necessarily involves economic equality. This call to symmetry and reciprocity lies at the heart of the admonition to esteem others as oneself and is the central component of Christ's unconditional love. His love is never limited because of the worthiness of the loved one, never fades, is not pretended, is not merely self-love disguised. It sees all others as equal in dignity and value and attempts to equalize the inequalities of status and treatment by means of individual sacrifice.

When the Book of Mormon inveighs against inequality, it is admonishing us, especially the priests and teachers and prophets and elders, that no person can claim to be the child of Christ unless filled with the love of Christ. And we cannot be full of Christ's love if we love ourselves, our riches, our comfort, our invulnerability, our superior status, our power, or our prestige, more than we love others, who are like us made in the image of God. Repeating this teaching again and again, the Book of Mormon leads to the climactic verses beginning with Moroni 10:21: "And except ye have charity [that is, charismatic love] ye can in nowise be saved in the kingdom of God. . . . "

Such admonitions mean that every member of the church should esteem every non-member as a member. Every bishop and stake president and apostle should esteem every other person as if he or she were called to a like calling. We believe it means that no priesthood leader should hear a confession of sins unless he is willing to confess his sins to the person whose confession he is about to hear. What is needed is a reciprocity and symmetry of power and a vulnerability between the confessor and the penitent. We believe too that true unconditional love and spiritual equality means that no priesthood leader should teach or admonish or counsel or criticize anyone unless he is open and available to be taught, admonished, counseled, and criticized by others.

The idea that priesthood leaders are above this admonition or that they are answerable only to their leaders and not to their followers is repugnant to the spiritual egalitarianism of the Book of Mormon. It is contradicted by such sayings as: "Think of your brethren like unto yourselves, and be familiar with all and free with your substance, that they may be rich like unto you" (Jac. 2:17). In the church today we must replace our notion of a priesthood chain of command with the concept of a priesthood circle of prayer. Instead of a priesthood pipeline operating within the church machine, we must think in terms of the body of Christ, wherein his blood touches every living member, and the head will not say to the foot, "I have no need of thee." The gift of the priesthood is no substitute for the gift of the Holy Ghost. The presence of the priesthood correlation program, which standardizes written materials and worship services the world over, cannot compensate for the absence of the integrated community of Saints.

At the heart of divine love is sacrifice — the willingness to be diminished so that another may be increased. This is the meaning of

Christ on the cross. God, who could have insulated himself from pain, descended to earth, assumed the aspect of his children, and bore the greatest pain in his own person. Rather than hoard the heavenly feast for himself, he invites beggars to his table. He breaks bread with us and drinks from the cup our lips have touched. When he speaks to us, it is no longer from a great white throne centered in a vortex of light, surrounded by celestial griffins, warding off the unwashed. He speaks to us eye to eye from a traitor's gibbet with his blood and sweat and shame upon him for all to see and with his wounds forever open. He comes not as king but as slave. He comes not as judge but as accused. He comes not as patriarch but as bastard. He comes not to punish us but to let us punish him. He does not ask us to love him until we are first certain that he loves us. He is the great failure who saves us from our success. He is the great fool who spares us from our wisdom. He is the rejected lover who will not in turn reject his love. He is a prophet without honor, a citizen of a despised nation, a poor relation, an unwanted guest. He is the voice of one crying in the wilderness of every human heart. He is the God of grief and sorrow who is the joy of our desiring. He is utterly good because he loves us in our sins and imperfections, because he freely made himself equal to us, and because he freely opened the way whereby we may be made equal to him. This is the equality of which the Book of Mormon speaks—the equality that lies at the heart of Christ's unconditional, undiminishing, unfeigned, perfectly symmetrical, and completely reciprocal divine love.

~ CHAPTER FIFTEEN ~

WOMEN AND PRIESTHOOD
IN THE BIBLE

If priesthood is a component of the gospel, if it is essential to sanctification, spiritual growth, and spiritual gifts, and if the Book of Mormon mandates spiritual equality for all people, then what justifies the
continued disenfranchisement of women from the priesthood?

Perhaps the chief argument is that women have been excluded from
priesthood roles as a matter of tradition and a time-honored interpretation of scripture. In our view, this interpretation is deficient. It ignores certain textual complexities which suggest that at certain critical
religious junctures, during dispensations of great spirit and knowledge —
such as the time of Sarah and Abraham, or Jesus and the Marys, or
Emma and Joseph Smith — women have been involved and even included
in the priesthood.

In the first part of this chapter, we wish to examine a number of
priesthood concepts embedded in the stories of Genesis — that strange
book so full of familiar tales, which when read are full of unfamiliar
and at times curious details. In doing this we will also draw upon Joseph
Smith's revisions of Genesis and his statements interpreting these stories. Our purpose is to focus upon the involvement of the matriarchs
in the transmittal of priesthood rights, authority, and power. In the
final section of this chapter, we discuss New Testament evidence suggesting that in early Christianity women functioned in priesthood roles.
In the following chapter we will treat Joseph Smith's views on women's
right to priesthood. In doing this, we do not assume that there existed
from Old Testament times down to Joseph Smith a true and consistent
theology of priesthood that completely supports either our view or anyone else's view of what priesthood should be. But we do think that
within the Judeo-Christian-Mormon tradition there are texts that contradict the view that women should be or always have been spiritually

disenfranchised. More importantly, we think these texts can serve as sources of empowerment for those women who wish to maintain allegiance to this tradition.

PRIESTHOOD AND THE MATRIARCHS OF GENESIS

Genesis presents us with the story of Abraham and Sarah. At age ninety Abram is visited by God, and God makes a covenant with him, changes his name to Abraham, makes Abraham a "father of many nations," and gives him Canaan as an everlasting inheritance. What is a little unexpected about the story is that God makes a distinct and separate covenant with Sarai. Her name is changed to Sarah ("princess"), signifying that she will become a mother of nations and that "kings of people shall be of her" (Gen. 17:16). The parallel suggests that God bestowed upon her blessings equivalent to Abraham's.

The first and perhaps most important question raised by these events is: What was the meaning of the covenant God made with Abraham and Sarah?

The answer according to Joseph Smith's Inspired Translation of Genesis 14 is that God covenanted or promised to bestow upon them a priesthood. That Sarah also obtained a promise of priesthood is implied by the fact that she is designated a mother of kings. In her day kings often claimed descent from a god or goddess and ruled by virtue of their priestly inheritance. To be a mother of kings was in essence to be a priestess with power to confer upon her children the legacy of priesthood.

It is easy to miss the involvement of the matriarchs—Sarah, Rebekah, and Rachel—with the priesthood if we read these stories with the patriarchal prejudice inherent in our religious training. But even with this bias, we usually become aware of certain angularities, certain curious statements or odd juxtapositions of ideas in the texts, which we are likely to pass over as merely irrelevant peculiarities or as errors in the text. If we were to pause on these portions, perhaps certain questions would present themselves to us.

For example: If Abraham had received the covenant and blessing of priesthood, wouldn't all of his sons be heirs of the priesthood? Why did the heir have to be Sarah's child as well? Abraham himself suggested as much when he says to God: "O that Ishmael might live before thee!" (Gen. 17:18).

The answer, we think, is that Ishmael though Abraham's son was not Sarah's son. God had not made his covenant with Abraham alone. Sarah too had to be considered. The chosen seed, those who were to inherit the right to the priesthood, were to be her seed as well as his. But the story suggests something even more revolutionary than this. It suggests that in the culture of Abraham and Sarah, the right to the priesthood was not passed down through the father but through the mother. This hypothesis explains to some extent why the Book of Genesis seems overstocked with stories of courtship and marriage and is so preoccupied with assuring us that Isaac and Jacob in particular married the right women. The evidence, we think, is sufficient to justify this hypothesis.

Let us turn first to the stories of Sarah and her suitors: Pharaoh, the king of Egypt; Abimelech, the king of Gerar; and Yahweh, the king of heaven.

In the twelfth chapter of Genesis, we are told that Abraham and Sarah journey to Egypt where Abraham tells the emissaries of the Pharaoh's court that Sarah is his sister. This is only half-true. Sarah was really his half sister as well as his wife. This strange detail—that Abraham and Sarah had different mothers but the same father—is important. It provides evidence that their native culture was a matrilineal one, where children of the same father but different mothers could marry. But what meaning could this have in light of the stories of Sarah and her royal suitors, who pursue her as a great prize even when she is old? We think the answer lies in understanding the ritual of the sacred marriage, the *hieros gamos*. During this period in this locale, it was not uncommon for a king to seek a ritual marriage with a priestess in order to imitate the divine union of the god and the goddess. Such a marriage was looked upon as a sacred ordinance guaranteeing peace, fertility, and prosperity to the kingdom. Both Pharaoh's and Abimelech's interest in Sarah, considering her age, is more plausible in terms of this custom. Both Pharaoh and Abimelech are presented as Sarah's suitors—suggesting not only that Sarah had great beauty but also that kings sought her for the priestly inheritance she could confer on her posterity.

These three stories suggest that Sarah was the priestess whose marriage to the king would bring about the *hieros gamos*, the sacred marriage which rejuvenates the kingdom. She is sought after by earthly kings for this reason.

Focusing on our current concerns about priesthood, the stories of Sarah and her suitors suggest that she and not Abraham was the vessel through which the rights of the priesthood were transmitted. This is further suggested by the portrayal in Genesis of Abraham's concern that Isaac marry a woman of the right family. To insure this Abraham sends his servant, Eleazar, back to his and Sarah's ancestral home (Gen. 24:2).

Abraham's brother is Nahor. Nahor married Milcah, and they had a son named Bethuel. Bethuel is Abraham's nephew, and Bethuel's daughter is Rebekah. One of the peculiar details about this story is that Rebekah is announced not merely as the daughter of Bethuel but as Rebekah, "the daughter of Bethuel, the son of Milcah, the wife of Nahor" (Gen. 24:24, 47). The text focuses on Rebekah's lineage through her mother. This focus is evidence that the story was not originally patrilocal and patrilineal but matrilocal and matrilineal, implying that Rebekah's inheritance comes to her from her grandmother.

After Rebekah meets and converses with Abraham's servant for the first time, the story says: "the damsel ran and told them of her mother's house" (Gen. 24:28). In a matrilocal culture one's house is the house of one's mother not one's father. Moreover, the negotiations for the marriage of Rebekah and Isaac are carried on with Rebekah's brother not her father (vv. 29–49). This is so even though her father is mentioned as joining in the negotiations in a secondary way (v. 50). In a matrilineal society the brother would hold this more favored position, because he would be an heir of his mother, even though he might not be able to pass on the inheritance unless he married an heiress. Also after Rebekah accepts the marriage proposal, Abraham honors with gifts not Rebekah's father but her mother and brother (v. 53). Finally we have Abraham's concern that Rebekah agree to leave home and live with Isaac (vv. 5–6). This would not be a concern in a patrilocal culture, where that was expected, only in a matrilocal culture, where the norm is for the man to leave his home and live in the house of his bride's mother. Moreover, when Rebekah arrives in Canaan, she sets up residence in Sarah's tent, suggesting that she is being ensconced in the deceased Sarah's place as her rightful heir (v. 63).

This evidence is fortified in the story of Esau and Jacob. Rebekah, like Sarah before her, is concerned about the right wife for her sons, both of whom are rightful heirs to the priesthood. But in this story, to Rebekah's displeasure, Esau marries into the wrong family (Gen.

26:34–35), while Jacob, in keeping with Rebekah's wishes, returns to the ancestral home and marries two of his mother's nieces (28:5–7). Then we are told the peculiar story of Rachel and her family's idols (31:34–35). Rachel considers these idols her inheritance and sits on them so that her father cannot find them. She takes them with her when she departs for Canaan with Leah and Jacob. Argument has been made that this story signifies that Rachel — as the youngest daughter — and not Leah was the rightful heiress of the priestly inheritance. It has also been suggested by some scholars that these idols were not worshipped but were holy objects, like the Urim and Thummim, used for divination (Teubal).

These stories show that the right to the priesthood, considered an essential prerequisite to the receipt and exercise of priestly authority, was passed on in matrilineal succession, possibly by right of ultimogenitor — through the youngest female — and that Sarah, Rebekah, and Rachel were heiresses of this right. Thus those males who received the priesthood had first to acquire the rights to it from their mothers.

Later in the time of Moses, a patrilineal priesthood right was conferred on the house of Levi and the sons of Aaron. But the existence of such a right was not necessarily exclusive. It could have existed side by side with the matrilineal right.

Lineal priesthood rights are recognized in Mormon scripture. Doctrine and Covenants 86:8 states: "Therefore, thus saith the Lord unto you, with whom the priesthood hath continued through the lineage of your fathers — for ye are lawful heirs, according to the flesh, and have been hid from the world with Christ in God — therefore your life and the priesthood have remained, and must needs remain through you and your lineage until the restoration of all things spoken by the mouths of all the holy prophets since the world began." Mormon scripture says nothing of a matrilineal priesthood except perhaps allegorically in Section 113, verse 7, which contains an answer to a question about the meaning of the phrase in Isaiah, "Put on thy strength, O Zion." According to this section, "to put on *her* strength is to put on the authority of the priesthood, which she, Zion, has a right to by lineage; also to return to that power which she had lost." Also the Mormon teaching that the Melchizedek priesthood is "without father, without mother" (Heb. 7:3) suggests the existence of a priesthood which belongs to or is derived from the mother as well as one that is derived from the father.

In the Old Testament the inheritance of priesthood rights was a prerequisite to further priestly dignities, whose transmittal was by appointment, blessing, or ordination. This is illustrated in the story of the birthright conflict between Rebekah's twins, Esau and Jacob. As they grew Isaac favored his elder son, while Rebekah favored her younger. This implies that the family was divided on the succession issue. Was it patrilineal and primogenitive and therefore did it point to Esau? Or was it matrilineal and ultimogenitive and therefore did it point to Jacob? God confirms the matrilineal concept. The story makes it clear that Rebekah and Jacob stole nothing. They were claiming their due. The text takes pains to tell us that while her sons were yet *in utero*, Rebekah was told by God that the younger should rule over the elder (Gen. 25:23). We are informed that later Esau sold his birthright to Jacob for a pot of lentil soup (vv. 31–32). Then comes the story of how Jacob dresses in skins to trick the blind Isaac into believing he is blessing his hairy son Esau, when it is Jacob in disguise (27:1–29). After Isaac learns he has been tricked, he does not curse Rebekah or Jacob (v. 37).

The point is that Rebekah, though quite certain of her position on the succession issue, does not deny, disparage, or denigrate Isaac's right to confer the priesthood by blessing upon one of her sons. In fact this blessing or ordination is so important that Rebekah is willing to deceive her husband and put herself and her younger son at odds with Esau in order to insure that Jacob gets it (Gen. 27:41–44). For her the inheritance alone is not sufficient.

Thus Jacob was blessed as Isaac (Gen. 25:11) and Abraham had been (14:19). Joseph Smith's version of Genesis contains a passage implying that the blessings given to Abraham, Isaac, and Jacob were in fact ordinations to the priesthood order: "And now Melchizedek... lifted up his voice and blessed Abram, being the high priest, ... and gave unto him riches, and honor, and lands for an everlasting possession" (JST Gen. 14:33–34, 36–37, 40). Abraham as an heir of the priesthood was blessed (that is ordained) to the priestly order by Melchizedek. Joseph Smith explained that "Abraham says to Melchizedek, I believe all that thou hast taught me concerning the priesthood and the coming of the Son of Man; so Melchizedek ordained Abraham and sent him away. Abraham rejoiced, saying, Now I have a priesthood" (TPJS, 322–23). In the Pearl of Great Price, the same story is told: Abraham, an "heir" because he had inherited the priesthood right, becomes a "rightful" heir by virtue of his ordination by Melchizedek (Abr. 1:2). But what is usually overlooked in these stories is the fact that Rebekah too is presented as the recipient of such a blessing or ordination. Genesis 24:60 states: "And they [her mother and her brother; cf. v. 55] blessed Rebekah, and said unto her, ... be thou the mother of thousands of millions, and let thy seed possess the gate of those which hate them." This is virtually the same language used to report God's blessing to Sarah (Gen. 17:15–16). Moreover in Mormonism "seed" is a code word for priesthood (Abr. 2:11).

However, there is little other evidence of the ordination of women in these stories. Elsewhere in the Old Testament certain women, Miriam, Deborah, Noadiah, and Huldah, are presented as prophetesses (Ex. 15:20–21; Judg. 4:1–10; Neh. 6:10–14; 2 Kings 22; 2 Chron. 34). In ancient times, of course, there was no clear link between the calling of a prophet or prophetess and priesthood ordination. But the modern church teaches that the ancient prophets held priesthood. There is nothing in the scripture to suggest that prophetesses should not also be considered priesthood figures.

The idea that certain priesthood prerogatives are transmitted by enrobing in priestly clothing is also suggested in the foundational stories. In Genesis 3:21 God makes coats of skins for Adam and Eve. In the Mormon temple ceremony, initiates are told that these skins were the garments of the priesthood and confer special powers on those ceremonially clothed in them as part of the endowment. Genesis 9:28 contains the story of Ham, who is punished for seeing his father's nakedness; in contrast Shem and Japeth cover him with a garment. Hugh Nibley suggests that this was the garment of the priesthood, which Ham had stolen from Noah (Gen. 10:27–32; Nibley 1978, 95). In the story of Esau and Jacob, Rebekah's trick involved clothing Jacob in skins so that he would seem to the blind Isaac to be the elder Esau. We wonder if this story, like that of Noah and Ham, is a parable about the priestly garment. Perhaps Jacob obtained the garment of the priesthood and its attendant priestly rights, and Isaac is portrayed as confirming or ratifying the transmittal of these rights. Nothing more is mentioned about a garment until Genesis 37:3, when Jacob gives his son Joseph a coat of many colors. Nibley explained that this coat was in fact an ornamented coat — a replica of the ancient priesthood garment. If so then this passage implies that Jacob had conferred upon the son he loved above all others certain priesthood blessings by this act of investiture. There appears to be no reference in the stories to a woman other than Eve having received the garment of the priesthood.

However, the Mormon temple endowment ceremony, an oral representation of the story of Adam and Eve, presents clear evidence that the garment of the priesthood with its attendant priestly rights and blessings is as much for women as for men. The ritual language of the ceremony attaches enormous significance to the garment and the other priestly robes.

Anointing, like investiture, is another mechanism of priesthood transmittal which appears throughout the Old and New Testaments — but not directly in the Genesis stories, where the word "anointing" is not used. However, in Genesis 28:18 Jacob dreamed of a ladder on which the angels of God ascended and descended, and in this same dream God appeared and promised to be with him always. When Jacob awoke, he was afraid and said: "How dreadful is this place! this is none other but the house of God, and this is the gate of heaven. And Jacob rose up early in the morning, and took the stone that he had put for his pillows, and set it up for a pillar, and poured oil upon the top of it "(vv. 17–18). Later after God appeared Jacob again set up a pillar of stone, "and he poured a drink offering thereon, and he poured oil thereon" (35:14). This suggests that the anointings were in the nature of libations and not ordinations. Yet in both instances the pouring of oil is associated with a theophany, a covenant from God, and the outpouring of a divine blessing.

In other books of the Old Testament, anointings appear prominently as a means of consecrating objects such as the tabernacle and its furniture (Exod. 30:22), shields (2 Sam. 1:21; Is. 21:5), as well as prophets (1 Kings 19:16), priests (Ex. 28:41), and kings (Judg. 9:8; 2 Sam. 2:4; 1 Kings 1:34). Oil becomes so important as a result that it is made a crime to compound it (Ex. 30:32–33). The anointing makes the anointed one sacrosanct (ibid.; 1 Sam. 24:7). In Psalms the anointing becomes a metaphor for the bestowal of divine favor (Ps. 23:5, 92:10). It signifies the outpouring of God's holy spirit (1 Sam. 10:1, 9, 16:13; Is. 61:1; and Zach. 4:12–14).

We have found no mention in these stories of the anointing of women. However, in the Mormon temple endowment the anointing is prominent not only in the initiatory ordinances but as the crowning blessing promised the initiates. Mormon ritual practice, more fully explored later, establishes the propriety of anointing women as priestesses.

The transmittal of the priesthood by an oath and covenant is common in the Genesis account. God promises the priesthood to an individual and seals it with his oath, which God swears by himself, since there is nothing greater to swear by. This pattern was followed with Abraham, with Isaac (JST Gen. 26:3), and with Jacob (Gen. 28:4, 13–22; 32:24–32).

The writer of the Epistle to the Hebrews clarified the concept of the oath and covenant as follows: "[W]hen God made promise to Abraham, because he [God] could swear by no greater, he swear by himself, saying, surely blessing I will bless thee, and multiplying I will multiply thee. And so, after he [Abraham] had patiently endured, he obtained the promise. For men verily swear by the greater; and an oath for confirmation is an end of all strife. Wherein God, willing more abundantly to shew unto the heirs of promise the immutability of his counsel, confirmed it by an oath. That by two immutable things [the oath and covenant], in which it was impossible for God to lie, we might have a strong consolation, who have fled for refuge to lay hold upon the hope set before us" (Heb. 6:13–18). Abraham, who had patiently endured his trials, received from God the priesthood by this oath and covenant.

Joseph Smith further clarified this concept in a number of revelations and statements. He taught, as we shall discuss at greater length in a subsequent chapter, that the oath and covenant confirms upon an individual "all that [the] Father hath" (D&C 84:38). Doctrine and Covenants 76, speaking of those individuals in the highest glory, states that they are "priests after the order of Melchizedek" (v. 57), and that the Father hath given them "all things" (v. 55). Section 132 confirms that both men and women are entitled to this blessing, for it says, speaking to men and women who receive the anointing to the fullness of the priesthood: "[They] shall come forth in the first resurrection ... and shall inherit thrones, kingdoms, principalities, and powers, dominions, all heights and depths; ... and they shall pass by the angels, and the gods ... to their exaltation and glory in all things, as hath been sealed upon their heads, which glory shall be a fullness and a continuation of the seeds forever and ever" (v. 19).

WOMEN AND THE PRIESTHOOD IN THE NEW TESTAMENT

With the advent of Christianity, the emphasis on lineal priesthood rights was eclipsed or supplanted. The exclusivity of the Hebrew claim to priesthood was swept away. Gentiles were given access to God's priesthood covenant through Jesus Christ, the messenger of the covenant proclaimed as a light not only to Israel but to Gentiles, slaves, and women. The apostle Paul expressed this sentiment in one of the earliest Christian texts, Galatians 3:28–29: "There is neither Jew nor Greek, there is neither bond nor free, there is neither male nor female: for ye are all one in Christ Jesus. And if ye be Christ's, then are ye Abraham's seed, and heirs according to the promise." Not only does Paul assert the essential spiritual equality mandated by the gospel, but he also promises all converts that by accepting Christ, they become Abraham's seed and "heirs according to the promise."

The inheritance promised to Christians is the inheritance promised to the descendants of Abraham and Sarah. That inheritance is the priesthood. The priesthood, once obtained by lineal right, now becomes the legacy of all those with faith in Christ. Paul explains to the Galatians: "Tell me, ye that desire to be under the law, do ye not hear the law? For it is written, that Abraham had two sons, the one by a bondmaid, the other by a freewoman. But he [Ishmael] who was of the bondwoman was born after the flesh; but he [Isaac] of the freewoman was by promise. . . . Now we [Christians] . . . as Isaac was, are the children of promise. But as then, he that was born after the flesh [the Jews] persecuted him that was born after the Spirit [the Christians]" (Gal. 4:21–23, 28–29). Christians, as heirs of the promise, are heirs of the priesthood.

Paul's announcement that the gospel and its associated priesthood inheritance is available to all believers follows from the way Jesus treated disenfranchised peoples. In his treatment of women, he deviated significantly from the norms of his time and culture. He did this not only by dealing with them in a spirit of great equality but also by including them in his ministry at all the important junctures of his life — his birth, his preaching, his miracle working, his crucifixion, and his resurrection.

During this period Jewish men thanked God each day in their prayers that they had not been born women. And yet in his public preaching and parable telling, Jesus compared himself to women such as the baker woman who leavens the loaf (Luke 13:20–21) and the housewife who finds the lost coin (15:8–10). Jewish men of Christ's time did not socialize with women and avoided contact with them, but Jesus initiated a conversation with a Samaritan women, announced to her his messianic mission, and asked her to take his message to her townspeople. Menstruating women were considered unclean, yet Jesus not only allowed such a woman to touch him without rebuke but healed her and sent her away with a blessing. Women of this period were not allowed to preach or study scriptures, and yet Jesus discussed Torah with Mary. Jewish law did not accept women as legal witnesses, and yet Jesus made women the witnesses of his resurrection. Even more striking, Jesus selected women to hear first the report of his rising from the dead and to announce his resurrection to the male disciples. This is especially important when we consider that in the primitive church the primary qualification for the apostleship was to be a witness of the ministry, death, and resurrection of the Lord.

Following his death Christ's egalitarian outlook toward women persisted in the early Christian church. For example, women were allowed to pray and prophesy in Christian meetings, something which was forbidden in Jewish worship (1 Cor. 11). Women also performed significant missionary work in the early church and were leaders of Christian households. In Luke and Acts the four daughters of Philip are referred to as prophetesses (Luke 2:22–38; Acts 21:9, 2:17). And in Romans 16, Priscilla, Mary, Tryphena, Tryphosa, and Persis are all commended by Paul for their important work.

Moreover in Romans 16:7, we read the statement of Paul: "salute Andronicus and Junia, my kinsmen and my fellow prisoners, who are of note among the apostles." Junia is the name of a woman. In spite of this fact, she is clearly included among the apostles of Paul's day in this scripture. Furthermore, the New Testament contains evidence of women serving as church deacons. Again in Romans 16:1–2, the text mentions "Phoebe our sister who is a servant to the Church." The Greek word for "servant" in this passage is *diaconos*, which means "deacon." It is significant that the Greek stem for this word is masculine, signifying that the term is not simply a descriptive adjective (which would have had a feminine suffix, *diacona*) but is probably being used to refer to a church office. It appears from this text that the office of deacon was most likely more important than it is in the modern church, since Phoebe is also called a *prostatis* of many. The Greek word *prostatis* could be translated "patroness" and implies that Phoebe had some kind of authority over church members. Her leadership role is also suggested by Paul's instructions that church members were to "assist her in whatsoever business she hath need of you."

In sum, the Old and New Testaments indicate various ways the priesthood has been transmitted: by inheritance, through lineage or through adoption into the family of Christ; by appointment or ordination; by investiture; by anointing; and by oath and covenant from God. The scriptures present some important evidence of the involvement of women with the priesthood from the earliest times, both as receivers and transmitters of priesthood authority, power, and blessing. Admittedly these scriptures are few and somewhat obscure. Nevertheless, it is clear that there are no scriptures which expressly prohibit women from the priesthood nor is there any statement suggesting that this privilege will forever be denied them.

CHAPTER SIXTEEN

A KINGDOM OF PRIESTESSES

Because for Mormons priesthood is indispensable, its inception has long been viewed as the most important aspect of the Mormon movement. Each May the church commemorates John the Baptist's restoration of the Aaronic priesthood and Peter, James, and John's restoration of the Melchizedek priesthood to Joseph Smith and others. However, little if anything is ever said about the bestowal of the fullness of the priesthood "by the hand of Elijah the prophet."[1] It appears that this priesthood still remains a mystery to most Mormons who connect Elijah's mission only with genealogy, vicarious ordinances for the dead, and temple sealings. In our view the priesthood restored by Elijah has a much more extensive significance for the LDS church. In the early years of Mormonism, when the leadership was struggling to define the nature, scope, and levels of priesthood and its relationship to callings and spiritual gifts, little was said about Elijah and the fullness of the priesthood. After 1836, however, the fullness of the priesthood concept began to emerge.[2] In the 1840s and especially during Joseph

---

[1] Significantly among the first revelations Joseph Smith received from the angel Moroni was the 1823 pronouncement that the priesthood would be revealed not by John the Baptist or Peter, James, and John but by Elijah the prophet. This revelation did not appear in print, however, until 1842. Section 110, dated 3 April 1836, reports the coming of Elijah the prophet together with other heavenly messengers including "Messiah" to restore the fullness of the keys of the priesthood. However, it was not until May 1842 that Joseph transmitted the keys of this priesthood to others (Quinn; Ehat; Buerger).

[2] The concept of the fullness of priesthood is claimed to have had an earlier provenance than 1836. The revelation known as Doctrine and Covenants 2, which refers to "the priesthood by the hand of Elijah the prophet," is said to have been received on 23 September 1823, but was first published on 15 April 1842 in the *Times and Seasons*. It

Smith's last two years, he seems to have been preoccupied by this subject.[3]

Church historical documents show that on 4 May 1842 Joseph "communicated" the keys of the fullness of priesthood to nine men by means of an "endowment."[4] On 5 May 1842 these men "communicated" to Joseph the same keys.[5] Eventually Joseph organized these newly en-

---

is also claimed in "the substance of a revelation given in Jackson County, Missouri, July 17, 1831, and reported by William W. Phelps, giving Joseph Smith and his associates instruction upon their arrival in Missouri to dedicate the land of Zion" that the Lord revealed: "Verily, I say unto you, that the wisdom of man, in his fallen state, knoweth not the purposes and the privileges of my holy priesthood, but ye shall know when ye receive a fullness by reason of my holy anointing" (Collier, 58).

[3] In remarks made by Joseph Smith during this period, he indicated his intention to proceed with the administration of ordinances necessary to elevate himself and others to the fullness of the priesthood. In a 16 July 1843 sermon, he said that he "would not prophecy any more, Hyrum should be prophet (did not tell them he was going to be a priest now, or a king by and by)" (HC 5:512). On 23 July 1843 he recorded: "Last Monday morning certain men came to me and said: 'Brother Joseph, Hyrum is no prophet—he can't lead the church; you must lead the church. If you resign, all things will go wrong; you must not resign; if you do the church will be scattered.' I felt curious and said: 'Have we not learned the Priesthood after the order of Melchizedek, which includes both Prophets, priests and kings... and I will advance your Propeht to a Priest, and then to a King—not of the Kingdoms of this earth, but of the Most High....' 'Thou hast made us unto our God, Kings and Priests, and we shall reign on the earth' " (TPJS, 318).

[4] The words "endow" and "endowment," used in the LDS church to refer to the temple ceremony, are not derived from the word "endow," meaning a gift or bequest, but from the word "endue," used in Luke 24:49. Endue means to lead into, to instruct, to introduce, to take in, to put on as a garment, to clothe or cover, to assume or take upon one's self, to put on garments, to overlay, to invest with dignities, possessions, honors, etc., to invest with property, to supply, and to bestow or grant (Oxford English Dictionary, s.v. "endue").

[5] This pattern of ordination was used from the beginning of Mormonism. In the reports of the bestowal of the lesser priesthood on Joseph Smith and Oliver Cowdery, Joseph was commanded to ordain Oliver first. Then Oliver ordained Joseph. Since Joseph was to restore the gospel and the priesthood, he was the first to administer an ordinance and then in turn would receive the same ordinance from whoever had received it from him. This made Joseph the first to confer priesthood keys in this dispensation. The same pattern was claimed with respect to the conferral of the higher priesthood. Though Elijah is said to have restored the fullness of the priesthood on 3 April 1836, no ordinations are mentioned. However, on 4 May 1842, the keys of the fullness of the priesthood were conveyed to Brigham Young, Heber C. Kimball, Willard Richards, Newel K. Whitney, James Adams, and George Miller. The following day these ordinances were administered to Joseph and Hyrum.

dowed men into a group known by various names: the "holy order," the "quorum of the priesthood," the "quorum of the anointing," the "first quorum," the "council pertaining to the high priesthood," and the "ancient order." Most commonly, however, this group was simply referred to by the shortened title of "the quorum."

More than a year passed before any other members were added. Then on the morning of 28 September 1843, five additional men were endowed. In the evening of the same day, Joseph Smith "was by common consent & unanimous voice chosen president of the Quorum & anointed & ordained to the highest order of the priesthood (& Companion — d[itt]o" (Faulring, 416; Ehat, 94–95; Quinn 1978, 85).

One of the most significant aspects of this event is contained in the parenthetical: "(& Companion — d[itt]o)." This refers to the fact that a woman — believed to be Emma Smith (Ehat, 95) — received the fullness of the priesthood through the temple ordinances. At some time prior to 28 September 1843 Emma had been endowed with the fullness of the keys of the priesthood. Then on that date she was anointed a "queen and priestess" and became a member of the holy order of God (ibid., 94). It appears that Emma was the first woman to receive the priesthood in this way. Thereafter she was in charge of dispensing these same ordinances to other select women (Newell and Avery, 162). Since that time hundreds of thousands of Mormon women have been endowed with the priesthood and its keys in the temple and have been promised that they with their husbands would be "anointed and ordained to the highest order of the priesthood." Thus, the doctrine that women have a right to the priesthood was established in the early days of the church, but it has been obscured and overlooked, rather in the same way Emma's ordination was anonymously reported in parentheses: "(and companion d[itt]o)." So women do hold the priesthood after all.

The offices of the Aaronic and Melchizedek priesthoods were eventually seen as a means to prepare males for the fullness of priesthood. There is no evidence that Joseph Smith ever ordained women to these offices. However, it appears that he intended to prepare them to receive the fullness of priesthood through a different instrumentality, namely the Female Relief Society of Nauvoo. This purpose was delineated by Joseph Smith in a series of discourses given by him to Relief Society members between 17 March 1842 and 31 August 1842. These speeches are our only direct evidence of his views on the subject of women and the priesthood, aside from the fact that he actually endowed and anointed women to priesthood and included them in the quorum of the anointed. For this reason we will review these discourses at some length.

The first of these speeches was given when the society was organized on 17 March 1842. Much of the meeting was taken up with choosing and ordaining a presidency and instructing in parliamentary procedure. Joseph suggested that the society elect a presidency and said he would ordain them. Church leaders later claimed that this was not an ordination to priesthood, a point stressed later by LDS church president John Taylor who at the time actually ordained the Relief Society presidency (*Woman's Exponent* 9:55). But Joseph explicitly compared the Relief Society to the ecclesiastical priesthood. He said that the presidency of the Relief Society, once elected, should "preside over the Society ... just as [the] presidency preside over the Church [and their officers should] be appointed and set apart, as Deacons, Teachers, &C. are among us." He stated further that the new presidency should serve during good behavior or "so long as they shall continue to fill the office with dignity, &C, — like the first Presidency of the Church" (WJS, 104).

After Emma Smith was elected the first president of the Relief Society, Joseph said that this action fulfilled the promise of D&C 25, where Emma was called an "elect lady" because she was "elected to preside." He explained that in July 1830, when this revelation was given, Emma was ordained "to expound the scriptures to all; and to teach the female part of the community; and that not she alone, but others, may attain to the same blessings — " (WJS, 105). Joseph's comment, on this occasion, that Emma was to teach the "female" part of the community takes away from the original scripture which contains no such limitation: "Thou shalt be ordained under his hand to expound scriptures and to exhort the Church according as it shall be given thee by my spirit" (D&C 25:7).

Elsewhere, however, Joseph did acknowledge this expanded sphere of woman's influence by saying to the Relief Society that although their administrations should be confined to their close acquaintances, their knowledge and preaching could "extend to all the world" (WJS, 118–19). This accords with D&C 25, where Emma is also told that "he shall lay his hands upon thee, and thou shalt receive the Holy Ghost, and thy time shall be given to writing and to learning much" (v. 8). Here Emma is also enjoined to "lay aside the things of this world, and seek for the things of a better" (v. 10). Emma Smith and Mormon women in general are called to learn, write, expound the scriptures, and exhort the church by virtue of their having received the gift of the Holy Ghost. They are not simply to stay in the home and content themselves with "the things of this world."

Joseph's second Relief Society discourse, delivered on 30 March 1842, taken with his sermon of 28 April 1842 contain the crux of his remarks on the relationship of women to the priesthood. Two main themes emerge. First, he stated that women would receive the keys of the priesthood. He approached this point with the preliminary observation that the society was to "be built up to the Most High in an acceptable manner" (WJS, 110) and that the society should be careful about which women were admitted as members. He wanted the society to make "a close examination of every candidate." He warned that "they were going too fast—that the society should grow up by degrees; should commence with a few individuals—thus have a select society of the virtuous, and those who will walk circumspectly" (ibid.). Although these remarks may appear elitist, the rest of the text contradicts this impression. It suggests that his emphasis on a careful selection of new members stemmed from his view of the purpose of the organization. The society was not just one more women's group dedicated to the reformation of morals. Its purpose was to prepare women to receive their endowment and the fullness of the priesthood. Joseph told the society that "All must act in concert or nothing can be done, that the society should move according to the ancient Priesthood, hence there should be a select society separate from all the evils of the world, choice, virtuous, and holy" (ibid.). The term "ancient priesthood" refers to the fullness of the priesthood of the Ancient of Days, Adam and Eve (TPJS, 157, 237; D&C 116), the only priesthood given to men and women jointly (D&C 132:19). Joseph's statement that the Relief Society should "move according to the ancient Priesthood" was a reference to the fact that faithful Mormon women would be given the same priesthood held by Eve.

Joseph then went on to connect the "ancient order" with the building of Zion. He told the Relief Society that "he was going to make of this society a kingdom of priests as in Enoch's day—as in Paul's day" (WJS, 110). The original version of this statement was later edited so that the word "society" was changed to "church." Perhaps this was done because it seemed incredible to later church members that Joseph would have actually said that he intended to give Relief Society women the priesthood. However, in Bathsheba W. Smith's account of this discourse, she wrote that Joseph "wanted to make us, as the women were in Paul's day, 'a kingdom of priestesses.' We have the ceremony in our endowments as Joseph taught' " (Madsen 1987, 84). Even if Joseph did use the masculine form "priests" instead of the feminine form "priestesses," perhaps he was simply drawing from the scriptural passage of Exodus 19:6, "ye shall be to me a kingdom of priests."[6]

The second theme Joseph sounded in this Relief Society discourse also echoed Paul in the New Testament. The theme was charity. He commended the women "for their zeal but said sometimes their zeal was not according to knowledge" (WJS, 110). When trying to root out evil, the Relief Society should be careful they were not destroying good, implying that we cannot always judge good and evil by the traditions of our culture. God may require certain behaviors repugnant to conventional morals. This is, undoubtedly, a reference to the practice of polygamy, which was at this time on Joseph Smith's mind.

In his 28 April 1842 discourse, Joseph Smith again directly addressed the question of woman's relationship to priesthood. His choice of subject seemed to have been prompted by the fact that some of the women had been giving blessings to each other at previous meetings. The feeling of many male church members was that this practice was wrong because blessings and priesthood were male prerogatives. To this objection Joseph gave a two-part reply. First, he said that women

[6]Jesus is reported to have made a similar remark which was recorded in the apocryphal Gospel of Thomas, a gnostic text. There Peter objects to Jesus' always being in the company of Mary Magdalene. In response to this criticism, Jesus is presented as saying: "I myself shall lead her in order to make her male" (Robinson, 130). This, however, does not mean that Mary would cease to be a woman but that she would become one with him. This fact is explained elsewhere in the text, where Jesus explains: "When you make the two one, and when you make the inside like the outside and the outside like the inside, and the above like the below, and when you make the male and the female one and the same, so that the male not be male nor the female female . . . ; then will you enter [the Kingdom]" (ibid., 121).

Some see this text as an example of the gnostic tendency to eliminate sexuality altogether and to see woman as valuable only insofar as they are desexed and mirror the male. However, we believe this passage can be interpreted to reinforce the importance of a mystical union of the sexes in which the man and the woman, while retaining their individual sexual natures, become one with one another and one with God. In this sense these passages are another way of expressing Paul's concept that "in Christ Jesus there is no more male and female" (Gal. 3:28). They become a compound in one, a whole or holy person, a "Man of Holiness" (Moses 6:57; 7:35). In this context "man" is used in the sense employed in Gen. 1:27 to embrace both male and female in mystical unity.

have the right to administer to the sick because of the ordination and authority they receive by virtue of obtaining the gift of the Holy Ghost. Joseph quoted Mark 16:16–18 and explained that spiritual gifts such as casting out devils, speaking in tongues, laying hands on the sick are given to all, "whether male or female," who believe and are baptized: "He ask'd the Society if they could not see by this sweeping stroke that were in [wherein] they are ordained, it is the privilege of those set apart to administer in that authority which is conferr'd on them — and if the sisters should have faith to heal the sick, let all hold their tongues, and let every thing roll on" (WJS, 115). The fact that God honors the administration of women by healing the person blessed, said Joseph, shows that there is no harm in the practice. "It is no sin for anybody to do it that has faith, or if the sick has faith to be healed by the administration" (ibid., 116).

But Joseph did not leave the matter there. He added a second justification. Women would soon have an even greater right to administer in spiritual gifts — the priesthood to be conferred upon them in the temple. Joseph said he was "turning the key" to them by revelation: "that the time had not been before that these things could be in their proper order — that the Church is not now organiz'd in its proper order and cannot be until the Temple is completed" (WJS, 115). Although the ecclesiastical offices and ordinances had been in place since Kirtland, Joseph did not consider the church properly organized until the ordinances of the temple were introduced (TPJS, 224). These ordinances would empower women to act as priestesses. He told the Relief Society: "I now turn the key to you in the name of God and this Society shall rejoice and Knowledge and intelligence shall flow down from this time — this is the beginning of better days to this Society" (WJS, 118).

The proper place for the conferral of the priesthood upon women was the temple. But since Joseph had premonitions of his death, he felt an urgency to begin this work before the temple was completed: "He said as he had this opportunity, he was going to instruct the Society and pour out the way for them to conduct, that they might act according to the will of God . . . He spoke of delivering the keys to this society and to the Church — that according to his prayers God had appointed him elsewhere" (WJS, 116). The term "keys" used here is significant, for in Mormonism "keys" implies priesthood prerogatives, rights, and presiding authority (*Mormon Doctrine*, 375–79). The keys mentioned in these passages are the keys of the fullness of the priesthood transmitted by way of the endowment ceremony.

Joseph said he intended for the women of the Relief Society to have the visitation of angels, a privilege of the fullness of the lesser priesthood: "If you live up to these principles [charity and virtue] how great and glorious — if you live up to your privilege the angels cannot be restrain'd from being your associates" (WJS, 117). He then told them that they could also be brought into the presence of God, a privilege of the fullness of the greater priesthood: "Females, if they are pure and innocent, can come into the presence of God, for what is more pleasing to God than innocence; you must be innocent or you cannot come up before God" (ibid.). Here Joseph Smith emphasized that women need no male intercessor; they have direct access to the divine. Righteousness alone is the prerequisite for priesthood blessings, and this applies to both men and women alike. For the "rights of the priesthood are inseparably connected with the powers of heaven, and that the powers of heaven cannot be controlled or handled only upon the principles of righteousness" (D&C 121:36).

The following statement from the "Manuscript History of the Church" also provides evidence that in these discourses Joseph was speaking of extending the priesthood to women: "At two o'clock P.M. I met the members of the 'female Relief Society' and . . . gave a lecture on Priesthood showing how the sisters would come in possession of the privileges blessings and gifts of the Priesthood and that signs should follow them, such as healing the sick, casting out devils &C and that they might attain unto these blessings by a virtuous life and conversation and diligence in keeping all the commandments" (WJS, 119).

In this speech Joseph then went on to raise the issue of charity, showing its connection to the spiritual gifts and the priesthood. He quoted 1 Corinthians 12 and 13, where Paul wrote that charity is the greatest of the spiritual gifts. This is so not because charity outranks the others but because it encompasses them. It is the greatest in scope not the greatest in status. It is like a mantle covering the body of Christ. Without charity the members could not function as they should. They would wrangle in "jarrings, and contentions, and envyings, and strifes, and lustful and covetous desires" (D&C 101:6). Joseph then applied the principle of charity to the Relief Society in two ways.

First, though the women did not yet have the fullness of priesthood, they were enjoined to be charitable, to wait and be patient until God called them higher. Joseph told them "it was the nonsense of the human heart for a person to be aspiring to other stations than [those] appointed of God — that it was better for individuals to magnify their respective callings, and wait patiently till God shall say to them come up higher" (WJS, 115). Joseph warned that when women actually received a higher position, they would be tempted with power and ambition much like the "great big Elders": "the same aspiring disposition will be in this Society, and must be guarded against — that every person should stand and act in the place appointed, and thus sanctify the Society and get it pure" (ibid., 116).

Second, Joseph told the women that although it is "natural for females to have feelings of charity," it is also true that the "female part of community are apt to be contracted, in their views." One of the problems, he explained, is that sometimes it may "appear that someone is doing wrong when he is in reality doing the will of God." The devil can make us think that which is right is wrong: "he will so transform things as to make one gape at those who are doing the will of God" (WJS, 117). Joseph told the women, "you must enlarge your souls toward others if you [w]ould do like Jesus, and carry your fellow creatures to Abrams bosom. . . . let your hearts expand — let them be enlarged towards others — you must be longsuffering and bear with the faults and errors of mankind. . . . You must not be contracted but you must be liberal in your feelings" (ibid., 118).

In his next two discourses to the society, Joseph focused entirely on the subject of charity. He said that charity brings unity of feeling, and unity of feeling brings us into union with God: "if one member suffer all feel it by union of feeling we obtain pow'r with God" (WJS, 123). Unity of feeling is, of course, an important concept. Once again Joseph seemed to be preparing women for higher temple ordinances, connecting charity or "perfect love" with calling and election: "Until we have perfect love we are liable to fall" (TPJS, 9).

In Joseph's view the love of God was more perfectly expressed when the priestly role of saving souls was added to the role of administering to temporal needs: "Away with self-righteousness. the best measure or principle to bring the poor to repentance is to administer to their wants — the Society is not only to relieve the poor but to save souls" (WJS, 124).

In light of the fact that women have an important and co-equal priestly calling, it should not be surprising to learn that Joseph Smith began to include women in a priesthood governing body in the months just prior to his martyrdom. In September of 1843 Joseph not only gave women the endowment and the fullness of the priesthood but included them in the quorum of the anointed, the holy order.[7] Although it has been argued that this quorum never functioned in the church and that it was simply the antecedent to an endowment company in today's temple practice, there is evidence to the contrary (Quinn 1978, 89).

If Joseph thought of the holy order merely as an endowment company, why did he not treat it as an ephemeral body? Why was it called a quorum? Why did he meet with them regularly? Why did he continue to instruct them? Why was he chosen as president of the holy order if the quorum itself had no special significance? Why did he allow this quorum to engage in activities beyond instruction in the temple endowment? The quorum conducted prayer circles not merely for the purpose of instructing the members in the details of temple prayer but for the purpose of addressing in prayer problems affecting the whole church. The quorum counseled together, partook of the sacrament, discussed the doctrines of the kingdom, heard lectures from Joseph Smith, and looked upon quorum meetings as an occasion for spiritual renewal. The following excerpt from Heber C. Kimball's journal reflects this: "On Sunday Morning at 9 Oclock all of the holy order will assemble fore prair and council. Our wives will come and pertack with us: the Sacarment will be administer[ed] . . . and spend the day in those thing[s] that the spirit shall teach. . . . " (Quinn 1978, 93).

Prayer, of course, was one of the primary functions of the quorum. Though this may not seem as important as administrative meetings, Joseph instilled in the minds of his followers the idea that the true order of prayer was the most effective means of bringing about change. Joseph did not have a managerial view, he had a sacral one. He believed (as perhaps did Thomas More) that the kingdom of God could be governed by prayer. For this reason prayer was not just another private devotional. It was an act of spiritual administration, asking God to bring about needed changes and needed action.

It is thus possible to view the holy order both as a prayer circle and as an administrative body of the church. Brigham Young claimed that it was by the true order of prayer that he kept the church together and the mobs at bay after the martyrdom (Allen, 48n; Kimball Journal, 21 Dec. 1845; HC 5:45). On one occasion in Nauvoo, Newel K. Whitney and Dr. John M. Bernhisel thought the quorum should meet to pray

---

[7] See, for example, Kenney, 1:337–52.

that the weather would change so that sickness would not spread among the Saints (Quinn 1978, 104). Joseph himself claimed that he had to be careful when he prayed for his enemies' destruction, since the Lord was likely to answer his prayers (WJS, 331). Because of this early stress on the importance of prayer in church governance, the tradition has persisted to this day that presiding quorums meet together to conduct prayer circles.[8]

Joseph Smith also taught the quorum that the true order of prayer was a means by which messengers and revelations could be tested, devils detected, and spirits discerned. Since for Joseph true religion always involved revelation and contact with the supernatural, the ability to discern the source of the contact was essential. According to George A. Smith, "there was no point upon which the prophet Joseph dwelt more than the discerning of Spirits" (Ehat, 33).

Joseph instructed the quorum that since they had the keys, they were to test the revelations of anyone claiming to have received one for the church. At the trial of Sidney Rigdon in August of 1844, two different members of the quorum used this argument to show that Sidney Rigdon's revelations were false. Orson Hyde said that Rigdon should have called the quorum together to have his revelation tested. In the same trial William Marks tried to defend Rigdon by saying that Rigdon did not know about this procedure: "As respects his [Rigdon's] not presenting his vision or revelation before the first quorum I can say that Elder Rigdon did not know that this order was introduced. Brother Joseph told us that he, for the future whenever there was a revelation to be presented to the church he should first present it to that quorum, and then if it passed the first quorum, it should be presented to the Church. But Brother Rigdon did not know this, for he was only just brought into the quorum before he left to go to Pittsburg" (*Times and Seasons* 5:664). Both Hyde and Marks were referring to the anointed quorum. It is also clear that the quorum had real if not supreme priesthood authority in the church, for this quorum, which Marks refers to here as the "first quorum," could pass upon the validity of revelations for the church.

This same view of the quorum was emphasized by others at Rigdon's

---

[8] In December 1845 Amasa Lyman told a group of newly endowed Saints: "You have now learned how to pray. You have been taught how to approach God, and be recognized. This is the principle by which the Church has been kept together, and not the power of arms" (Heber C. Kimball Journal, 21 Dec. 1845).

trial. For example Heber C. Kimball indicated that although Sidney Rigdon had held high church office, he did not have as much authority as others who held the fullness of the priesthood and participated in the "council pertaining to the High Priesthood": "[Sidney Rigdon] has no authority only what he receives from the church, if he was one with us, why was he not in our councils? He was not in the council pertaining to the High Priesthood until just before he started for Pittsburgh. Brother Phelps was the means of bringing him in, but he has not got the same authority as others; there are more than thirty men who have got higher authority than he has" (*Times and Seasons* 5:663).

In Heber C. Kimball's mind, to have the fullness of priesthood and to participate fully in the "first quorum" was equated with having the highest authority in the church. This view is substantiated by evidence that Joseph Smith conducted important church business in a meeting of the "first quorum" held on 1 October 1843. There Joseph anointed William Law and Amasa Lyman as counselors in the First Presidency of the church, in spite of the fact that Sidney Rigdon had not yet been officially released from his position in the presidency according to church procedure. When questioned how ordinations could be valid, Joseph answered cryptically: "Why, (said he) by the same rule that Samuel anointed David to be King over Israel while Saul was yet crowned" (Ehat, 119).

It appears that from the time Joseph organized the quorum until his death, he relied more and more upon it to test out his doctrinal innovations and to disclose his most important decisions (Ehat, 41). Joseph's focus on this quorum made up of couples holding the fullness of the priesthood underscores the importance of the priesthood power of both women and men for the full redemption of the individual and society. The outer city of God could not be built until the inner temple in each man and woman was reconstructed. It was by the last anointing to the fullness of the priesthood and by the acquisition of the powers of heaven that each man and woman was brought to this place. That Joseph saw this as his culminating work is seen in the phrase he used when he referred to this dispensation not just as the "dispensation of the fullness of times" but as the "dispensation of the fullness of the priesthood" (HC 5:14). This was part of the restoration of all things; the priesthood operative at the beginning of the world had to be restored in the end of the world (Moses 6:7). For as Bishop Whitney stated, "without the female all things cannot be restored to the earth — it takes all to restore the Priesthood" (Newell 1987, 116).

That Joseph Smith held this view is corroborated by ancillary evidence. For example, in an 1843 patriarchal blessing given to Leonora Taylor, wife of Apostle John Taylor, Patriarch Hyrum Smith said: "You [Leonora] shall be blessed with your portion of the Priesthood which belongeth unto you, that you may be set apart for your Anointing and your induement [sic]" (Madsen 1987, 101). Zina Card in a blessing given to her by Patriarch Joseph Young was told that she would have power over the adversary and over all kinds of diseases, that she would be "full of the spirit of the Father" and that she held "the blessings and the power according to the holy Melchizedek Priesthood, you received in your endowments" (Madsen 1987, 101).

The symbols and ordinances of the temple also evidence that the endowment was understood to be a bestowal of priesthood on both men and women. Both wear the garments and robes of the Aaronic and the Melchizedek priesthoods and are instructed that with the robe in the proper position, they can officiate in all of the ordinances of both priesthoods. Women perform priestly duties in the temple and actually administer priesthood ordinances.[9]

However, Joseph's vision of priesthood faded quickly after his death. And so did the importance of the quorum, the place of women in it, and the role of women as priestesses in Zion. Ironically, though the Twelve Apostles succeeded to Joseph's place because of their anointing to the fullness of the priesthood, they shifted the preeminent authority away from the quorum of the anointed to the quorum of the twelve. An apostolic dispensation ensued.[10] Perhaps Brigham Young did this

---

[9] In ancient Israel entrance into the holy sanctuaries of the temple was forbidden to anyone but the priests, and only the high priest could enter the holy of holies. In Mormon temples women have access to all the inner sanctuaries, even the holy of holies, where the highest ordinance of the temple, the second anointing, is administered.

[10] In the decades following the death of Joseph Smith, the concept of the fullness of the priesthood was divorced from the quorum of the anointed and associated instead with the quorum of the twelve. In a sermon given in the Salt Lake tabernacle on 6 April 1853, Brigham Young stated: "The keys of the Eternal Priesthood, which is after the order of the Son of God, are comprehended by being an Apostle. All the Priesthood, all the keys, all the gifts, all the endowments, and everything preparatory to entering into the presence of the Father and the Son, are in, composed of, circumscribed by, or I might say incorporated within the circumference of the Apostleship" (JD 1:134).

Apostle George Q. Cannon's speeches on this subject take the concept a step further. He does not speak of the fullness of the priesthood but the "fullness of the

consciously because he believed that the time for Zion was not yet. Perhaps he was angry at the women of the church, especially Emma Smith, for opposing polygamy, or perhaps he did it because necessity dictated this course of action. Whatever the reason, under the administration of Brigham Young, the anointed quorum and the concept of woman's role in the priesthood both received quick death blows (Derr).

Just after the apostles assumed the leadership of the church, they "conversed about [the Quorum and] voted no women . . . to be admitted in the Quorum — till times will permit" (Ehat, 206). The ostensible reason for this action was fear that a mob would make an attempt on the lives of all members of the anointed quorum, but still the exclusion of women points to a pattern of closing doors to women. In fairness to Brigham Young and other leaders, we should add that during the period from the death of Joseph to the completion of the Nauvoo temple, even the entire body of male members of the anointed quorum seldom met together. Instead they gathered in smaller groups for prayer circles. Also individual women were occasionally allowed to receive the fullness of priesthood with their husbands. However, when the male

---

Apostleship," suggesting that the office of king and priest belongs exclusively or at least primarily to the members of that quorum rather than to all members of the church. No mention is ever made of the relationship of this priesthood to women. The reminiscences related here are urged upon the members of the church for the purpose of reinforcing the claim of the quorum of the twelve to the succession after the death of Joseph Smith. An argument could be made that Joseph did not in fact lay the kingdom on the shoulders of the twelve but on the shoulders of the men and women of the Holy Order, of which the twelve were members. Cannon himself said: "Prior to the completion of the Temple, he took the Twelve and certain other men, who were chosen, and bestowed upon them a holy anointing, similar to that which was received on the day of Pentecost by the Twelve, who had been told to tarry at Jerusalem. This endowment was bestowed upon the chosen few whom Joseph anointed and ordained, giving them the keys of the holy Priesthood, the power and authority which he himself held, to build up the Kingdom of God in all the earth and accomplish the great purposes of our Heavenly Father; and it was by virtue of this authority, on the death of Joseph, that President Young, as President of the quorum of the Twelve, presided over the Church" (JD 13:49).

On 8 October 1877, he further stated: "Was it necessary for the Prophet Joseph Smith to set apart Brigham or Heber or Willard, or any of the rest of the Twelve Apostles? No, for the same reason, they had received the fullness of the Holy Priesthood, the full endowment and the keys, and the authority, and the fullness of the Apostleship. . . . The blessing of such men or by such men, would not bestow upon him any additional authority or any more keys, presuming that he had received the fullness of the Apostleship" (JD 19:235).

members of the quorum began meeting again regularly in the Nauvoo temple, they did not include their wives at their first few meetings. That the women felt a sense of loss during their period of exclusion is reflected in Heber C. Kimball's statement that Brigham Young's decision to include the women once again in the 7 December 1845 meeting of the anointed quorum "gave great joy to our wimmen" (Quinn 1978, 93). The quorum of the anointed met on a few more occasions in December 1845, with an ever-increasing number of new members as more and more of the Saints received their endowments. Then at the end of that month, the quorum ceased its separate meetings.

Perhaps Brigham Young felt it was unnecessary to continue these meetings since the temple was completed and the endowment was being administered there and since important church business could be taken care of by the twelve. By early December 1845, Brigham Young no longer conducted church business in quorum meetings. For example, on 11 December 1845 the anointed quorum met in the Nauvoo temple for a prayer circle. After they were finished Brigham Young called some of the men out of the group for a private meeting in which they discussed some information relevant to the Saints' going west. Then this smaller group prayed again in the true order about these concerns (Quinn 1978, 89–90). This procedure contrasts with the way the anointed quorum was conducted by Joseph, who trusted all members with confidential matters.

With the disbanding of the anointed quorum, women were no longer included in prayer circles, except at that point in the endowment ceremony when instruction on prayer circles is given. Men, however, continued to participate in prayer circles — not only church leaders but also lay members who were invited to be members of specially constituted prayer circles. According to Michael Quinn, "the available records of the special and ecclesiastical prayer circles from the 1850s to the 1950s describe only one instance in which women met with their husbands in prayer circle meetings" (1978, 95). In a meeting in 1896, the First Presidency and Quorum of the Twelve discussed whether the sisters should be allowed to hold their own prayer circles and also whether they should be permitted to join their husbands in prayer circles. These leaders decided both questions in the negative: "The subject of permission to the sisters to meet in prayer circles was discussed, as the question had been asked whether it would be right or whether they could be permitted to meet with their husbands in a prayer circle, seeing that sisters had been admitted to prayer circles in the Nauvoo

Temple. It was shown, however, that on such occasions it was for the purpose of teaching the order of prayer as it is now the custom in the Temples. It was decided that if the sisters desired to meet for prayer they could do so as members and officers of Relief Societies in their regular places of meeting, but that it would not be advisable for them to meet at circles or to participate in prayer circle meetings" (ibid.).

These men thus reasoned that the only purpose of the prayer circles in Nauvoo was to give instruction in the true order of prayer. If this is true, then the instruction itself becomes meaningless since it leads to nothing outside itself. What good comes from receiving the keys to ask and get an answer if a person is never allowed to exercise those keys. Obviously these church leaders in 1896 felt that men could and should engage in the true order of prayer, since prayer circles for church leaders and for other male church members abounded at this time. But these same leaders saw no need for women to utilize these same keys, which they also had received. The implication is that the concerns of women are too trivial to be addressed in the true order of prayer. This 1896 decision serves also as a statement against the necessity of the union of the sexes. One of the purposes of the true order of prayer is to promote unity of feeling and belief, and yet it has not been considered important to include women in prayer circles from 1846 to the present.

Besides disbanding the anointed quorum and excluding women from prayer circles, Brigham Young decided to "defer the operations" of the Relief Society in 1844. This decision also shut doors for women and cut off official channels for operating in their priestly roles. John Taylor thought this was done because Emma Smith had been using the Relief Society as a forum to oppose Brigham Young and the doctrine of plural marriage. She may have preached against polygamy to the sisters even while Joseph Smith was alive. Perhaps Brigham Young felt that a spirit of dissension was operating in the society. But as John Taylor remarked, other women had done much good "and should not be deprived of their rights and privileges because others have done wrong" (Woman's Exponent 11:54).

It was not until 1867 that Brigham Young officially reorganized the Relief Society on a churchwide basis, although during the interim local Relief Societies had functioned in Utah as charitable institutions. For example, Native American Relief Societies were made up of anglo women whose business it was to see that the Native Americans of Southern Utah were properly clad. Unfortunately the enterprise seemed doomed to failure because the Mormon work ethic would not allow these clothes to be given without some return effort. Most of the clothes wound up in the hands of white settlers, and the Indians, we may suppose, remained unclad (Jensen).

With the reorganization of the Relief Society in 1867, the focus of the society was much more temporal than spiritual. The ever-practical Brigham Young felt he needed the services and resources of women to stabilize the economic and social structure of the Mormon kingdom and to stave-off the encroaching Gentiles with their unwanted worldly influence.

Though Brigham Young's purpose for reorganizing the Relief Society coincides with the women's original purpose in Nauvoo (a charitable institution to fortify community morals), this purpose falls short of the vision Joseph Smith had for the society: to expand women's spiritual horizons and make of them a "kingdom of priestesses." Leaders after Joseph were quick and deliberate in limiting women's sphere of action in the church. A 21 December 1845 Heber C. Kimball journal entry of a meeting in the Nauvoo Temple illustrates this. Seventy-five persons were present, and Heber C. Kimball presided in the place of Brigham Young, who was absent from Nauvoo. On this occasion instructions and explanations about the endowment were given. The women present were told by George A. Smith that they "ought to be in subjection" to their husbands and by Amasa Lyman that "the man . . . has covenanted to obey the law of God, and the woman to obey her husband" and by Heber C. Kimball that women should be "in subjection to their husbands, [for] the man was created, and God gave him dominion over the whole earth, but he saw that he never could multiply and replenish the earth without woman; and He made one and gave her to him. He did not make the man for the woman but the woman for the man" (*Woman's Exponent* 12:26, 34).

This comment demonstrates that, by this time, a fundamentally negative and restrictive interpretation of the endowment as it touched upon the role of women was being developed by church leaders to ensure that women did not avail themselves of the priesthood privileges extended to them by Joseph Smith. Instead of seeing that women were being given priesthood in which to function in spiritual matters, they could only speak of women in terms of subjection to men. It is as if these remarks were motivated by a fear that women would see themselves as the spiritual equals of men and, therefore, had to be reminded to stay in their proper place. There is little if anything left here of the tone of Joseph's discourses to the Relief Society in which he told Mormon women that he was "turning the key to them," or in other words opening up doors. By December 1845 we see those doors beginning to close.

But in spite of these limitations, Mormon women in the nineteenth century continued to express their religious devotion by holding prayer circles among themselves, by anointing and healing the sick, by speaking in and interpreting tongues, and by prophesying. Those who had participated in the anointed quorum and the Relief Society of Nauvoo believed that they had the right to do these things by virtue of their anointings as queens and priestesses (Madsen 1981; Newell and Avery 1981).

It is ironic that some men and women today look back at these women and their enjoyment of spiritual gifts as though they lived in a golden age, when in reality they lived and served under restrictive conditions and within a framework that had greatly narrowed since the time of Joseph Smith. But, of course, from our perspective, these women did live in favored times, for by the outset of the twentieth century, the enjoyment of spiritual gifts had nearly ceased among women of the church and, sadly, among men as well. By this time, women no longer thought of themselves as having a rightful and equal claim upon the fullness of the priesthood. This was due, in part, to the fact that the ordinance of the holy anointing to the highest and holiest order of the priesthood was falling into disuse. There was also lost the idea that this priesthood and these ceremonies were indispensable to full salvation (Buerger).

Where does all this lead? Is there a paradise to be regained? If there is, it was never realized in this dispensation, even during the lifetime of Joseph Smith. There never was a Mormon golden age. Though Joseph may have had the vision of a Zion society, where men and women were united together and held "all things in common," he certainly did not bring such a society into being. He was, as Isaiah prophesied, a "rod" that bore no fruit, but who may yet be the "Branch" that brings again Zion (11:1).

Zion cannot be built without the equality of priesthood set forth in the doctrine of the fullness of the priesthood restored by the prophet Elijah. Without this the "whole earth would be utterly wasted" at the coming of the Lord. In spite of the fact that the modern church sees the fulfillment of Malachi's prophecy of the return of Elijah in terms of genealogy work and of temple marriage, for us Elijah's mission was to reveal the fullness of the priesthood and the temple as a place to receive the keys of that priesthood and an anointing to the power of an endless life so that we may be transformed thereby in the divine image and stand in the presence of God.

This chapter was first written as a paper entitled "The Missing Rib: The Forgotten Place of Queens and Priestesses in the Establishment of Zion." When our close friend, Gregg Alvord, heard this title, he said caustically, "What about the forgotten place of kings and priests?" Of course, he was right. Most men and women in the church today are not struggling for the right to exercise spiritual gifts and priestly powers. As Mormons, we live in an age when the spiritual powers seem to be at their nadir. How many, today, care about spiritual gifts? About the establishment of Zion? Is it not already here? Do we not, as one Mormon wag has acerbically pointed out, have Zion's Bank?

Here, of course, is the problem we face. In order for women to take their rightful places as queens and priestesses, both men and women in the church must first accept a redefinition of priesthood in spiritual rather than strictly temporal or corporate terms, to accept the unseen as well as the seen, the sacral as well as the secular. If women simply demand ordination to ecclesiastical or priesthood offices as a means of seizing power in the church structure, then they are questing after the wrong objective and are fighting the wrong battle — the battle of the sexes, which is really a struggle for power, for the whip handle, for the number one spot, for the management of the corporation.

This is not to say that women should not hold priesthood and church offices. We have often argued that women should be included in *all* the offices and councils of the church, including the First Presidency. Our point here is that priesthood should not be defined in terms of competitive or coercive power. This is unrighteous dominion, a form of oppression and denigration of life. Rather, we must see priesthood in terms of the power of God, the power of life, the power of divine love, the power that restores, unites, atones, and balances extremes. This is the priesthood power that both men and women should be encouraged to seek.

Joseph Smith told the Relief Society, in every speech he ever gave them, that for this to come about it was essential to have charity, the pure and sacrificial love of Christ. What will happen if the women of the church argue for and seek with patience, determination, and love their priesthood rights? In Joseph's words, "God shall say to them, come up higher" (WJS, 116).

CHAPTER SEVENTEEN

THE OATH AND COVENANT
OF THE PRIESTHOOD

From time to time in the LDS church, especially in priesthood meetings, reference is made to the "oath and covenant" of the priesthood, a concept derived from an 1832 revelation now found in Doctrine and Covenants 84.[1] In discussions of this concept, two troubling constants seem to emerge: first, the oath and covenant is assumed to be the exclusive province of males; and second, the teaching seems to defy

---

[1] The revelation given on September 22–23, 1832, reads:

33. For whoso is faithful unto the obtaining these two priesthoods of which I have spoken, and the magnifying their calling are sanctified by the Spirit unto the renewing of their bodies.

34. They become the sons of Moses and of Aaron and the seed of Abraham, and the church and kingdom, and the elect of God.

35. And also all they who receive this priesthood receive me, saith the Lord;

36. For he that receiveth my servants receiveth me;

37. And he that receiveth me receiveth my Father;

38. And he that receiveth my Father receiveth my Father's kingdom; therefore all that my Father hath shall be given unto him.

39. And this is according to the oath and covenant which belongeth to the priesthood.

40. Therefore, all those who receive the priesthood, receive this oath and covenant of my Father, which he cannot break, neither can it be moved.

41. But whoso breaketh this covenant after he hath received it, and altogether turneth therefrom, shall not have forgiveness of sins in this world nor in the world to come.

42. And wo unto all those who come not unto this priesthood which ye have received, which I now confirm upon you who are present this day, by mine own voice out of the heavens; and even I have given the heavenly hosts and mine angels charge concerning you.

The date comes from the original manuscript in the handwriting of Fredrick G. Williams (Revelations).

analysis and ready understanding. Our purpose in this chapter is to address four questions that often arise in discussions of this doctrine: What is the nature of the oath and covenant? To whom and by whom are they administered? To what priesthood do they belong? And what purpose do they serve?

In respone to the first question, we have heard some Mormons conjecture that the terms "oath" and "covenant" are either synonyms or else comprise a single term of art. In either case, they refer to a two-party contract between God and a priesthood bearer made at the time of the man's ordination in which he promises God to obey all of the commandments and thereby qualify himself to receive "all that [the] Father hath." If the man fails to keep the commandments, he is guilty of breaking his "oath and covenant." Others suggest that the phrase "oath and covenant" refers to God's promise of "all that [the] Father hath" as a condition of and an inducement for a man's future obedience. Still others believe that the two terms "oath" and "covenant" are not synonyms but separate labels for the two sides of a bilateral agreement or contract entered into by a man when ordained to the Melchizedek priesthood. A man's promise to obey the commandments (the "covenant") is given in exchange for God's promise (the "oath") to give him priesthood power and blessings.

In our view none of these explanations is correct. In the first place the words "oath" and "covenant" are not synonymous. They describe legal notions which are entirely different. An oath is the ritual of swearing or attestation; a covenant is a promise but not a contract (*American Heritage*, s.v. "oath"; Corbin). In fact, in modern American law a bare covenant is not enforceable.[2] It takes the exchange of two or more covenants to make an enforceable contract. Under ancient rules of English law, a single covenant given without consideration (that is given unilaterally without a return promise, performance, or forbearance)[3] could

---

[2] "No society compels its members to keep every promise they may make. At the same time, the good of society demands that certain promises must be followed by performance, . . . [for this reason each society] perfects forms and procedures by which it can guarantee those promises. Those procedures are in the beginning of law most closely connected with religion, and are known as *oaths* . . . which [are] conditional self-cursing[s],. . . appeal[s] to the gods to punish the promisor if he defaults.. .. At the present time the oath is merely an 'ancient ruin still standing' " (Mendenhall, 53).

[3] In law the *act* of making such an exchange of comparable valuables is referred to as "consideration"; also the valuables themselves are referred to as "consideration." Sometimes the Latin phrase *quid pro quo* is used in place of the word "consideration."

be enforced if the person making the unilateral promise sealed the covenant with an oath. A promise sealed by an oath is a formula going back to the third millennium before Christ (Mendenhall, 50–52).[4] The Hebrew word *berit*, from which the term "covenant" is translated, can refer to a one-sided obligation assumed by one party without expectation of return.[5]

It appears that Joseph Smith's concept of an oath and covenant fits into this last category. Doctrine and Covenants 84:38 states that all the Father has will be given to the faithful priesthood bearer by way of a unilateral promise of God, a promise binding because it is made under oath. This is reminiscent of Hebrews 6:13–18, where Abraham is presented as the recipient of God's blessings. There we are told that Abraham had patiently endured his trials and was accounted a suitable candidate to receive the promise of "all that [the] Father hath." The writer of Hebrews states that God wished to show Abraham and his posterity that the divine promise was immutable. So God confirmed

---

[4] Anciently the actual oath which accompanied and upheld the promise and made it binding upon the promisor could take any of a variety of ritual forms: eating together, the use of oil and water, or drinking from a cup (Hillers, 40). Oath swearing might also entail an exchange of gifts, the shaking of hands, or the eating or spilling of salt (McCarthy, 4). "The most widely attested form of swearing a covenant, however, involved cutting up an animal" (Hillers, 40). It has been noted that slaughtering animals at the time of covenant making was considered a sacrificial offering and added solemnity to the occasion (Weinfeld, 184), creating a mystical relationship between the parties involved (McCarthy, 32–33).

[5] Some scholars have analogized the covenant that God made with Israel at Sinai (Ex. 20) to Hittite suzerainty treaties in which the vassal is obligated by an oath to obey the king. This is an ancient form of adhesion contract in which the terms are dictated by the stronger party. Some scholars have even speculated that the Sinai covenant was recast in terms of the verbal formulas of the Hittite treaties in order to give legal impetus to the Decalogue. In other words, to make the Ten Commandments respectable from a Hittite point of view (Mendenhall, 66; McCarthy, 72). But the Decalogue lacks the witnessing by the gods, the cursing and blessing formula, and the requirement that the covenant be re-read periodically, as found in the suzerainty treaties. More importantly, in the Sinai covenant "God does not force himself and his covenant on the people . . . all texts . . . concerned with the covenant [at Sinai] are shot through with persuasion; the people are never compelled to enter into the relationship" (McCarthy, 55). Furthermore, the Sinai covenant was predicated on sacrificial rites, covenant meals, and the creation of mystical familial relationships. All of these facts indicate that there was, rather than a Hittite influence, "a very strong cultic element . . . " There is a greater sense of quid pro quo in Exodus than in Genesis. The Abrahamic covenant is discussed below (ibid., 72).

this covenant or promise with an oath. But because God could swear
this oath by no greater person, God swore upon God's own name, thus
giving Abraham and his posterity (that is, the faithful) the assurance
that God would fulfill his covenant to confer eternal life, an endless
priesthood, and joint-heirship with Christ.[6]

Mormon texts indicate that Abraham was not the first to receive
such an oath and covenant. God had previously granted it to others, to
Enoch (JST Gen. 14:30) and Melchizedek (vv. 25-29, 33) and later to
Isaac (Gen. 26:3) and Jacob (28:4; Weinfeld, 196-99; Hillers, 103).[7]

---

[6] In Abraham 1:18-19, God promises to give Abraham the priesthood. In Abraham
2:7-13 and Genesis 12:2 of Joseph Smith's Inspired Translation, God promises to
bless Abraham's posterity with the right to hold the priesthood and to give Abraham
and his seed the right of adoption so that all those who accept the gospel would be
accounted the seed of Abraham too. In JST Genesis 14:40 and 15:2 we are told that
God conferred on Abraham the blessings promised him by Melchizedek—including
the blessings of honor, riches, and an everlasting possession. In JST Genesis 15:21
God promises to give Canaan to Abraham's posterity as an everlasting possession.
And in JST Genesis 17:8-11 God promises to give to Abraham a son, Isaac, through
whom will be realized all of Abraham's other blessings relating to posterity. It is difficult to tell in exactly what sequence if any these promises were made. It is possible
that these different accounts are referring to only one or two covenants. But whether
one or many, God not Abraham makes the promises.

In the Genesis 15 account, God also swears to keep his promise. "It is He,
accompanied by a smoking oven and a blazing torch... who passes between the
parts [of the sacrificial animal] as though he were invoking a curse upon himself"
(Weinfield, 196). "The author is discreet; he does not flatly say that Yahweh invokes a curse on himself. But the version he has related makes the literal restatement unnecessary, and the imagination of the reader can supply: 'Just as this heifer
is cut up, so may I...'" (Hillers, 103). It is similar to the oath in "the Abba-El-
Yarimlim deed where Abba-El, the donor, takes the oath by cutting the neck of a
lamb... saying, '[May I be cursed] if I take back what I gave you'" (Weinfeld,
199).

The covenant which God made with Abraham is "completely different [than
other Old Testament covenants].... it is clearly stated or implied that it is Yahweh
Himself who swears to certain promises to be carried out in the future. It is not
often enough seen that no obligations are imposed on Abraham. Circumcision is
not originally an obligation, but a sign of the covenant, like the rainbow in
Genesis 9. It serves to identify the recipient(s) of the covenant, as well as to give a
concrete indication that a covenant exists. The covenant [at Sinai] is almost the
exact opposite. It imposes specific obligations upon the tribes or clans without
binding Yahweh [whereas the covenant of God with Abraham binds God alone]
(Mendenhall, 62).

[7] In Genesis 28:13-22, the granting of the blessing to Jacob is presented in a way
that involves a stone, a pillar, the House of God, and an anointing with oil—all ritu-

Joseph Smith asserted that it was God's intention to make this oath and covenant with each descendent of Abraham, Isaac, and Jacob at Mount Sinai (JST Gen. 14:25–34, 40). However, as a result of unfaithfulness, the greater promises of God, "the priesthood . . . my holy order, and the ordinances thereof" (JST Ex. 34:1–2), were withheld from the house of Israel as a people; and the law of carnal commandments was given in place of the higher priesthood blessings. The house of Israel did not become a "kingdom of priests" (Ex. 19:5–6; cf. Pet. 2:9; TPJS, 322).[8]

Joseph Smith apparently viewed the oath and covenant as a priesthood blessing administered by God, but it was a blessing reserved for recipients of the fullness of the priesthood not for those who had been ordained to that portion of the Melchizedek priesthood commonly held by men in the LDS church. In his revision of Genesis, Joseph Smith connected the oath and covenant with the fullness of the priesthood held by Enoch (JST Gen. 6:32; 14:24–31, 40). This priesthood was delivered not by man but by God's own voice. God promised to Enoch by an oath and covenant that he should have power over nature. Melchizedek, a descendant of Enoch, also received this power. Melchizedek, in turn, ordained and blessed Abraham pursuant to this covenant.

According to Joseph Smith: "Abraham says to Melchizedek, I believe all that thou hast taught me concerning the priesthood and the coming of the Son of Man; so Melchizedek ordained Abraham and sent him away. Abraham rejoiced, saying, Now I have a priesthood" (TPJS, 322). Elsewhere he said: "What was the power of Melchizedek? 'Twas not the Priesthood of Aaron which administers in outward ordinances, and the offering of sacrifices. Those holding the fullness of the Melchizedek Priesthood are kings and priests of the Most High God, holding the keys of power and blessings" (ibid., 322–23).

"King and priest" was the calling of Melchizedek. It was by the keys and powers of this calling, we are told, that he ruled the people of

alistic symbols. In Genesis 35:9–15 the oath and covenant is linked with Jacob's receiving a new name—Israel—by which his descendants would be known throughout history.

[8] It is to be noted that 1 Samuel 16:13 and Psalm 89:20–37 indicate that God did later make an oath and covenant with David. Joseph Smith, however, explained that "although David was a king, he never did obtain the spirit and power of Elijah and the fullness of Priesthood" but received something less than the full blessings given to the ancient Patriarchs (TPJS, 339).

Salem. It is said that by this power he blessed them with endless lives (TPJS, 322), and they were translated into heaven to join the City of Enoch (JST Gen. 14:33–34). Abraham, who was blessed and ordained by Melchizedek, was likewise raised to this calling. He held the right belonging to the ancients to sanctify his people and administer endless life to them. Joseph Smith also said, "the Levitical Priesthood . . . [is] made without an oath; but the [fullness of the] Priesthood of Melchizedek is [made] by an oath and covenant" (TPJS, 323).

Joseph Smith sometimes referred to Melchizedek as a king and priest (TPJS, 322–23) and sometimes as a "high priest after the order of the covenant God made with Enoch" (JST Gen. 14:27). These are not inconsistent descriptions. The term "high priest" can refer to any number of distinct priesthood offices. In the Old Testament the "high priest" was the presiding figure of the lesser or Aaronic priesthood (Lev. 1:10; Heb. 7:11, 8:3–5). As used in the modern Mormon church, the term refers to a member of the high priest quorum, which President John Taylor explained was "instituted for the purpose of qualifying those who shall be appointed standing presidents over the different Stakes scattered abroad. A sort of normal school, if you please, to prepare men to preside, to be fathers of the people" (JD 19:242; 9:87–88).

The term "high priest" also refers to one holding power over nature (D&C 93:17). Jesus was called a high priest (Heb. 3:1), and Abraham, ordained by Melchizedek, refers to himself as a "High Priest." He is also called a "prince of peace," the title by which Jesus was known (Is. 9:6), as well as a "rightful heir" with the "right belonging to the fathers" (Abr. 1:2). The point of this is that Joseph Smith connected the oath and covenant to more than clerical duties associated with priesthood office. As already shown, he envisioned queens and priestesses also, as well as kings and priests. In Section 84, we find further evidence for the view that the "oath and covenant" belongs to the fullness of the priesthood:

First, verse 33 mentions the "two priesthoods spoken of." The first of these is clearly the lesser or Aaronic Priesthood. According to Joseph Smith, no oath and covenant is connected with this priesthood (TPJS, 323). The greater priesthood is that which was passed down from Abraham, that is, the fullness of the priesthood.

Second, verse 33 connects the greater priesthood with the doctrine of sanctification. This connection echoes the teachings of the Book of Mormon prophet Alma, who stated that those taking "upon them the high priesthood of the holy order" (Al. 13:8) were like Melchizedek, the "high priest after this same order" (v. 14). They were "sanctified," and their garments were washed white through the blood of the Lamb" (v. 11). This suggests that the greater priesthood of Section 84 is the same as the "priesthood of the holy order" of Alma 13 — in other words, the fullness of the priesthood.

Third, verse 34 connects the greater priesthood with the concept of election, which Joseph Smith described at length (TPJS, 150–51). The "elect of God" are described in Section 76 as "they who are the church of the Firstborn" and "they into whose hands the father hath given all things." They are "priests and kings, who have received of his fullness, and of his glory; And are priests of the Most High, after the order of Melchizedek, which was after the order of Enoch, which was after the order of the Only Begotten Son. . . . These shall dwell in the presence of God and his Christ forever" (D&C 76:54–57, 62).

Fourth, verses 1–5 refer to the city of the New Jerusalem and to the temple. This is important because it is in the temple that the fullness of the priesthood is conferred. Joseph Smith explained: "If a man gets a fullness of the priesthood of God he has to get it in the same way that Jesus Christ obtained it, and that was by keeping all the commandments and obeying all the ordinances of the house of the Lord" (TPJS, 308).

Fifth, verses 36–39 refer to heirship, which is often linked in the scriptures with the fullness of the priesthood. For example, when Abraham receives that priesthood, he accounts himself a "rightful heir" (Abr. 1:2). Paul declares that Abraham became the "heir of the world" (Rom. 4:13) and that those who suffer with Christ and are glorified with him are "heirs of God and joint-heirs with Christ" (8:17). Joseph Smith revealed that "they who are of the Church of the Firstborn" are priests and kings "into whose hands the father has given all things." They are heirs (D&C 76:54–57).

We should observe here that the original version of this revelation contains a passage deleted from the present version: "And woe unto all those who come not unto this priesthood which ye have received, which I now confirm upon you this day, viz. the 23rd day of September AD 1832. Eleven high priests save one, by mine own voice out of the heavens; and even I have given my angels charge concerning you" (Revelations). These ten men were probably not at this time elevated to the fullness of the priesthood but received the office of high priest. Joseph Smith taught that all priesthood was Melchizedek but that there were varying degrees of it (TPJS, 180). That portion of the Melchizedek priesthood taken from the children of Israel was the fullness of the priesthood (JST Deut. 10:1–2; JST Ex. 34:1–2). It was restored in Jesus' time but then lost again. Beginning in 1829 the priesthood was restored to Joseph Smith by degrees: first, the Aaronic or lesser priesthood (D&C 13), then the higher priesthood. This was followed by a period of development in which priesthood quorums, offices, and keys were defined in the growing church organization. Then on 3 April 1836 Jesus, Moses, Elias, and Elijah appeared to Oliver Cowdery and Joseph Smith as they kneeled in prayer behind the veils of the presidency's pulpits in the priesthood assembly room of the Kirtland temple (ibid., 110). During this visitation Joseph and Oliver received additional priesthood keys vital to the development of the church (TPJS, 224). From 1836 until his death, Joseph Smith stressed the need to build temples, where the fullness of priesthood could be bestowed upon Latter-day Saints to prepare them for the personal visitation of God.

One allusion to the bestowal of this priesthood was made by Oliver Cowdery to Parley P. Pratt at the time Pratt was ordained to the first LDS Quorum of Twelve Apostles. Cowdery said, "Your ordination is not full and complete until God himself lays his hand upon you" (HC 2:195–96). Both Wilford Woodruff and Orson Hyde, as well as other apostles, emphasized that it was in the winter of 1843–44, when they were endowed, not in 1835, when they were ordained, that they received the fullness of the keys and powers of the priesthood (Kenney, 2:341–42, 344–48, 393; MS 5:109; JD 1:134, 13:49; 19:232, 233, 235, 266; *Times and Seasons* 5:651, 648, 661, 663, and 666; TPJS, 237, 326, cf. D&C 124:95–97). On 6 August 1843 Woodruff reported that "[Brigham Young] remarked that if any in the Church had the fullness of the Melchizedek Priesthood, he did not know it. For any person to have the fullness of the priesthood, he must be a king and priest. A person may have a portion of that priesthood, the same as governors or judges of England have power from the king to transact business; but that does not make them kings of England. A person may be anointed king and priest long before he receives his kingdom" (HC 5:527).

Joseph Smith made it clear that the fullness of the priesthood was not just for leaders: "We calculate to give the Elders of Israel their washings and anointings and attend to those last and more impressive ordinances, without which we cannot obtain celestial thrones. But there must be a holy place prepared for that purpose.... So that men may receive their endowments and be made kings and priests unto the Most High God, having nothing to do with temporal things" (TPJS, 362–63).

When planning the westward move of the church shortly before his martyrdom, Joseph Smith wrote to the elders who were to go west as an advance party: "I want every man that goes to be a king and a priest. When he gets on the mountains, he may want to talk with his God" (ibid., 333). Again asserting his intention to elevate others to the fullness of priesthood, Joseph Smith declared that it was God's purpose "to make of the Church of Jesus Christ a kingdom of Priests, a holy people, a chosen generation, and as in Enoch's day, having all the gifts as illustrated to the Church in Paul's epistles" (ibid., 202). We have already argued at length that Joseph's intent was that women should share in this priesthood.

This notwithstanding, a practice was instituted in the early days of the church of ordaining individuals to *become* kings and priests or queens and priestesses rather than actually bestowing these titles and offices directly on them.[9] This promissory and conditional ordination was referred to in an address given in the Nauvoo Temple by Apostle Heber C. Kimball: "We have come to this place and all your former covenants are of no account, and here is the place where we have to enter into a new covenant, and be sealed, and have it recorded. One reason why we bring our wives with us is that they may make a covenant with us to keep these things sacred. You have been anointed *to be* kings and priests, but you have not been ordained yet. And you have got to get it by being faithful" (Kimball Journal; Cannon).

Ordination to the fullness of priesthood is presented in Mormon texts as a multi-step spiritual journey: A person must be spiritually born into the family of Jesus Christ by faith and through grace (D&C 84:33; 76:53). Then a male must receive the Aaronic and Melchizedek priesthoods available in the church. Both males and females must be endowed with the priesthood and the fullness of the keys thereof and be sealed in marriage in the new and everlasting covenant (ibid. 84:33; 131:1–3; TPJS, 308). The sealed couple must be anointed king and priest and queen and priestess, thus becoming members of the holy order of God, and they must magnify that calling by manifesting to

---

[9] On 2 August 1883 Apostle George Q. Cannon stated to the School of the Prophets in Provo, Utah: "in the washing that takes place in the first endowment, they are washed that they might become clean from the blood of this generation — that is, I suppose, in the same way they are ordained to become Kings and Priests — that ordinance does not make them clean from the blood of this generation any more than it makes them Kings and Priests. If they fully receive of another endowment, a fullness of power, the promises are fulfilled in the bestowal of power upon them" (Minutes).

God a willingness to sacrifice all earthly things to become one in Christ
(D&C 84:34). By this means, these individuals become sanctified by
the Spirit, thereby becoming the children of Moses, of Aaron, the seed
of Abraham, the church, the kingdom, and the elect of God (v. 37).
They may receive the visitation of angels. But eventually, either in life
or death, they must also obtain the visitation of Christ, who is the
Father and the Son—the "second comforter" spoken of in John 14 (vv.
36–37). They must receive from Christ the Father the promise or covenant of "all that [the] Father hath," a promise that is sealed by God's
own oath "out of the heavens" (vv. 38–40). Finally, they may also receive the fulfillment of the promise of the Father by actually obtaining
power over nature as a token of their inheritance in the world to come
(vv. 63–67; cf. Luke 22:29–30).

If these experiences are not realized in mortality, then apparently
they may be realized in the after life. The ordinances by which men
and women are ordained kings and priests and queens and priestesses
may be done by proxy for the dead in the temple. These steps cannot
be taken suddenly (1 Tim. 5:22). Faith in Christ, endurance of affliction, and submission to all his ordinances, including the covenant of
marriage, are presented as fundamental preconditions for receiving the
fullness of priesthood (D&C 50:26–29; 76:53; Eth. 12: 6–9; D&C
101:4–5; JST Gen. 14:26–27). Those anointed to the fullness of the
priesthood have authority to administer in all the ordinances of the
gospel and of the priesthood (TPJS, 337), to officiate in any of the offices of the church and kingdom of God, including the apostolic office
(D&C 107:1–10), to bear witness of the Father and the Son (84:63–64),
to pray in the true order, to detect the source of revelations (124:95,
97), and to assist the presidency of the Holy Order in anointing other
kings and priests and queens and priestesses.[10]

---

[10] Heber C. Kimball reported in his journal the remarks of Brigham Young given
on 26 December 1845: "Pres. Young said when we began [temple ordinance work]
again he would pay no respect to quorums every man comes in is washed & anointed
by good men and it makes no difference. Every man that gets his endowment, whether
he is High Priest or Seventy, may go into any part of the world and build up the kingdom if he has the keys—or into any island. We have been ordained to the Melchisedek
Priesthood, which is the highest order of Priesthood, and it has many branches or offices—and those who come in here and have received their washing & anointing will
be ordained Kings & Priests, and will then have received the fullness of the Priesthood,
all that can be given on earth, for Brother Joseph said he had given us all that could be
given to man on earth."

Though the second anointing is the highest ordinance conferred in the church, this ordinance must be sealed by God. This sealing is the oath and covenant. Joseph Smith explained this teaching in his discourse on Elias, Elijah, and Messiah: "The spirit of Elias is first, Elijah is second, and Messiah last. Elias is a forerunner to prepare the way, and the spirit and power of Elijah is to come after, holding the keys of power, building the temple to the capstone, placing the seals of the Melchizedek Priesthood upon the House of Israel, and making all things ready. Then Messiah comes to His temple, which is last of all" (TPJS, 340). In other words the spirit and power of Elias refers to the work associated now with the Aaronic and Melchizedek priesthoods — proclaiming faith and repentance, baptizing for the remission of sins, laying on hands for the gift of the Holy Ghost; in short adopting new members into the family of Christ (TPJS, 335–36; Eth. 3:14).

After this the faithful are to receive, under the keys of Elijah, all the blessings of the temple. This is when the "seals are put upon the House of Israel." Individuals so sealed and so empowered to seal others have all that can be conferred upon mortals by mortals. Then they are prepared to be visited by the Messiah ("Messiah comes to his temple") and to receive from him the oath and covenant of the Father (2 Ne. 9:41). This is the final confirmation from the godhead of their promise of immortality, eternal life, and an everlasting possession of all that the Father has. This blessing is the capstone on the temple, "which temple," said Paul, "ye are" (1 Cor. 3:17). This is the crowning component of the fullness of priesthood, by which the anointed are made joint heirs with Jesus Christ and saviors on Mt. Zion (HC 6:184, 364–65). Within the world view of Joseph Smith, this was a supernatural event through which recipients of all gospel, priesthood, and temple ordinances realize their calling, election, anointing, and coronation. They become numbered among those whose lives are "hid . . . with Christ in God" (D&C 86:8–9; cf. 101:39–42; 103:9–10; Matt. 5:13). These individuals have entered into their exaltation, awaiting only the time of the resurrection to be glorified and made one with the Most High.

CHAPTER EIGHTEEN

WOMEN, ORDINATION, AND HIERARCHY

The assertion that women should hold priesthood, be ordained to priesthood and church offices, and participate fully with men in the Mormon hierarchy is objectionable to many Mormons. In this chapter we explore the most common objections. We do not expect that our responses will be satisfactory or convincing to those who are deeply committed to the status quo on these issues. Nevertheless we hope our arguments may serve at least as a starting point for further discussions by those uncomfortable with the official posture.

If God wanted Mormon women to be ordained to the priesthood, God would reveal it first to the president of the church, and therefore we have no right to discuss the issue or request a change in policy.

This objection, the one most frequently raised to our view on women and the priesthood, assumes that we Mormons can rest assured that even though members may err from time to time, the church and its leaders are always right and do not need input from the membership. But is this true? Is the church fool proof and fail safe? The Book of Mormon repeatedly warns that we should not think that "all is well in Zion" (2 Ne. 28:21). We are told that the Nephite church went astray because of false traditions and pride. The people of Lehi's Jerusalem were wrong to think that they were unerring and invulnerable. In spite of these messages, Mormons feel confident that the church could not err on a doctrine as far reaching as women's relationship to priesthood. If we were wrong on this, God would appear to the living prophet, as he did to Alma the Younger and Paul, and set the church straight.

Though this is a comforting view, the scriptures taken as a whole demonstrate that such intervention is the exception rather than the rule, even for prophets. Our own experiences and life's struggles tell us that revelations are not easy to get. And once obtained they are not easy to understand or put into practice. In one text we are explicitly told that revelation comes through questioning (D&C 9:7). Even divine answers apparently must be preceded by questions. Most of Joseph Smith's revelations came in answer to questions. The Aaronic priesthood was restored, we are told, because Joseph Smith and Oliver Cowdery had a question about baptism. The whole restoration movement, it is said, began with the question: "Which church is right?" And Jesus said, "Seek and ye shall find; knock and it shall be opened unto you." Questioning is fundamental to revelation. But questions arise only when we face problems. We cannot see problems in the church if we believe that everything we are told by the institution comes straight from God.

The Book of Mormon tells us that this life is a probationary state—a time when we learn by trial and error, by the things that we suffer. If we know anything about how God works, it is that God does not routinely intervene to prevent mistakes, pain, or even sin. We are often left to live with the consequences of our actions and omissions. We spend most of our lives chastening ourselves with our own misperceptions of reality. God does not force upon us any particular world view. In Moses' time, for example, God wished Israel to be a kingdom of priests and priestesses and for everyone to come up into the mountain and talk with him face to face. But, we are told, the people wanted a religion similar to the one they had known in Egypt (Ex. 32). God did not force them to accept a greater revelation, and Israel was given a lesser law (JST Ex. 34:1–2; JST Deut. 10:1–2). Peter, the chief apostle, was told in a revelation not to call unclean what the Lord had made clean and to send the gospel message to the Gentiles. And yet for nearly fifteen years, he and the other apostles refused to do this. God did not force them to obey but called on Paul, an outsider, to perform this work anyway. Paul's effort was so inspired and revolutionary that the leaders of the church at Jerusalem had to reassess their position and change their minds.

Clearly we live in an imperfect world, where our culture can blind us to the will of God. Our traditions do not usually seem wrong to us. But if adhered to rigidly, traditions can obstruct change and growth. The church has always struggled in its imperfections. This was true of the primitive church as it wrestled with its prejudice against the Gentiles. It was true in Joseph Smith's day, when there was constant rivalry and resistance to new ideas. Is it possible that we are in a similar situation today with respect to women and the priesthood?

Consider the 1978 revelation extending priesthood to black males. Mormons often assume that it was God's will that the priesthood be withheld from blacks until 1978. But we think this denial may well have been contrary to the will of God, the consequence of our prejudices, our unwillingness to extend full equality to a disenfranchised group. The historical evidence shows that the doctrinal basis for refusing blacks the priesthood was at very best vague. The policy seems to have grown up during the early Utah period. In 1836 Joseph Smith allowed a black to be ordained to the Melchizedek priesthood. Would God have opened the way for other blacks to have received the priesthood earlier if we as a people had been willing to receive them and to ask for the change? Was the ban lifted in 1978 because we had a prophet who, for the first time, wanted a change, in part to resolve the problem of mixed ancestry? Have women been denied the priesthood all these years for the same reason the Gentiles were denied the gospel? For the same reason perhaps that blacks were denied priesthood? Because of tradition?

Another common objection to women holding priesthood is that priesthood is by nature patriarchal.

In his 1989 "Tribute to Women," Elder Boyd K. Packer said: "From the beginning the priesthood has been conferred only upon men. It is always described in the scriptures as coming through the lineage of the fathers" (Packer, 73). Elder Packer is correct in part. In the scriptures priesthood is set out in patriarchal terms and is rarely connected to women. But it is only fair to point out that the scriptures rarely connect the gospel to women either. Faith, repentance, baptism, the gift of the Holy Ghost, and the whole process of spiritual rebirth and maturation are referred to scripturally in predominantly male-oriented language. Yet in spite of this we know the gospel was meant to apply to women. The church has always understood this. And women have learned to read the scriptures and identify with them in spite of their dominant male orientation.

The scriptures contain nothing claiming priesthood is inherently and unalterably linked with maleness. Clearly the qualifications for priesthood set forth in Alma 13 (exceeding faith, repentance, and a desire to choose righteousness) apply equally to men and women. We could easily imagine a feminine application for priesthood verses just as we have done with gospel verses. We should consider that the priesthood, like the gospel, was made available to anyone having faith in Jesus Christ and accepting the ordinances. The writer of Hebrews emphasizes this when stating that the Melchizedek priesthood is "without father, without mother, without descent, having neither beginning of days nor end of life" (Heb. 7:3). Though one implication of this passage is that priesthood can be transmitted through a lineage of mothers, the more important point is that the Melchizedek priesthood is not restricted to any particular sex or lineage. It is not the priesthood of an elite group. The point of Hebrews is that because Christ our Great High Priest sacrificed his life for us, we can now all enter "boldly" (Heb. 4:16) as priests or priestesses of God into the holy of holies.

The Messiah opened the way to salvation and priesthood for all who accept the salvific work of Jesus Christ. This means that the Patriarchal, the Aaronic, and the Levitical priesthoods — as well as all other intercessory priesthoods — have been superceded by the fullness of priesthood, which is offered to both men and women without concern about lineage and without restriction. Each person can receive the full power of God and stand as his or her own priest or priestess: "For this is the covenant that I will make with the house of Israel after those days, saith the Lord; I will put my laws into their mind, and write them in their hearts: and I will be to them a god and they shall be to me a people: And they shall not teach every man his neighbour and every man his brother saying, Know the Lord: for all shall know me, from the least to the greatest" (Heb. 8:10–11; Jer. 31:31–34; D&C 1:20).

Another objection to women holding priesthood is that the church has always been governed by men.

Of course this is true. And traditions concerning church governance tend to reinforce the prevailing attitude that women should be barred from ordination. This is nowhere more evident than in solemn assemblies and in general conferences of the church, where voting takes place according to priesthood quorums, starting with the First Presidency and then proceeding to the Quorum of the Twelve, the First Quorum of Seventy, and down through all the quorums of the priesthood, ending with the deacons. After all the males have voted, the women and children are asked to vote simultaneously. The message is loud and clear: an adult woman stands slightly below a twelve-year-old boy in the hierarchy. Though this procedure has little practical significance, it is psychologically damaging.

Of more practical consequence is the fact that the great majority of decisions affecting wards, stakes, and regions of the church are made in priesthood councils, where women have no "vote" or say at all. It is not surprising then that many Mormon women feel disenfranchised from the church. Without their holding priesthood, their voices will not fully be heard, their gifts will not fully be magnified, and they cannot enjoy full fellowship in the "kingdom of God." The fact that a condition prevails or a tradition is long-standing is no guarantee that it is God-approved. The purpose of revelation is to correct tradition when it is false. Objections based on tradition in a church that accepts the doctrine of continuing revelation are hardly objections at all.

Another objection is that women who desire priesthood are power hungry.

This objection comes from two opposing quarters: feminists and traditional Mormons. Traditional Mormons argue that women who want the priesthood are simply trying to get control. But is this the reason why men want priesthood? The institutional answer is no. God wishes men to hold priesthood not to rule but to serve. If this is true for men, why should it not also be true for women? Might God wish women to hold priesthood authority and exercise it within ecclesiastical and priestly hierarchies to enhance their service to God?

Some feminists, on the other hand, argue that women seeking priesthood are male-identified and are dishonoring their sex by opting for a corrupt male power structure. But how can women dishonor their sex by seeking spiritual blessings? And why should a woman's desire for priesthood necessarily signify a lust for power that corrupts? Why can't a woman's desire for priesthood be compared to her desire for the Holy Ghost? We have already discussed how these are closely connected. Why can't Mormon feminists and traditionalists acknowledge that many women desire priesthood not because they wish to seize unrighteous power or equalize the inequities of the past but because they wish to bless, inspire, comfort, and administer to others — their daughters, sons, husbands, and friends. Why cannot a woman's desire for priesthood be compared to a desire for a good marriage?

Church teachings to the contrary, a good marriage is not possible when one spouse commands and the other sustains. Peace and harmony between husband and wife and between men and women in the church are based upon mutuality of love and equality of dignity and esteem. The gifts, inspiration, and talents of each must be appreciated and given scope to develop, and room must be allowed for role reversals and balanced interdependence.

Being a church member is like being in a marriage, but at present the marriage is not a very good one. Mormon women are not full partners with Mormon men. They do not participate in the most significant church councils and their influence is not adequately felt.

If women hold priesthood, would not the church be exposed to the disruptions feminism has caused in the world?

An integration of masculine and feminine is taking place in society at large. Women are being encouraged to assume leadership roles in the marketplace and in professions, while increasingly men are assuming responsibilities in the home. Arguably these changes have not all been beneficial. Women have sometimes been forced to become competitive and aggressive; children have been neglected; and some men have been left bewildered. People fear that by opening the priesthood and its offices and callings to women, similar disorientation will result in the church.

This is an important concern, and it suggests rightly that change creates new problems even as old problems are resolved. But we believe that most of these complications can be turned in the long run to the benefit of the church. Consider, for example, that many children are already neglected — by fathers overwhelmed by burdensome church positions and full-time jobs. Children need the influence of both parents. If women and men shared priesthood offices and callings, perhaps they could also more equally share the responsibility of the home and the welfare of their children.

One possible way to balance the duties of home and church is to allow each presiding office of the church to be a dual office, to be held by both husband and wife acting in concert. The office of bishop or stake president could be filled by a married couple. Thus we would have co-bishops, co-presidents, co-apostles, co-prophets, co-seers, and co-revelators with equal votes. This is not to say that singles should be excluded from these offices, but when a married person is selected to fill a church leadership position, his or her spouse if ready and willing should be called to the office too.

Allowing church offices to be filled by married couples could lessen the strain on the families of church leaders. Rather than the man always being at church and the woman always being at home, they could share or alternate their responsibilities. This may have positive effects on the congregation as well. Women might feel more comfortable discussing some personal problems with a woman, and men with a man. Also a leader would not be required to keep confidences from his or her spouse. Both could be involved in the ministry together. They could counsel together, plan together, pray over their flock together. Where appropriate their children could be included in discussions and plans so that all of this joint service would have the ancillary benefit of encouraging the joint spiritual development, not only of the wife and husband but of their entire family.

As for the concern that priesthood callings would take women away from their duties in the home, remember few offices held by priesthood bearers are more time-consuming than that of Relief Society president or Primary president. Women are already dedicating large amounts of time to the church. Holding priesthood office would not greatly increase this commitment, although it would give greater prestige, authority, and scope to their work.

Rather than give priesthood to women, some individuals concerned about abuse of priesthood authority have suggested priesthood hierarchy be eliminated altogether.

Of course there have been abuses. Some members have been disillusioned and others do not feel valued. This is true not only for women but for men outside the leadership circle. Exclusivity arises when priesthood is viewed as an institutional privilege rather than as a spiritual gift. But because priesthood as hierarchy has had destructive effects on the development of both the individual and the community does not mean that all hierarchy is bad. If we accept Jesus as our Lord and King, we automatically acknowledge a certain type of hierarchy. Eliminating priesthood would probably not eliminate leadership. It would only further desacralize the church. Moreover, the idea of gradations and degrees is apparent in our individual gifts and levels of knowledge and competence. The principle that we are equal in value and dignity is fundamental, but the church needs both a democratized priesthood and a hierarchical structure to maintain order.

Another objection is that women are just as spiritual, even more spiritual, than men. Why should not they be content with spiritual gifts, which are independent of priesthood?

It is very well to say that women are just as spiritual as men. But unless their spirituality is given scope, it has no impact on the church. As we have said, the priesthood is made up of inner spiritual power and outward authority: "the rights of the priesthood are inseparably connected with the powers of heaven" (D&C 121:36). Certainly women can receive and use the powers of heaven as they preach, teach, comfort and serve others. But they are prohibited from administering ordinances, presiding in the church, making policy decisions, managing resources and money, directing spiritual affairs, and making important doctrinal decisions and contributions. In other words the church tends to separate what should be "inseparably connected." Though we can dichotomize the rights and powers of priesthood intellectually, in reality priesthood is one. We cannot have the fullness of priesthood without both its inner and outer and its female and male aspects. Men cannot simply exercise authority without spirituality. And women cannot be expected to be spiritual without authority.

Western thought has tended to denigrate matter, body, and form — to see these as inferior to spirit. Traditionally the male principle has been connected with spirit or essence, while the female principle has been associated with body or form. Thus to be female is to be relegated to a lower order of things. If we deny the importance of outer forms, we will perpetuate a system esteeming maleness over femaleness. In reaction to previous centuries, our own century has tended to value form over content, but this has not corrected the problem. It has only continued the swinging of the pendulum from one polar opposite to the other. What we most need now is reconciliation, appreciation of diversity, acceptance of opposites. In the church today we are impoverished spiritually in part because we have failed to embrace all these manifestations of God's creation.

The failure to accept both inner and outer aspects of priesthood, however, has had positive as well as negative effects. On the positive side is the fact that because spiritual gifts are not seen as the exclusive domain of priesthood, women are able to render spiritual service. Praying in meetings, teaching doctrine, and speaking (occasionally) in general conference are now seen as activities permitted to women. On the negative side, however, such outward priesthood functions as giving blessings and casting out devils are still considered the sole property of priesthood holders, in spite of Joseph Smith's teaching that anyone with the Holy Ghost could do these things.

Another negative effect of splitting the "rights of the priesthood" from "the powers of heaven" is the growing tendency in the church to see priesthood as solely the authority to preside and manage and to equate ordination with spiritual competence. As leaders put less emphasis on religious feeling, imagination, knowledge of doctrine, compassion, and aptitude for the inner dimension of the religious life, the members follow suit, putting less significance on the spirit and more emphasis on control.

We do not mean to say that church governance is unimportant.

Our personal inclination is not toward temporalities, but we understand there must be a balance between the temporal and spiritual. The physical management of a temple, for example, will very much affect its spiritual operations. If the temple is disorderly or in bad repair, it can negatively affect the spiritual experience of those who attend. But if the temple is overly efficient and statistics-driven, this will discourage meditation, prayer, and spiritual renewal. In time this will ironically have a negative impact on statistics. Too much emphasis on forms at the expense of substance will ultimately deaden the forms.

For this same reason equal emphasis must be placed on both the inner-spiritual-private and outer-temporal-public dimensions of priesthood, an idea reflected in the scriptural teaching that to receive a fullness of joy, the body and spirit must be united (D&C 93:33). When the inner and outer priesthoods come together, the power and blessings flowing from it are increased. For these reasons we feel it is a mistake to relegate the priesthood of women to the inner aspects only. In order for women's priesthood to flower, it needs to be named and acknowledged.

But if women receive priesthood, will not this destroy important distinctions between male and female?

The notion of women holding priesthood is threatening to some because it forces us to re-examine some of our most cherished ideas about gender and sexuality — concepts which support self-identity. Feminists have been divided about whether essential differences between the sexes exist. Some stress the common humanity of men and women; others the unique nature of each sex. As always we find ourselves taking a middle view. We try to balance the two positions because we accept that men and women are both genuinely similar and genuinely different. Jungian psychologists tell us that each of us has both a male and female component to our nature. This makes the entire gender issue extremely complex. In trying to define precisely what is male and what is female, we are likely to create rigid gender roles forcing us to deny parts of our being. Though gender roles may be necessary, it is also vital to exchange roles. Priesthood can actually facilitate this process. Moses, for example, was told that he should be a nursemaid to the children of Israel; and Jesus acted as our mother in giving birth to a new spiritual creation. Women also can play the part of father by planting the seed of spiritual life through preaching the gospel. Such reversals are healthy, because they help us to avoid alienation and to encourage mutual understanding.

To ordain women would be to destroy an already existing balance: Men have priesthood and women have motherhood; and women should not be ordained until men can have babies.

Actually men do have babies all the time. Men have fatherhood and women have motherhood. Motherhood is not the equivalent of priesthood any more than fatherhood is. Just as fathers need priesthood, so do mothers. Priesthood in males is equivalent to priesthood in females. Both are necessary to bring about spiritual rebirth and maturation. Through the priesthood men are able to serve as spiritual fathers. And through the priesthood women are able to serve as spiritual mothers. It is a mistake to confine women to a temporal role in the private sphere, while reserving the spiritual role in the public sphere to men. This is especially damaging to children. If they are to grow up spiritually healthy, they must accept the male and female in themselves and see how those principles are actualized in the real world and in the church. Though men and women share a vast majority of human characteristics in common, we believe, there is still something essentially different between them. Because of this difference the priesthood may be manifest differently through males than it is through females. Thus without the contribution of female priesthood holders on every level, the church cannot be complete and whole. Both male and female manifestations of the priesthood are essential. One cannot replace the other. The male and the female in their priestly functions must act together to bring about spiritual fullness and completion.

In the Egyptian myth of Isis and Osiris, the god Osiris is tricked by a brother god and killed. His body is cut to pieces and strewn over the whole landscape. There appears to be no hope for him until the goddess Isis, his sister-wife, goes into mourning and wanders through the earth gathering his body piece by piece. Because of her vigilance, devotion, and love, he is brought together again and raised from the dead. This can be a metaphor for Mormonism. The future of the church rests not solely with the male priesthood holders but with the female priesthood holders as well. Like Isis, Mormon women must mourn and then wander and find all the forgotten portions of our history and the lost promises and hopes and expectations and bring them back together again. By the power of the love of God, we must seek to revitalize what is dead. This task is not easy, since women are not connected directly to the church's power structure. This is a great frustration. Though women can gather together and speak and feel and know, they cannot directly bring about change, and many are left wondering what we can do.

Even if we agree that women should have the priesthood, why should we waste our time worrying about it, since there is nothing we can do?

On the contrary there is something we can do. We can first of all change the way we see ourselves. If women and men see themselves as members of Christ's body, endowed with priesthood (even though the priesthood of women is not generally acknowledged and even though their priesthood is not given scope in the ecclesiastical institution), this will change how we view ourselves and how we act. Even unendowed women and men, when they see what God has promised by way of the Holy Ghost, experience a change in themselves.

Second, we can act together and independently as men and women. We can teach, share ideas, draw upon each other's gifts of knowledge and discernment. Women can approach God as priestesses and act as instruments of God rather than seeing themselves as appendages to the church or their husbands.

Third, we can have courage to face opposition and adversity without rancor. We can refuse to give up or give in. This may seem a small thing. But it is crucial. People in and out of the church long believed that blacks would not get the priesthood, but God opened the way for them. We must not despair, although we get discouraged. We must continue to hope and pray for guidance and look at what has been promised us and when and by whom. We can reach out with our hearts and see in our minds a church with a truly lay priesthood, with privileges and blessings available to all. We can envision a community of Saints, where both women and men hold priesthood office and have equal voice in governing the church. We can see a parliament of prophets and prophetesses, where member-representatives of local congregations meet with general authorities to work out the policies and practices of a church governed by spiritual gifts and characterized by community and consent.

Moses said, "Would that all God's people were prophets." This is our hope: Would that we as Mormons held and magnified the fullness of the priesthood. Would that we were a kingdom of priests and priestesses and of prophets and prophetesses, a kingdom where equality of dignity and value was the rule, where we esteemed our sisters and brothers as the very image of God, where we accepted the divine union of female and male as our true priesthood.

Without a proper apportionment of the spiritual contributions of both male and female, of both inner and outer aspects of priesthood, there can be no birth, no rebirth, no inner life, no continuing contact with God, no significant revelation, no balanced manifestation of spiritual gifts, no mature counsel, no reliable effort to bring good out of chaos, no attempt to hold all things in common. In short there can be no City and Kingdom of God, here or hereafter. It is into the seamless cup of balanced and spiritually regenerated union that God, male and female, have promised to pour the fullness of the priesthood, which is the power of an endless life.

~ CHAPTER NINETEEN ~

ZION: VISION OR MIRAGE

Many religious traditions talk about the doctrine of the two ways—the "Way of Life" and the "Way of Death." To follow in the Way of Death is to maximize power and to seek gratification through control. It is to accept that the greatest mechanism of control is death and that the most efficient way to resolve the most intractable human problems is by taking human life—the way Cain resolved the problem of Abel (Moses 5:47–50). This has been an operative principle of the modern world, where, in the name of progress, tens of millions of political murders, assassinations, and terrorist killings have been committed in this century, more than in any other period of recorded history (Johnson, 184–86, 298–305, 413–22, 430–31, 481–84, 497–500, 548). To be in the Way of Death is to be in the heart of darkness, in the grip of fear, and to respond to others as objects to be subdued and superintended.

To follow in the Way of Life, on the other hand, is to tread the Via Dolorosa. It is to live outside oneself, to be vulnerable to others. It is to love one's enemies rather than liquidate them, to celebrate and transcend differences rather than to eradicate them, to bear annoyances, discomforts, uncertainties, and risks rather than to pass them on to others. It is to take responsibility for pain caused, to forgive wrongs endured, and to accept forgiveness for wrongs committed. To be in the Way of Life is to have a heart purified by love and to accept others without condition.

Both as individuals and as societies we are called frequently to choose between these two ways: Are we to be the oppressors or the oppressed? Are we to bear affliction or afflict others? Sometimes this choice is clear, sometimes obscure. Sometimes it is dramatic, sometimes commonplace. Usually we are not consistent in our choosing. For this reason, most of us are simultaneously the oppressors and the oppressed. The most powerful of us cannot maintain complete control and deflect all suffering at all times, and the weakest of us have some power over certain aspects of our lives, even if it is only the power to utter the eternal NO, to refuse to participate in what we believe to be evil.

On a societal level, those in the Way of Death are referred to scripturally as Babylon, while those in the Way of Life are called Zion. Our modern world, like most of us, partakes of both ways. As a culture, we — particularly in the West — are impressed with such self-centered values as competition, achievement, and success; but we are also deeply troubled by the plight of the impaired, the powerless, and the poor. Though for the most part we gauge our worth by our economic growth, our popularity, and our net worth, we also admire those, like Mother Teresa, who freely make personal sacrifices for the weak, the helpless, and the downtrodden. As for the technique of killing to get gain, we deplore it, but it is by no means alien to our culture. Of course, most people do not resort to outright murder to avoid suffering or to secure for themselves a comfortable life-style. There are more subtle ways of administering the blows of death. We can kill with achievement won at someone else's loss, with success purchased with someone else's failure, with empowerment paid for with someone else's disenfranchisement, with preference attained by invidious discrimination, with wealth acquired at another's cost, with hope and joy secured with another's despair. As citizens of the world, we learn to inflict death by a thousand humiliations, by "the thousand natural shocks that flesh is heir to." It has ever been so.

For this reason, throughout history, philosophers, visionaries, and mystics of nearly all cultures have addressed the question of how society should be rightly ordered. This is the theme of Plato's *Republic*, which contains his design for the just state. It lies at the heart of the Jews' longing for their promised homeland. It fires our romantic infatuation with King Arthur's Camelot. It illuminates the Christian vision of the New Jerusalem, prophesied in the Revelation of St. John.

Mormonism was meant to be a new revelation of the Way of Life, with both personal and societal ramifications. On a personal level, Mormonism is a revelation of the power and ordinances of God by which individuals might be spiritually healed and made holy. On a social level, Mormonism was to be the instrument by which Zion would literally be established on the American continent (D&C 124:28–47). The failed Puritan hope of a city on a hill in New England was to find its fulfillment among the Mormons, in the mountain-valleys of the American west.

This concept of a literal kingdom of God on earth was the primary ideological force that shaped the consciousness of the Mormon pioneers. It was their avowed intent to create an actual kingdom in the Rocky Mountains. Its crown would penetrate north into Alberta, Canada. Its head and neck was to comprise Montana and Idaho. Its heart would be in Utah, and its trunk would consist of parts of Nevada, Arizona, Colorado, and New Mexico. One leg would reach down into old Mexico. The other would kick westward beyond Las Vegas to San Bernardino, stretching toward the coast for a toehold on the sea.

The Kingdom of God loomed large in the minds of nineteenth-century Mormons, who, after having been driven out of state after state, were determined to build a city that would serve as a refuge for the saints and an ensign to all people. It was to be the fulfillment of the prophecies of Isaiah. The mountain of the Lord's house would be the ensign to which all nations would flow. And the nations would say, let us fear Zion, for she is as clear as the sun, as fair as the moon, and as terrible as an army with banners. In Zion there would be no rich and poor, no bond and free. For, there, all would be free, everything would be held in common, and all would be partakers of the heavenly gift (4 Ne. 1:3). Zion would be the community of the pure in heart, the body of Christ. Every citizen would seek "the interest of his neighbor" and would do "all things with an eye single to the glory of God" (D&C 82:19). In due course, the boundaries of Zion would increase beyond the Great Basin until they embraced the whole of the United States. Then we Mormons would reclaim our abandoned lands in Jackson County, Missouri. There we would build the center stake of Zion, the templed City of the New Jerusalem. Eventually, Zion would grow to encompass all of North and South America and, in time, would reach beyond the seas. In the end, Old Jerusalem would be redeemed, the wicked would be destroyed, and Christ would return to usher in the millennium of peace.

This vision, so elegant and inspiring, has stirred the hearts and captured the minds of Latter-day Saints for over 150 years, with each generation longing, perhaps expecting, to enter the promised land. And when we and many others of our generation were young, and energetic, and students in college in the late 1960s and early 1970s, we too nourished this same hope, this same expectation. Back then, the nation was in the throes of anti-war protest and counter-cultural idealism. Most young Mormons did not participate much in these movements. But many of us shared in the national fervor in another form. We believed in Zion. We believed we were part of that chosen generation whom the prophets had foreseen and, perhaps, envied — the generation that would usher in Zion in preparation for the second coming of Christ. We had reassurances from many of our leaders that this was so. It would happen, we were told, if we were worthy and loyal, if we held to the iron rod, remained on the straight and narrow, and avoided the corruption of the world. The possibilities were thrilling. The future seemed bright. Some of us took as our motto the catchphrase proclaimed by LDS church president John Taylor, "The Kingdom of God or Nothing!"

Of course, except for the correlation program that was intended to bring all the departments and functions of the church under direct priesthood control in anticipation of Christ's second coming, Zion has never been an official goal or program of the twentieth-century church. There has not been a call to return to Jackson County, Missouri. In the late 1960s, Alvin R. Dyer, an ordained apostle and member of the First Presidency, was called to be "the watchman over the land of Zion" — an event that caused some stir when it was announced. But nothing came of it.

The unwillingness of the modern church to marshall and commit its resources to the building of Zion was not particularly discouraging to the zealous of our generation because we understood that Zion was not for everyone. Not all were worthy. Not all were pure in heart. Our leaders had to provide milk before meat. But many of our generation were hungry for meat. And the call of Zion was strong. So, like knights in search of the holy grail, we set out in pursuit of the City of God, each in his and her own way.

Some of us prolonged our educations, putting off the inevitable day when we must choose careers. We did this not because we were lazy or afraid, but because we were waiting for opportunities that would accord with our dream. We did not want to go into business or pursue professions. We wanted to become more spiritual, to draw closer to God. On Sunday mornings many of us could be found sitting in our singles-ward or student-ward chapels, singing fervently with our peers the words of the hymn (n. 114):

More purity give me,
More strength to o'er come,
More freedom from earthstains,
More longing for home;
More fit for the kingdom,
More used would I be,
More blessed and holy,
More, Savior, like thee.

Building Zion would not be easy. We knew that. It would require personal effort, wisdom, and sacrifice. It would require humility and suffering perhaps. Not all of us would endure. But we wanted to endure. We had faith. We had youth. We had leaders to show us the way.

Time marched on.

Some of us became writers and artists to avoid the taint of the world. We gardened, grew our own herbs, canned our own fruit, and ground our own wheat. We made bread with our own hands. And some of us wove our own cloth. Others of us kept our children in home schools and engaged in home industry. We worried about the acid rain, the strength of the dollar, the menace of shortages, the growing nuclear arsenal, the Mid-East. We saw signs everywhere. Would we be ready? Were we pure? Were we prepared? Would we be chosen?

Twenty years passed.

We are older now. Married and single. Some surrounded by children. Some alone. Others alienated. All burdened with the daily task. Our energy reserves are low or spent. We are, perhaps, wiser, or sadder, or angry, or confused. For us, as for our progenitors before us, Zion hovers, in the distance, out of reach—a shimmering mirage in the desert.

Like so many heroes and heroines in Mormon fiction, we "came to realize." And what we realized was that there is no escaping the world. It had seeped into everything long ago. We realized that the university, though exciting, is no less corrupt than the marketplace and that the arts, though inspiring, are no less materialistic than the professions. Teaching, we realized, is absorbing and enriching, but it is no purer than other work and for the most part subsists on the support of those who earn their money by competition and acquisitiveness. Some of us retired to communes where we found a temporary peace, but where we also discovered that we could exist only if we had something to sell to the world outside. Like the Mormons of the nineteenth century, we realized that we had to trade with the Gentiles and that, even if we thought

we could not live with them, we certainly could not survive without
them. Yes, we grew some of our own food and baked our own bread. It
was good. But we had to rely on the real world for water, seeds, land,
for heat and light, for books, and for money. Some of us refused to eat
meat out of respect for animal life only to discover that, in order to
live, we had to kill plants for food, for fiber, and for shelter. We tried
not to abuse the environment, but we went on using it. We loved our
children and tried to protect them; but every night they went to bed a
bit older and a bit more messy with the world; and every morning they
woke to their own dreams — not ours. Some, in desperation, opted for
extreme solutions: separatism, survivalism, fundamentalism — anything
that promised purity, superiority, spiritual election — and realized, perhaps too late, the heartlessness of those who prize their certainty and
rectitude above love, above family, above friends.

Mostly, what we realized was this: We are part of the world, part of
the environment, part of the food chain, part of the problem. We are
called to endure the crosses of the world, and despise the shame of it (2
Ne. 9:18).

Perhaps, most disillusioning of all was the realization that our dream
of Zion itself was flawed. The city of God, like the Way of Life it springs
from, can be wrongly understood. It can be seen in a narcissistic and
elitist way. It can create in believers a "we-they" mentality, a judgmental
puritanism, an arrogance that inevitably breeds jarring, contention,
envy, and strife. The City of God, we realized, cannot be founded on
simple-minded notions of idealism and naive concepts of election. Unfortunately, too many of these sentiments contaminated our dream.
Some of us confused Zion with the capitalist quest for material success. Others, with the socialist agenda of a closed and protected community. Somehow, we managed to combine some of the worst of the
West with some of the worst of the East.

On reconsideration, it seemed to some of us that, perhaps, the failure of nineteenth-century Mormons to create the political Kingdom of
God in the State of Deseret was a blessing rather than the curse we had
been taught it was. Because of that failure, we twentieth-century Mormons have been forced to accommodate, to participate in the secular
American culture, to accept for ourselves and to accord to others certain guarantees of individual freedom, and to abide by the nation's
commitment to the rule of law, to civil rights, and to the separation of
powers. We had to learn to live in harmony with a people suspicious of

religious zeal.In sum, what many of us realized is that though the brightness of Zion is peace, the shadow of Zion is tyranny.

This was not a pleasant insight. For us it had been "The Kingdom of God or Nothing." We were not adequately prepared for something worse than nothing, for a rude awakening from a beautiful dream, to a cold, grey, imprisoning reality, where every light casts a shadow and nothing is ideal. Everywhere, it seems, even in our most cherished causes, we find self-delusion, corruption and failed hope. We thought the resolution of our problems and dilemmas was in our ideal of Zion. But that ideal was unreal. What we embraced as Zion was an unachievable purity, an unreachable holiness, and an impossible dream. We were willing, but blind; determined, but proud; certain, but wrong. Now some of us feel deceived. Others are silent. Many wear faces haunted by a vague sense of loss. And in our hearts we can hear the distant echo of that doleful scripture: "Zion is fled" (Moses 7:69).

We should have known better. We should have seen this coming. Not because Zion is too good to be true, but because the failure of Zion had been predicted plainly by no less an authority than Joseph Smith and in a text no more obscure than the Doctrine and Covenants. In Section 101 a parable is related regarding "the redemption of Zion." In the parable a nobleman instructs his servants to cultivate a plot of land with olive trees, surrounded by a protective hedge and guarded by watchmen in a tower. But the servants cannot see the need for the tower and dispute whether or not to proceed with its construction, concluding they can better invest the money with exchangers. They become "slothful" and disobedient until one night an enemy breaks through the hedge and destroys the vineyard. When the nobleman learns what has happened he vows to avenge himself and reestablish the fortified vineyard, although at a future date when he can muster sufficiently loyal troops to accomplish the task.

How is this parable to be interpreted? Why is Zion represented by the symbol of a tower? Does this symbol have any connection to the tower of Babel? If so, what can we learn from the positive and negative applications of this symbol? And what is the meaning of the watchman on the tower? Is it a reference to Joseph Smith? To some later church president or leader? Or does the watchman represent something quite different, such as the priesthood, the Holy Order, the body of men and women who have trod the path of spiritual maturity and received the fullness of the priesthood? And who are the Lord's servants? The leaders of the church? The members? Both? Why were they at variance one with the other? Is this a reference to a dispute over doctrine? Church governance? Church practice? Or was it a dispute resulting from the attempts of some to impose an orthodoxy unacceptable to others? How did the servants become slothful? Did they cease doing good works? Did they stop searching the scriptures? Or did they become spiritually indolent and retreat into the comfort of a secularized religious organization? In what sense did these servants give the money for Zion to the changers? Does this symbolize an actual misuse of church funds? Or does it represent the acquisition of beliefs and values alien to the central purpose of the restoration? What is the hedge that was broken down? The church? The nation? The protecting spirit of the Lord? What is the nature of the enemy? Is it a person? A people? An ideology? How is the enemy to be routed? By force? By persuasion? By love? And finally, how is Zion to be redeemed and when?

We do not have definitive answers to these questions. Nor can we provide a description of what Zion will be. However, we can say that, as Mormons, our failure to realize Zion resulted, in large part, because, our dream was contaminated. In the words of the parable, with no watchman on the tower to alert us, we were invaded by enemies — not by gentiles, unbelievers, or apostates, but by a predisposition toward elitism, narcissism, self-righteousness, authoritarianism, and — perhaps worst of all — by a blindness to the reality that Zion must be a paradox of liberty and order, rather than just another Mormon town.

We seem always to have visualized Zion as our city: a Mormon fantasy land, built on our assumptions, brimming with our values, dedicated to our aspirations. For us Zion was always the land of the pure and the home of the pure, a place open only to the righteous — a city of the Mormons, by the Mormons, and for the Mormons that would not perish from the earth. For us, Zion meant us: "the only true and living Church on the face of the whole earth" (D&C 1:30). In asserting this position, we ignored the Book of Mormon's insight that in Mormon usage the word "church" should refer to the "saints" who hold membership in the ecclesiastical structure, and also to "the covenant people of the Lord — scattered upon all the face of the earth" (1 Ne. 14:14). The City of God must include more than the inner circle, for the foundation of Zion is not moral rigidity, but charity — the love of God. We forget that God could not be love if God were unmerciful; and God could not be love if God were unjust. The message of the Judeo-Christian tradition is that God burns with love for humanity and pursues our salvation with a passion brighter and fiercer than any desert sun, a passion that is a searing paradox of justice and mercy. As mortals, we can never be good enough to satisfy God's desire for righteousness. As mortals, we can never be bad enough to dampen God's unquenchable ardor to be reunited with us. The purity of Zion, then, is not purchased with achievement, nor is it fashioned out of self-righteousness. This means that the citizens of Zion are pure not because they have excluded the impure, but because they have recognized their impurities, have been forgiven of their sins, have forgiven others, have received the love of God, have stood ready to impart love without partiality or condition, and have received the imputation of holiness through the grace of Christ Jesus. Because we have not understood these things, we have failed to see that Zion is not only a city of justice, but a city of refuge, an open city, a city of mercy.

Moreover, as Mormons, we have traditionally pictured Zion as a city of order. Rarely do we speak of it as a city of freedom. Because we think Zion's natural state is one of social harmony, we rarely consider that, in such a place, men and women must have both the longitude for growth and the latitude to err. Our experiences should have informed us that if, in Zion, law, order, and harmony were to be imposed by force, it would be a prison, not a sanctuary. If we are to be happy in Zion, we must be free with a freedom that embraces the liberty of conscience, of religion, of speech, of assembly, of participation in the governance of the community, the freedom from arbitrary compulsion, the freedom to hold property apart from the community for the maintenance of the personal power to act beyond the scrutiny of government to explore, develop, and disseminate ideas and to engage in criticism and dissent.

Because we think of Zion as a venue beyond corruption, we rarely consider how political power will be managed there. But our experiences should have taught us that power corrupts and absolute power corrupts absolutely. In Zion, as elsewhere, political power must be limited, divided, and balanced, subjected to checks and counter-checks, and exercised only with the consent of the governed. If Zion is to be a refuge for the oppressed, we as its inhabitants cannot be subject to the arbitrary dictates of leaders regardless of their political, social, economic, ecclesiastical, or spiritual standing. Zion must be governed by the rule of law. There, we should be required to obey only fixed, prepublished, properly legislated rules of conduct that apply equally to all and invidiously discriminate against none — laws whose effect, for good or ill, on specific individuals cannot be determined at the time of enactment. The power of the majority must be further limited by the deep and abiding commitment of the entire community to the concept of unalienable, sacrosanct personal rights that vest in each individual and that may in no wise be abridged, even by democratic processes. Furthermore, in Zion individual freedoms may not be curtailed by the technique of making crimes out of behaviors that are disapproved by the majority. The list of crimes must be limited to deliberate or criminally negligent actions that can be shown to involve the use of arbitrary force, or to have been committed with intent to do damage to or with a reckless disregard for person or property, or to have been perpetrated through the misrepresentation of facts. Thus, it would not be possible, in Zion, to outlaw a race, an alienage, a religion, a political affiliation, or mere membership in a particular class or group. We should have learned that, if tyranny is to be avoided in Zion, its citizens must be committed to the principle that no person should be deprived of life, liberty, or property without a public hearing, an opportunity to make a defense, to call and cross-examine witnesses, and to receive a judgment predicated on proper evidence and mandated by law. To avoid oppression in Zion, we, as its citizens, must demand and obtain open government, free access to all information bearing upon the public welfare, and the prohibition of excessive influence upon the organs of government by power cliques, factions, and special interest groups.

Unfortunately, our failure to understand Zion as a city of freedom has prevented us from understanding Zion as a city of order. We have not seriously examined the principles around which the community of Zion would cohere. What would constitute the minimum requirements for citizenship in Zion? Faith? Repentance? Baptism? Rebaptism? A demonstration of the gifts and fruits of the spirit? Birth in the covenant? Ownership of property within the geographical boundaries of Zion? A family connection to one or more of its citizens? Economic ties? Consecration? Covenant? And what would constitute grounds for expulsion or exclusion from the group? Apostasy? Lack of valiance? Immorality? Disinterestedness in the religious aspects of the community? Laziness and indolence? Upon expulsion from the community, what would become of family ties, property, cultural connections? Who would make the decision to expel or exclude? How would that decision be made and in what forum? What guarantees would there be against arbitrary or even malicious uses of authority? How would community values be protected from powerful individuals? How would individual dignity and freedom be protected against the power of the group?

And what would the economics of Zion be? How would the expectation of private wealth be balanced against the expectation of community prosperity? What would prevent the citizens of Zion from becoming slaves to a cult of acquisitiveness and greed? Would Zion be simply market driven? Would private property be discouraged in favor of communal ownership? How would such rights be defined and by whom? What would prevent social planning and control of community resources by the powerful? How is disclosure and accountability to be ensured? How would the activities of government, banks, large corporations, trusts, and holding companies be aligned with the goals of the community? How would individual gifts be protected against the aspirations of potent enclaves within the society?

We Mormons appear to have no clear answers to these questions. This is understandable. Less defensible, however, is our apathy in seeking and sorting out answers. We seem static, frozen almost in our own arrogance. We are not flexible and dynamic. We move, but slowly. We change, but as little as possible. As a people, we are not famous for our eagerness to reevaluate, reassess, repent, forgive, grow, and learn from our own spiritual, intellectual, emotional, political, economic, cultural, and domestic experiences. If ever we were such a people, we are not that now.

Paradoxically, however, there is a positive side to our failures. The scriptures, including the above-quoted parable of the redemption of Zion, seem to say that the City of God is to arise out of the ashes of failure. This is not so far-fetched. As contemporary psychotherapist Scott Peck has observed, true community can flourish only among those who have matured beyond pseudo-community, who have seen the error of their ways, who have been humbled by the reality of their limitations (Peck).

We Mormons have wrongly assumed that Zion would either be thrust upon us or else constructed by us. We have not yet considered the possibility that Zion might flower among us only to the extent that we pursue the Way of Life, the way of spiritual growth and development. The revelations suggest this alternative when they tell us that Zion will not be redeemed until we have been "taught more perfectly, and have experience" (D&C 105:10). We believe that Zion is not to be realized by imposition — not even divine imposition. It is to be realized as our relationship with God develops and matures. It is to be realized by a process of growth from inchoation, through differentiation, to integration.

An observation about the development of the priesthood may make this process clear. In the earliest days of Mormonism, priesthood was perceived in inchoate terms, as the authority of God bestowed upon the first Mormons. No one then seemed concerned with the nature of priesthood, its parts, its limitations, its functions, its operating principles. After a number of years, however, the growth of the church and the demands of ecclesiastical administration required a clarification of these points. As a result of experience and revelation, the priesthood began to be differentiated into degrees, orders, callings, and offices with enumerated functions, operations, and limitations. The result was a complex, male-identified priesthood structure. Later, in the Kirtland and Nauvoo periods, this highly articulated organization began to be integrated into a single concept of authority that eventually culminated in the anointing of men and women to the fullness of the priesthood, which was intended to embrace and, therefore, supercede all the extant priesthoods and their departments. Unfortunately, this later concept was largely abandoned after the death of Joseph Smith, and the church retreated back to the more familiar concept of a differentiated priesthood.

The establishment of Zion, too, is apparently to follow this pattern. For the earliest Mormons, Zion was envisioned inchoately. It was simply the earthly analog of heaven. Later, the Mormon pioneers attempted to force Zion without, perhaps, a clear understanding of how Zion should be constituted. They failed. Since then, attempts to achieve Zion privately have also failed. As a result, we, as a church, have accepted the tradition of Zion postponed, while refusing to admit, revisit, or learn from our failures. We have not yet differentiated. We have not yet extracted from our experiences the revelations that God has hidden in the ruins of our mistaken concept of the holy city. We have never moved beyond our inchoate dream of Zion. We have not yet discovered, examined, or understood the principles by which a true community of saints may cohere and endure. We have not yet accepted the fact that the call to Zion was meant to lead us first to a discovery of our weaknesses, then to repentance, and finally to spiritual growth, maturity, and community.

Many of us who have felt the call to Zion in our blood and in our bones wrongly thought we had been called to be "a marvelous work and a wonder," to realize the fulfillment of all the promises. But this was too great an expectation. God has made too many promises. We should have known we could not see with the eyes nor speak with the tongues of angels. We unwisely let our expectations inflate; and then, perhaps, we lost faith and became cynical when faced with the meagerness of our contributions and the puniness of their results.

In our youth, we were tempted to believe that we could build the holy city. Our temptation now is to believe that our alienation is the only reality and that life is no more than survival in a cold world, where cruelty hides behind masks of indifferent courtesies and where the meaning of our cities is to make and vend our merchandise. This, however, is also a temptation, not an insight. We were too blind in youth to see the coming darkness, but we need not be too blind in age to see the coming light. True community is possible. The Way of Life is real. "By small and simple things are great things brought to pass" (Al. 37:6).

We must come to accept that the redemption of Zion, like our personal redemption, is not a matter of achievement, but of grace, and of spiritual growth. If we, as a people, do not have this vision, then we are bound to perish—in a kaleidoscope of mirages. There will be no Zion for us until we grow from grace to grace, until we accept and trust the revelations God has given to us through our own experiences, until we acknowledge to ourselves and others that the concept of community we have heretofore so persistently pursued neither was nor could have been the City of God. We must come to accept that Zion is no mirage and that the mirage we saw was not Zion.

PART V

Sex Roles,
Marriage Patterns,
and the Temple

CHAPTER TWENTY

SEX ROLES

In previous chapters we addressed both the paradox of male and female as well as the dualistic view that accepts the superiority of the masculine over the feminine. In this chapter we again raise this theme. However, our focus here is on the complexity involved in the relationship between the genders and on the power of myth to illuminate and even resolve some of the convolutions and tensions between the sexes by acting as a "mediation between two polar extremes" (Kirk, 44).

We already noted the widespread tendency to divide the world into metaphysical opposites and to connect each with one or the other sex. Even common objects can be associated with the sex with which they share some obvious characteristic. The female as the universal container of life is symbolized by the womb and associated with the vessel, the cup, the well, the scabbard, the temple, the cave, the earth itself which receives, holds, and gives birth to all. The male, on the other hand, is connected with phallic symbols — the rod, the scepter, the staff, the sword, the plow, the sickle, the tree — and all that comes from heaven including rain, lightening, thunder. These latter associations are reflected in many ancient mythologies, where sky deities were often male and earth deities female. On a more abstract level, male and female are associated with other dualities:

Substance	Form
Spirit	Body
Truth	Light
Day	Night
Justice	Mercy
Symbolic	Literal
History	Myth

Conscious	Subconscious
Secular	Sacral
Rational	Intuitive
Square	Compass
Linear	Circular
Individual	Community
Freedom	Obedience
Culture	Nature
State	Church
Above	Below
Active	Passive

This catalog is obviously not exhaustive. Listing pairs of opposites is relatively simple. More difficult is deciding which of each pair should be linked with the female principle and which with the male.

Archetypically, certain pairs have been clearly tied with one sex or the other: spirit is usually connected with male, body with female; day with male, night with female; justice male, mercy female; rational male, intuitive female; active male, passive female. Other pairs, however, are more difficult to align: culture and nature, symbolic and literal, history and myth. Is nature feminine, as suggested by the term "mother nature," or is it masculine, as suggested by the popular belief that men go adventuring into nature while women keep the home fires burning? Is history a muse and therefore female? Or is it male and linked with the rational and scientific? Even those pairs traditionally associated with one sex or the other are sometimes reversed, not just by moderns who want to erase sexual stereotypes but by earlier thinkers. For example, the connection between the masculine and the spirit was reversed by the Romantics who, influenced by notions of chivalry, put women on pedestals and linked them with spiritual qualities. This happened anciently as well. Philo, the first century Hellenistic Jewish philosopher and theologian, wrote of the two-fold nature of God, manifest as the masculine and feminine principles. He saw the father manifestation of the divine as begetter, creator, and reason and the mother as bearer, nurturer, and practical wisdom. This we might have predicted. But surprisingly Philo assigns "soft" qualities such as "gentleness, beneficence, and goodness" to the father and "hard" qualities such "the legislative, chastising, and correcting powers" to the mother (Patai 1978, 74–75). Philo believed that since the mother maintains order, she must reprove.

These examples show that it is not clear which principles or characteristics should be linked to which gender. And it never has been clear. Moreover, most attempts to create precise delineations turn out to be simplistic, rigid, moralistic, and short-lived. This is true in Mormon culture, where for years there has predominated the black and white assertion that males are masculine and females are feminine. Though the church still gives lip service to this rigid view, a growing recognition of the ambiguity inherent in gender roles can be detected in some of our church manuals.

In one Relief Society mother education lesson, for example, women were encouraged to "obtain as much schooling as they wish and to excel in all their pursuits." Women were also told to seek a career both for their personal fulfillment as well as for the support of their families should the need arise. Mothers were advised to help both their sons and daughters develop certain characteristics such as "faith in God, compassion for others, respect for themselves and each other." This lesson implied that it is now officially acceptable for boys to learn homemaking skills and girls to enjoy sports. But in spite of these modest improvements, the overall tone of this lesson was condescending. In its treatment of the relationship between husband and wife, it reasserted the old truisms. The man is to preside, provide, and protect through his role as wage earner and priesthood holder. The woman is to support, sustain, and strengthen through her role as homemaker and mother. The lesson quoted a church authority: "He [your husband] needs to know that he is protecting you. He needs to feel that he is the leader in the family. . . . He needs to feel dominant." These words imply that by harboring or admitting negative feelings about their role as homemakers, women may undermine the superior position of men, upset the divine plan of God, and help the adversary destroy the family — which is a heavy burden of guilt for women to bear.

This lesson is checkered and troubling. We disagree that the differences between the sexes can be translated willy-nilly into sex-roles, many of which are stereotypical, artificial, contrived, rigid, and repugnant to the spiritual feelings and experiences of many church members. But we agree with the lesson's assumption that sexuality is eternal, that the image of God is reflected in both male and female, and that there are fundamental differences between the sexes. The lesson contained an important statement by President Spencer W. Kimball on this point: "The bodies of men and the bodies of women were created differently so they complemented each other, so that the union of the two would bring conception which would bring a living soul into the world. . . . " The eternal nature of our sexual differences is what creates the need for bonding or sealing. We see this process as symbolic of a deeper metaphysical truth. According to one scholar, "Sexual love is the most universal form of man's obscure search to eliminate duality for a short while, to existentially overcome the boundary between ego and not-ego, between self and not-self. Flesh and sex are the tools for an ecstatic approximation of achievement of unity" (Evola, 44).

Unfortunately these differences, which should be a source of celebration and wonder, have too often been the cause of animosity, jealousy, and invidious discrimination. For example, the historical denial to women of avenues of education is abhorrent and has had deleterious effects on society. And the notion that only a male can be a proper presider and provider and only the woman can be an effective sustainer and nourisher makes little sense within the complex relationships many modern married couples share.

The question is: how can we maintain a belief in the fundamental and eternal differences between the sexes when most attempts to define those differences in practical terms seem to degenerate into superficial descriptions of male and female sex-roles and rigid prescriptions of how individuals should act? The answer is that we must take pains to avoid thinking about gender differences in static and inadequate terms. Because the relationship between the sexes is living and dynamic, we can never settle upon any one fixed model of what the sexes should be. The paradox is that we can know the sexes are different, but we cannot know precisely or completely the metaphysical nature of this difference.

In the next paragraphs we wish to introduce several conceptual touchstones we have found helpful in sorting out some of the ambiguities and uncertainties which arise whenever we attempt to understand the elusive nature of the sexes. The first of these touchstones is succinctly stated in the Book of Mormon: "all things must needs be a compound in one" (2 Ne. 2:11). This idea suggests that unity can be formed by the conjunction of opposites. Day is made up of light and darkness, love is spiritual and physical, the earth is *firmamentum* and *fundamentum*. But the light of day is itself a composite of morning and evening, as night is a composite of evening and morning. Spiritual love is love of God and love of humanity. Physical love is the need to enjoy another and the need to be enjoyed by another. The firmament is clear and cloudy. The fundament is land and sea. Thus each component is a conjunction of opposites, containing in it the characteristics of the opposite member. The fact that each opposite contains something of the other makes possible in part the union of the two into a single compound.

Thus male and female each contains some characteristic of the other sex, which makes the bonding of the sexes possible. Although "opposites attract," similarities also draw us together. In the language of the Doctrine and Covenants: "[I]ntelligence cleaveth unto intelligence; wisdom receiveth wisdom, truth embraceth truth . . . " (88:40). Gandhi understood that within the female could be found a male component. Thus he was able to use the masculine aspects of passivity, and the weapon of passive resistance was born. A tree, usually thought of as a phallic symbol, also contains a female symbol of fertility in its leaves. The point is that the whole seems always to be a compound comprised of male and female components, each of which seems, in its own right, to be a compound of the male and female and therefore a reflection of the whole.

Remember, in each male there is both a female and a male principle, just as there is in each female. This means that a single female or a single male is not just half a person. Standing alone, each is capable of being a whole. The problem is that most of us are not whole because we have denied parts of ourselves, including parts of the male and female within us. We are in need of healing. Marriage is given by God as part of the healing process, which is why it is an ordinance of sanctification. We can be made whole (holy) if we let the opposites in the other bring forth those same characteristics in ourselves. But if we continue to deny parts of ourselves and project those parts on our spouse, expecting that person to make up for our lack of wholeness, then the marriage will be very troubled. For example, a man may fail to accept his own "soft" or feminine qualities — such as his sensitivity. If he projects this quality onto his spouse with the expectation that she is somehow to make up for his lack, then ironically he will begin to resent her sensitive nature out of envy. Or perhaps he will despise her for possessing a quality which he holds in contempt because he does not possess it. The same can happen if a woman denies her aggression and power (Scarf).

The unity created by marriage cannot be healthy if each partner in the marriage is unwhole. This can be illustrated by the symbol of the halved circle and the symbol of the Star of David. Marital union is not like two half circles that come together to make a perfect ring. Such an arrangement implies that an incomplete person is completed only by another incomplete person. Of course this happens in marriages, but if the situation persists, each partner will begin to resent the other for the dependency each partner feels. Marital union was not intended as a substitute for personal wholeness. Rather it was meant to allow whole and healthy individuals to combine to make something entirely new. The Star of David illustrates what we mean. Each triangle is whole and complete in itself. Each represents a kind of perfection. And yet when the two triangles are brought together to form the six pointed star, something beautiful and wonderful is created, something different from the parts which comprise it. And perhaps most remarkable: the parts are not obliterated in the new creation. They are still there, visible in their perfection, intertwined, interdependent, a "compound in one."

This Book of Mormon idea of everything being a compound is complicated by another concept: "there must needs be an opposition in all things" (2 Ne. 2:11). In other words the opposites we have described are equally necessary. However, in our culture people tend to prefer one part of the duality over the other. Most Westerners would prefer to be active and aggressive rather than passive. Passivity in the West is thought of as a weakness and aggressiveness a strength, an essential pre-requisite for accomplishing anything significant. This is what we tell our sons and now our daughters. It is a bias present even in certain groups within the women's movement, which has usually decried this concept of duality because it so often casts the female in the inferior role. And yet, the passive is not merely the failure to be assertive, but the positive capacity to be receptive, cooperative, and serve as a coun-terfoil to the active. A right-handed person, without the use of the left hand, would find it virutally impossible to accomplish even simple tasks without the left hand to hold things still or to receive the action. The passive, then, is the complement to, not the default of, the active.

However, as we have said before, the problem is not the concept of dualism but our predisposition toward favoritism or prejudice. There would be no harm in believing that women and men are opposites, if each is equally valued. This is the crux of Lehi's statement. Each entity is a composite, a compound of two different elements which are equally necessary: "for there must *needs* be an opposition in all things."

The preference for one opposite over another results in part be-cause we tend to confuse *necessary* opposites such as individual and com-munity with *rival* opposites such as health and sickness. *Rival opposites* consist of two contrasting qualities, one of which we see as bad because it consists of the corruption or contamination of the other, as with rain and acid rain. In contrast *necessary opposites* consist of two different mixtures or arrangements of the same qualities, as with bass and treble, inward and outward, up and down. Thus a devil is the opposite of a god in quite a different way than a goddess is the opposite of a god. God and Goddess are extremes on the same continuum, as are low "C" and high "C" in music. These sounds are extraordinarily similar, but because each causes different elements of the overtones series to resonate, the notes also sound very different. But the devil is the opposite of God in the same way sour milk is the opposite of good milk (to use C. S. Lewis's analogy). The devil is a fallen god, but a goddess is not. Moreover, the devil can also include a female counterpart. In Jewish legend, for example, Adam's fallen wife Lilith becomes a female demon.

But the matter is even more complicated, for the degenerated component of a rival pair is not necessarily devoid of value. For as good can generate evil, so evil can generate good. The hard-earned wealth of parents can become a bane to children. Industry can become obsessive and destructive. Pleasure sometimes leads to emptiness and pain. Conversely suffering may build character, sickness may promote an appreciation of health, death may be a welcome blessing, and sour milk can be used to make good biscuits.

Certainly the relative value we assign sex-linked characteristics often depends upon our cultural biases. For example, upon reading the *Odyssey* many people, male and female, are taken back by Odysseus' public, inconsolable, and tearful lamentation over his losses. The negative reaction occurs if we assume that real men do not stoop to public displays of sentiment. Rather than question our culture's prejudice on this point, many conclude that Odysseus was really not such a great hero after all. The ancient story exposes our own predilection for a certain type of ideal male. It shows us that in the view of another culture, an admirable man can have characteristics which we do not admire. This tells us that we are apt to generalize in simplistic ways.

This human tendency to seek simple solutions can distort our pictures of reality. There are numerous ways we can oversimplify. When it comes to issues of sex and sex roles, we often confuse the characteristics of a sex with the characteristics which that sex desires. As Carolyn Walker Bynum has noted about medieval mystics, "males seem to have been attracted to female images and women to male images" (162). In this period, the soul was viewed as a feminine principle, and therefore, as the object of the desire of males: "If the God with whom male mystics wanted to unite was described in male language, it became difficult for them to utilize metaphors of sexual union. Some monks solved that problem by depicting themselves or their souls as the brides of Christ, but others did so by making God the female parent with whom they could achieve physical union in the womb or at the breast" (161). Thus, males and females sometimes have sought God in terms of images of the opposite sex. But this statement is complicated by the fact that men and women may desire a bonding with their own sex as a reaffirmation of what they are or to supplement or reinforce what they desire. For this reason some women feel they need a goddess to reaffirm the importance of the feminine and to seek a model for what women should be. Men have had a god who has served this purpose for a long time.

Another way in which we oversimplify the relationship between the sexes is by our quick and easy moralizing about sex and sexuality. We do not like to admit our sexual feelings and needs, let alone talk about them. We tend to hide behind asexual masks. For example, many Bible stories contain a sexual component, either as part of the narrative or as part of the symbology. We deal with these by ignoring the sexual aspects and instead drawing from the story a simple moral: don't steal; don't lie; don't cheat; don't commit adultery or anything like unto it. But what is the moral of the story of Rahab the harlot? Or of Abraham and Sarah in Egypt? Or of Hosea marrying the prostitute? Or of David and Bathsheba?

Some time ago we heard a church high councilman tell some young people that King David had a "pornography problem." The naked body of Bathsheba, he thought, was a temptation or an obscenity, and all of King David's problems stemmed from his ogling her from the balcony. The speaker's point was that young men should avoid looking at naked women. But this story is not about a man with a fetish for pornography. It is about a king who happened to see a woman naked and was filled with desire for her and then used his royal authority to rid himself of her husband so that he could marry her. Like so many others in the Bible, the story does not condemn sexual desire but the abuse of authority. It is hard to read the story in this way, however, if one is afraid of sex and enthralled with power. The point is that if we engage in this type of denial and projection, we can only see sex, sexuality, and sex roles simplistically—in rigid, categorical, and often sentimental terms.

Our final conceptual touchstone is that any model of the relationship between the sexes or sex-linked principles is dynamic and not
static. It is a model in motion. In other words any description of sex
roles is complicated by the fact that the sexes can and sometimes must
undergo role reversals. As with the Star of David, the positions of the
triangles can be rotated without altering the pattern of the star. The
male does and sometimes must become the female, and the female does
and sometimes must become the male. Unless this happens a rigidity
effectively stifling creativity and life will result.

Role-reversals occur in many guises: child becomes parent, stu-
dent becomes teacher, host becomes guest, king becomes beggar. Becoming a parent can make one a more sympathetic child. Teachers, by
becoming students again, become better teachers. Students, by becoming teachers, become better students. The guest who has never been a
host will be a poor guest. The wise who have not seen their folly become arrogant, and the king who has never been a beggar becomes
tyrannical. In myth we find the ubiquitous role-reversal motif of the
good king who has gone in disguise as a pauper among his people:
Odysseus, Henry V, and of course Christ himself. In some cultures this
reversal is solemnized as the ritual humiliation of the king and forms
part of the coronation ceremony and yearly rites.

With the man and the woman, role-reversals are no less important.
Through such an exchange a proper balance can be maintained between the sexes. Reversals allow each to better comprehend and sym-
pathize with the other, to see the world from the other's point of view.
In the writings of Jeremiah there is a passage which hints at this process: "For the Lord hath created a new thing in the earth, a woman shall
compass a man" (Jer. 31:22). The Hebrew word used here for "compass"
is *sawvav*. It means to revolve, surround, be about on every side, whirl
around, to turn oneself about, to lead. The New English Bible renders
this passage as follows: "The Lord has created a new thing in the earth:
a woman turned into a man." And in the Oxford Annotated Bible: "For
the Lord has created a new thing on the earth; A woman protects a
man." This suggests a woman taking what has been viewed as a man's
role, to lead and encompass or include him, to protect him — a reversal
of Paul's statement that "woman was made out of man" (1 Cor. 11:8).

Men are also asked to take traditional female roles. In Numbers
11, Moses, troubled with the burdensome task of caring for the children of Israel, asks the Lord: "Am I their mother? Have I brought them
into the world, and am I called upon to carry them in my bosom, like a

nurse with her babies . . . ?" God's answer to this question is yes. But he tells Moses he will not have to bear this burden alone. So Moses assembles seventy elders (apparently to be nursemaids), and then God appears to confer upon them the same nurturing spirit given to Moses.

Having discussed some of the complexities involved in any consideration of sex-roles, we wish now to consider sex-role reversals in two biblical narratives: the story of Abraham and Sarah and the story of Adam and Eve. Isaiah puts the story of Abraham and Sarah into the context of mythic or religious paradigm: "Listen to me, all who follow the right and seek the Lord: look to the rock from which you were hewn, to the quarry from which you were dug; look to your father Abraham and to Sarah who gave you birth" (Is. 51:1–2). Abraham is the rock and Sarah the quarry. Both are models for us. And what patterns emerge from their relationship? First, as we have mentioned before, God makes a covenant with both. Sarah is to stand as a queen or princess in her own right, independent in the sphere in which God has placed her. She is a Princess of Peace. Both Abraham and Sarah are sealed to the Lord through covenant: the sign of Sarah's sealing is Isaac, the child of promise. The sign of Abraham's sealing is the circumcision. Here we have another reversal. In giving birth to Isaac, Sarah bled. In circumcision, Abraham also bled, symbolizing his covenant or marriage to God. In many tribes circumcision is linked with pre-marital rites, and in some tribes boys even wear girls' clothing when they are circumcised (Frazer, 263). So Abraham and Sarah both play the role of woman before God. And in turn both Abraham and Sarah play the part of priest. For though at times she looks to him for salvation, at other times he looks to her.

There is an apocryphal story, which takes place before Abraham and Sarah make their sojourn into Egypt. In a dream Abraham sees a pine tree, which would have been chopped down and used for firewood if it had not been for a palm tree which in some way spared its life. Abraham is told that he is the pine tree and Sarah the palm. Because of Sarah, Abraham's life would be spared. This came to pass when Pharaoh honored Abraham as the brother of Sarah, Pharaoh's intended spouse. Obeying God's command, Abraham had disclosed to Pharaoh only his relation to Sarah as brother, hiding his relationship as husband. Though Abraham was spared by this device, Sarah was put to the test: her virtue was placed on the lion couch, the sacrificial bed. She was willing to give up her virtue to save her husband. However, her sacrifice, like her husband's, was arrested. For every time the

Pharaoh approached her sexually, he was warded off by a disease. Eventually he learned the truth, and after chastising Abraham for the whole scheme, he counted himself lucky not to have angered their God and then let them both go.

Sarah through her sacrifice not only saved Abraham but provided us with a symbol of the truth that both the male and the female may serve as priest. Both may be called to make sacrifice, which is the chief priestly function. Both have power to confer life on the other. Both play a role in salvation.

The story of Adam and Eve also illustrates the complexity of male-female relationships. Though this story is often used to justify male dominance, the story itself, both in the Bible and in the temple drama, contains elements of sex role reversals. In the Garden of Eden, it is Adam who plays the passive and receptive role, while Eve is the active protagonist. It is Eve, not Adam, who recognizes the necessity of partaking of the forbidden fruit. She perceives that it is only by experiencing both good and evil that they can indeed become like God. Eve takes the initiative and is first on the scene. While Adam sleeps, Eve waits for him. And upon awakening, the first person Adam sees is Eve, whom he rightly recognizes as the Mother of All Living. Eve is the first to understand that they cannot stay in their paradise forever. It is she who quickly comprehends the necessity of opposition to bring about eternal life and joy. It is she who realizes the necessity of their remaining together and who uses this argument to persuade Adam to follow her into mortality. She is the first to recognize the true identity of Satan. And finally, it is her seed who will crush the serpent's head. Because, as we have noted, the word *seed* is linked with priesthood, this statement may mean that it is the priesthood of Eve or the woman which will crush the serpent's head. Perhaps this is a prophecy about the active role of women against the adversary in the end time, as may be reflected in Revelation 12. In any case, we have no retiring woman in Mother Eve.

In the Garden of Eden, Eve initiated the sojourn of humanity into the temporal sphere, while Adam yielded to her work. After the fall and expulsion from the Garden, these roles are presented as being reversed. Adam becomes active in the world in a way he had not been before, while Eve assumes a more passive role and yields to him. These role reversals, we believe, are not meant to be applied on a domestic level to reinforce traditional sex roles. Rather, this story must be seen mythically and cosmically. In the eternal drama of the sexes, each will sometimes be passive, sometimes active. But whatever the case, each is always required to act spiritually and to be personally responsible to God.

Even in the administration of gospel ordinances, role reversals take place. Although men perform the initial ordinances of salvation — baptism and confirmation — the last rites pertaining to the fullness of the priesthood are administered by women. This ritual pattern is apparently based upon the anointing and washing of Jesus by one of the Marys "against the day of my burying" (John 12:7; Luke 7:37–50). Heber C. Kimball believed that the woman performs this rite in order to have claim upon her husband in the resurrection (Kimball Journal). Although this statement may be interpreted to mean that the woman is dependent on the man for her resurrection, it can also mean that the man must look to the woman for the power of an endless life, which power is the fruition and completion of the gospel covenant. Thus, the woman is the vehicle through which the man obtains the power to come forth from the tomb, even as she is the vehicle by which he is brought forth from the womb. This idea is also suggested in the Egyptian myth where Osiris' resurrection is dependent on the efforts of Isis, and in other Egyptian ceremonies, where a woman had to be present at every "awakening."

The paradox is that the first shall be last and the last shall be first. Sometimes the woman is first, other times the man. Sometimes he leads, other times she does. Sometimes she is on top, other times he is, and at times they repose in perfect harmony. So long as each sex takes its turn in yielding to the other as the other assumes various roles, it should not matter in any given situation who is first and who is last. A few women lingered last at the foot of the cross and later were the first witnesses of the resurrection, while the apostles though first to preach the gospel, were the last of Christ's intimates to witness the risen Lord. And, of course, being last is not the same as being subordinate or inferior. Jesus saved the good wine until last. And at the last comes the healing of the wounds.

This shifting of roles, this exchange of natures, this interplay between opposites is the very stuff of life; the cup of one must empty that the cup of the other may be filled, that both may pour out their abundance to receive an even greater fulness. It is not in the elimination of extremes that life comes forth, but in their tension and balance, where contraries come into accord. The sex act itself, with its fluctuations and alterations of below and above, full and empty, inward and out-

ward, rest and motion, union and division, is the perfect symbol of
this dynamic marriage of necessary opposites that liberates the creative forces that are, in this world, the source of new life and, in the
next world, the source of eternal life — spinning and moving and living
from eternity to eternity. And those who behold this fearful symmetry
may, with John Donne, be moved to sing:

> My face in thine eye, thine in mine appeares,
> And true plaine hearts doe in the faces rest,
> Where can we finde two better hemispheares
> Without sharpe North, without declining west?
> Whatever dyes, was not mixt equally;
> If our two loves be one, or, thou and I
> Love so alike, that none doe slacken, none can die.
> ("The Good-Morrow," 8).

CHAPTER TWENTY-ONE

MONOGAMY, POLYGAMY, AND HUMILITY

In the 1830s, Joseph Smith secretly introduced polygamy into Mormonism. At first this practice was restricted to only a few individuals. During the period when the church was headquartered in Kirtland, Ohio, suspicions and suppositions regarding Joseph's involvement in polygamy spread and led to difficulties for the church and its leadership. During the 1840s, in Nauvoo, Illinois, polygamy, though still clandestine, grew more extensive. Consequently, it could not be kept secret. The city of Nauvoo buzzed with troubling rumors about various romantic liaisons, while in the surrounding non-Mormon communities moral outrage fueled the opinion that the Mormons had to be expelled from the state.

Mindful of these developments, Joseph Smith, Brigham Young, and other church leaders were contemplating moving the church to another settlement — perhaps to Texas, Wisconsin, Mexico, or the Rocky Mountains — some place where the Latter-day Saints could practice their religion unmolested by the attitudes and actions of others. In 1847, three years after Joseph Smith was murdered by a mob, Brigham Young led the Saints across the plains to the Great Basin. There the practice of polygamy remained a well known secret until August 29, 1852, when on instructions from Young, Apostle Orson Pratt officially made public the practice of "plural marriage" (JD 1:56). Thereafter, polygamy became a rule of the church.

For ten years, a minority of Mormons engaged in this practice under a growing cloud of public censure that linked polygamy and slavery as the twin relics of barbarism. Finally, in 1862, Congress enacted a law that defined polygamy as bigamy and made it a crime in the territories. This was the first attempt by the federal government to eliminate this practice. Mormons considered the law unconstitutional and refused to obey it. In March 1863, Brigham Young was arrested on a charge of bigamy and placed under a $2,000 bond, but a trial was never held.

In the late 1860s, public opinion, freed from the concerns of the Civil War, again turned a frowning face westward toward the last barbarity—polygamy. In 1870, Mormon women held a large mass meeting in Salt Lake City to protest anti-Mormon and anti-polygamy legislation pending in Congress. In 1871, Young was again arrested, this time on a charge of unlawful cohabitation. The case went on until April 1872, when it was dropped due to a United States Supreme Court decision that overturned a number of Utah court proceedings.

In 1879, two years after the death of Young, the Supreme Court upheld as constitutional the 1862 anti-bigamy law. This was the beginning of the end for the LDS practice of plural marriage. In March 1882, Congress passed the Edmunds bill, which defined polygamy as "unlawful cohabitation" and disenfranchised from the vote those who continued its practice. A few months later the commission authorized by the Edmunds Act arrived in Utah territory to enforce the disenfranchisement of most of the Mormon population. In 1885, prosecutions of polygamists continued, while the church leadership, for the most part, was forced into hiding. By 1886, in spite of another mass meeting held by Mormon women to protest these actions, the crusade against polygamy continued, and many Mormons fled to sanctuaries in Canada and Mexico, where they could continue the practice. Also in 1886, according to most modern Mormon fundamentalist polygamists, church president John Taylor authorized several men, not church authorities, to keep polygamy alive, even if the church itself abandoned the principle.

The year 1887 saw the passing of the two staunchest defenders of plural marriage, John Taylor, third church president, and Eliza R. Snow, plural wife of both Joseph Smith and Brigham Young and president of the Mormon women's Relief Society. By the end of the 1880s, even Mormon opinion began to turn against the practice. In 1890, church president Wilford Woodruff issued the "Manifesto," a document declaring that no new plural marriages had been contracted with church approval during the previous year, that plural marriage had not been officially taught in that time, and that the avowed intent of the president of the church was to submit to the constitutional law of the land. It also advised church members to refrain from contracting any marriages forbidden by law. The Manifesto was accepted by the majority vote of the general conference of the church on October 6, 1890. This event marked the beginning of the reconciliation between the church and the federal government that eventually led to statehood for Utah in 1896. However, church members continued secretly to contract polygamous marriages in the United States and to openly practice polygamy in the Mormon colonies in Mexico.

In 1904, church president Joseph F. Smith issued the "second manifesto" outlawing polygamy throughout the church and invoking upon those who disobeyed this injunction the penalty of excommunication. Some have argued that this action was taken in order to palliate the U.S. Senate, which had refused to seat duly elected Utah senator and church apostle Reed Smoot on grounds that Mormons in Utah had not really abandoned plural marriage. After three years of hearings, Smoot was allowed to assume his seat in February 1907. In spite of all this, polygamous marriages continued to be contracted, sometimes by or with the approval of church leaders in the highest echelons, leaders such as Apostle Matthias Cowley, whose allegiance to the principle led to his resignation from the Council of the Twelve in October 1905 and church president John Taylor's son, John W. Taylor, an apostle excommunicated in March 1911 for refusing to abandon the principle and to refrain from performing plural marriages.

Although some Mormons continued to marry polygamously after 1910, the practice became less and less common. In the late teens and throughout the twenties, many church members, though uninvolved in the practice, remained loyal to the principle of polygamy by continuing to honor those who had sacrificed for it and by looking forward to its restoration as a church practice. Others were glad to see its demise. And others, so humiliated by the entire experience, left the church and Utah for refuges like California, where they could find a respite from religious zeal. By the early 1930s, only a small minority of Mormons, convinced that the church had been wrong ever to abandon the practice at all, continued to marry in polygamy.

The official attitude of the church toward these individuals became increasingly severe. In the 1930s, J. Reuben Clark, Jr., counsellor to church president Heber J. Grant, took measures to eradicate the practice once and for all among church members. As a result, polygamists left or were excommunicated from the church, only to claim that a rival priesthood authority derived from church president John Taylor allows them to continue the practice. Today, these groups are shunned by the church and its leadership (Foster; Quinn; Van Wagoner).

In light of this turbulent history, we can say without overstatement that, for over one-hundred and fifty years, polygamy has been the nemesis of Mormonism. Church leaders no longer attempt to justify or explain this part of Mormon history. Official pronouncements are confined to clarifications that true Mormons do not practice polygamy and to statements that distance the church from those who do. The emphasis of the church is on promoting monogamous marriages and happy, well adjusted families as the basic unit of a stable and prosperous society. As for church members, we rarely discuss polygamy in church meetings, and when we do, many of us are left feeling troubled and disoriented.

For many, polygamy remains the most embarrassing element of our history and doctrine. We find ourselves still having to explain to outsiders that the LDS church abandoned this practice long ago. We despise the fact that others think we are living outside mainstream, conservative American marriage patterns. Because we want to be seen as respectable, we react to inquiries about or accusations of polygamy with denials and repression. Officially we try to cover up our past. Most converts to the church have only the vaguest understanding of our history on this issue. Though most Mormons are aware that Brigham Young had multiple marriages, many do not realize the extent of Joseph Smith's involvement with this practice. And those who do, often try to believe he did not have sex with any of his plural wives. Most Mormons are unaware of the polyandrous aspects of marriage practices in Nauvoo, or that Joseph married women already married, sometimes without the knowledge of their husbands. Most Mormons do not know that plural marriages continued to be contracted long after the Manifesto was accepted by the church. They believe that everybody happily complied with the new mandate without reservation. Many want to believe that those who continued the practice of polygamy did so out of lust and rebellion. Many are further confused by the current practice of temple sealings which allows a man after the death of or divorce from his wife to be sealed again to another woman, also for eternity, thus reinforcing the notion that in the next life polygamy will continue. Women especially have had problems with the implication that polygamy might be an essential part of celestial marriage and wonder whether they are to be part of a future celestial harem — a picture that does not comport with the image most women have of an ideal heaven.

For our part, we frankly admit that we have no clear answers to many of the questions raised by the polygamy issue. We can say that we are not attracted to Mormon fundamentalism, largely because we believe it is authoritarian, patriarchal, and oppressive. On the other hand, we find somewhat disingenuous the mainstream American and Mormon intolerance for alternative marriage patterns when so many traditional marriages are themselves not strictly monogamous and that, in practice, most people either as a result of death or divorce reach the end of their lives having been involved in more than one marriage. We are both committed to the idea of fidelity and consider promiscuity to be unhealthy primarily because it is rooted in egocentricity. Paradoxically, however, we do not subscribe to the romantically enthralling myth of "the one and only." We think many people would be psychologically capable of having a loving relationship with more than one person. However, we think most such persons would agree that there is no way to develop and sustain such multiple relationships. In our culture and with our limitations, attempts to do this would undoubtedly shipwreck on the shoals of jealousy, envy, and fear. Nevertheless, though we understand that it is the tendency of most people to accept only that which accords with their received sense of ethics and their need for comfort and security and to reject whatever does not, we also recognize that in the history of the world, different sexual and marital arrangements have arisen in different cultures and that these, in their own way and in their own time, served as well as monogamy.

Confronted as we are with these troubling historical and psychological issues, what sense can be made of Mormonism's experience with and teachings on plural marriage? Was the entire episode merely the result of one man's weaknesses and temptations? Was it a moral test posed by God to the first Mormons — a test which they failed? Or was it truly a divine revelation? And, if so, what meaning could such a revelation have for us, who do not practice polygamy? As we have said, we have no clear answers to these questions. We pose them here principally to guide us through the discussion that follows.

Let us first observe that the revelation on polygamy in Doctrine and Covenants 132 was not written until July 12, 1843, some years after the practice of polygamy was first introduced. This text is, nevertheless, important because it contains the only authoritative scriptural defense of the teaching. The primary element in this defense, we think, is the assertion that God's command to practice polygamy was to the church what God's command to sacrifice Isaac was to Abraham: "Abraham was commanded to offer his son Isaac; nevertheless, it was written: thou shalt not kill. Abraham, however, did not refuse, and it was accounted unto him for righteousness" (vv. 34–36).

This comparison suggests that an understanding of the meaning and purpose of the arrested sacrifice of Isaac will illuminate our understanding of the meaning and purpose of polygamy. For this reason, we turn once more to the Abraham story, keeping in mind our initial questions: Was the sacrifice of Isaac the result of Abraham's weaknesses and temptations? Was it a moral test posed by God—a test which Abraham failed? Or was it a divine revelation? And, if so, what was its meaning and purpose for those of us who have not received such a command?

From the Mormon scriptural texts dealing with Abraham, there is little doubt about Abraham's attitude toward human sacrifice. Although Abraham had inherited from his forefathers the notion that animal sacrifice was to be carried out in "the similitude of the sacrifice of the Only Begotten of the Father" (Moses 5:7), Abraham himself, who nearly became a sacrificial victim, viewed human sacrifice with revulsion. Moreover, the texts do not present Abraham as a father who attempts to sacrifice his son out of weakness or temptation in order to control him, or to avoid pain, or as an act of vengeance or propitiation, or as the concoction of a religious fanatic bent on proving his worthiness to God. Nor is the sacrifice presented as a test of wills in which Abraham is torn between his moral repugnance for murder and God's seemingly senseless command that Isaac be butchered on a stone in the mountain. True, Abraham is grieved that his son must suffer and die, but there is nothing in the text to suggest that Abraham is impaled on the horns of a moral dilemma. He does not agonize over his troubles as does, for example, Job. Nowhere does the text indicate that Abraham was later blessed because he refused to go through with the sacrifice. In fact, the texts agree that Abraham never refused to go through with it. For all intents and purposes, he accomplished it. He not only poised the knife over the breast of his son, he was in the very act of plunging it into him when the angel came and stopped him. Significantly, God never chastises Abraham for this act nor scolds him for going against his own moral scruples. On the contrary, more than one text indicates that Abraham was blessed for his faithfulness in carrying out God's command. It is because he was willing to sacrifice his son that he is called "father of the faithful." God's direct appearance and command is presented in the story to eliminate the issue of uncertainty about the source of the command. The story of Abraham and Isaac begins with the appearance of God. Our modern tendency to disbelieve in direct contact with God obscures the point the story asks us to accept: that because of God's initial intervention Abraham and Isaac are involved in circumstances beyond control. This, then, is not the story of a good man who must prove himself worthy, but of a man who must endure the inevitable and who does so in faith, only to find in the end that God is not only as good as Abraham believed, but is better than he had ever dreamed even in his wildest imaginations. If this had been a story about morality, Abraham would have been a moral failure. But it is, instead, a story about faith, sacrifice, and atonement.

We conclude that the sacrifice of Isaac proceeded from a divine revelation whose principle purpose was to establish or reinforce the mythic notion that the king must willingly die for the sake of his people. Isaac was the child of the covenant, the miracle child, the king who was, in Abraham's mind, destined to atone for the sins of others. It was only when the angel of God appeared to stop the ritual that Abraham and Isaac learned this was not to be, that there was another greater sacrificial victim who would come to make atonement.

It is hard for many of us, nourished as we are on twentieth-century positivism, to see the necessity of Christ's sacrificial death. So we tend to interpret it only as a supreme act of love and devotion for humanity, which was performed in a way that would call out of us a corresponding outpouring of love and devotion for God. But for many people in the ancient world it was much more; it was the fulfillment of the myth of the dying god whose death and resurrection were considered essential to the sustaining of life from year to year. The New Testament writer seems to have held this same world view when he quoted Jesus as saying: "Except a corn of wheat fall into the ground and die, it abideth alone; but if it die, it bringeth forth much fruit" (John 12:24; 1 Cor. 15:36). Seen in this way, Jesus was the seed which fell into the earth and died and then became the tree of life, "which giveth life to all things . . . " (D&C 88:13). This was the message of the story of the arrested sacrifice: "And if thou [Abraham] shalt die, yet thou shalt possess it [the promised land], for the day cometh, that the Son of Man shall live; but how can he live if he be not dead? he must first be quickened" (JST Gen. 15:11).

This leads us back to our central question. If plural marriage was to the church what the arrested sacrifice of Isaac was to Abraham, then we may assume that it was not merely the outgrowth of Joseph Smith's personal weaknesses and temptations and that it was not merely a moral test which the church failed. Could polygamy in some way be a revelation in a historical setting of some important divine truth or pattern?

In Moses 6:63, we read: "And behold, all things have their likeness, and all things are created and made to bear record of me, both things which are temporal and things which are spiritual; things which are in the earth, and things which are under the earth, both above and beneath: all things bear record of me." In other words, in earthly things are reflected the image of heavenly things. Could polygamy, like the arrested sacrifice and the law of Moses, have been meant to point us to something else, something higher?

In our view, polygamy was a revelation of the pattern of the sacred marriage, the *hieros gamos*, that was thought by people in ancient cultures to insure fertility. Today, we think of fertility mostly in terms of reproducing offspring. This is not a very pleasant notion to our overcrowded world and to many women of childbearing years. But ancient cultures saw fertility as positive. It signified an abundance of those things which make life pleasant and meaningful: food and drink, land and water sources, flocks and herds, goods and chattels, wisdom and good counsel, poetry and song, and a source of energy sufficient to make the world work and cohere.

At the heart of the sacred marriage with its promise of prosperity was the concept of union with God. In the story of Abraham and Sarah, this union occurs when God becomes a partner in the marriage. When Sarah realizes she is barren, she humbles herself and offers her maid, Hagar, to Abraham. Sarah does this in order to "obtain children" from Hagar (Gen. 16:2–3). This was a common practice in Mesopotamia at that time. When a wife gave her handmaid to her husband, the maid in a sense became the wife by assuming her identity. Therefore, the children born to the maid were counted as the offspring of the original wife. In this story, however, Hagar does not cooperate nor does she identify with Sarah. Instead, after Hagar conceives, "her mistress [Sarah] was despised in her eyes." Sarah, in turn, reacts jealously towards Hagar and begins to treat her harshly. Finally, Hagar runs away to escape Sarah's ill-treatment. The tragedy of this situation is that neither woman's suffering seems to make her sensitive to the plight of the other. Note also that the quarrel between them is not over the affection of the common husband, but over their ability to produce an heir.

But God has compassion on them both and gives them both a blessing and a promise that they will each have a son and be the mother of nations. Additionally, we are told, God makes a priesthood covenant with Sarah and her posterity, as well as promising her that kings would spring from her lineage. Thus, Sarah, the priestess and princess, becomes the candidate for the sacred marriage. She is chosen to give birth to the miracle child of promise.

But what has all this to do with polygamy? Several scholars have pointed out that the stylistic details of the story of the conception and birth of Isaac fit into the mythic ritual pattern of the sacred marriage rite of the Mesopotamian culture. The implication of this is that the birth of Isaac is the result of the deity's having sexual intercourse with Sarah. George Widengren comments: "This interpretation would imply an Israelitic adoption of an ancient Canaanite tradition of the visit of a deity to the queen, the sacred marriage, the oracle about the birth of the royal-divine child, the naming of the child, and the prophesying of its future great deeds, and last of all the account of the birth itself" (Hooke, 184–85). Savina Teubal also interprets the conception of Isaac in terms of the sacred marriage rite. She points out that in the statement, "And the Lord visited Sarah as he said and the Lord did unto Sarah as he had spoken," the Hebrew word for "visit" can have a sexual connotation, for it is used elsewhere in the Old Testament in this sense (126). What emerges from this story is an interlocking marriage pattern that is truly polygamous, involving the many marriages among Abraham, Hagar, Sarah, and Yahweh. We believe that nineteenth-century Mormon polygamy was intended to mirror this pattern — the pattern of the *hieros gamos*.

But why? What purpose could there be and what benefit could inure to the church by the attempt of the early Mormons to replicate these strange arrangements? Perhaps the answer lies in the story. Perhaps the polygamous relationship among Abraham, Hagar, Sarah, and Yahweh was essential if the humans involved were to overcome their limitations. Perhaps God sought to expand and purify these souls by requiring them to grow beyond the natural boundaries of their affections. Like seeds, they had to burst beyond their shells in order to grow into trees of righteousness, pillars in the temple of God (Is. 61:3; Rev. 3:12).

Both the Abrahamic story and the historical practice of polygamy among the early Mormons press us to reexamine our moral assumptions and to come to terms with the connections and contradictions that exist among our deepest feelings of divine love, sexual love, love of offspring, and love of friends. Both challenge our complacency and our comfortable moral and emotional categories. Both remind us of the need to expand our capacities, to move beyond the restrictions and limitations of our traditions. Both teach us that we cannot attain what

God wants for us unless we are willing to be enlarged beyond the context of relationships we have defined. Both tend to instill in us a commitment to the creation of a unified community out of diverse nations, kindreds, tongues, and people.

In Galatians 4, the apostle Paul refers to the story of Abraham's two sons and uses it to chastise the Jewish Christians for their elitism, their refusal to accept into the church the Gentiles on an equal footing with themselves. Paul says that Hagar the slave woman represents the law and Sinai, while Sarah the free woman represents the covenant and the heavenly Jerusalem. Paul then turns the tables on his opponents. He says that Ishmael, the child of the slave woman and "born after the flesh," represents the Jews, whereas Isaac, the child of the free woman and born "by promise" or covenant, represents the converted Gentiles. Paul argues here that if the Jews base their claim of election on their being lineal descendents of Abraham in the flesh, then they must be the children of Ishmael, Abraham's natural son, whom they have always despised. His purpose in making this argument is to destroy the Jewish saints' exclusive claim to the covenant of God and to remind them that God's relationship with humanity is not based upon an elite status, it is not confined to one people alone. God is the God of Ishmael as well as Isaac.

If the purpose of polygamy was to expand the human capacity to love and to accept, then it is significant that Joseph Smith connected polygamy with two other important principles: the law of consecration and stewardship and the concept of the fullness of the priesthood. The idea behind the law of consecration and stewardship is that men and women cannot be equal in heavenly things unless they are first willing to be equal in earthly things. The idea behind the doctrine of the fullness of the priesthood is that the full range of divine gifts and powers can be realized only when men and women are united with each other and with God on an equal footing. These doctrines share common themes: the transcendence of human limitations through the intercession of God, the estimation and love of others as self, and ultimate union with the divine.

But even if we acknowledge that polygamy had a divine source and purpose, we also must acknowledge that people unpersuaded of this could and indeed have raised legitimate theological objections to its practice. Many people feel that polygamy threatens fidelity while monogamy strengthens it. Though we share this concern for fidelity in love relationships, we are not convinced that fidelity will be better insured in monogamous relationships. We agree that if a relationship is to be more than fleeting and superficial, if it is to endure and deepen, it must be based on mutual promises, commitment, sacrifice, and maturity. The question is whether it is possible to be faithful to more than one person. Those who practice polygamy affirm that this is possible, although we wonder how many such marriage relationships can be sustained and developed within the context of the ordinary limitations of time, energy, and resources. However, we agree that we cannot subdivide love like we can time. The addition of a new child, for example, does not diminish parents' love for their other children. But some have argued that the love of parents for their children cannot be equated with the love of spouses for each other. Perhaps there is something to this, but it appears to us that simultaneous fidelity and loyalty to more than one beloved is possible. This is particularly illustrated by men and women whose spouses die and who remarry. The new marriage relationship is not a betrayal of the old (even for Mormons who believe that the old marriage continues).

This very realization occurred to Hyrum Smith, Joseph's brother. When the principles of eternal marriage and ordinances for the dead were introduced to him, Hyrum wanted to be sealed to his first wife who had died. And yet he also wanted to be sealed to his living wife. He loved them both. He could not choose between them. He realized that both relationships involved fidelity. This experience, more than any other, convinced Hyrum that it was possible to be polygamous and faithful. And for this reason he was able to accept the doctrine of plural marriage as morally sound. Thus infidelity is not necessarily inherent in every polygamous marriage any more than fidelity is in every monogamous one. But in spite of these observations, we agree with those who think that polygamy is likely to attract individuals entirely unsuited to it, people who are, perhaps, seeking to escape one relationship by entering another.

Another common objection to polygamy is that it cannot possibly have divine origins or spiritual purposes because of the sexual nature of the doctrine. Is it not just an excuse for lust? The fact that we can accept the idea of expansion of love in terms of children and friends, but not marriage partners, demonstrates our prejudice that a person who has sexual relations with more than one person is morally reprehensible, even in the confines of plural marriage. This is substantiated by the long-standing debate about whether or not Joseph Smith was intimate with his plural wives. Many say they could accept these marriages if Joseph did not have sexual intercourse with the women. What does this say about our attitudes toward sex? As Terence L. Day has pointed out, we as products of Western culture are to some extent uncomfortable with sexuality (8).

In spite of Mormonism's emphasis on the positive aspects of sex and the finite and anthropomorphic nature of deity, many Mormons share this discomfort. It is difficult for many of us to accept the sexuality of our parents, and some of us can barely stand to see our children become sexually mature. At the same time, incest is within the church a growing problem that is very destructive of spiritual, sexual, and psychological growth. We seem to have no wholeness about our sexual nature. We associate the absence of sexuality with purity, and the presence of it with degeneracy. We tend to see sexuality and spirituality as opposites and want to deny the erotic part of our being. We sense a sort of schizophrenia among our people. This is true of the larger American culture as well. But where many Americans today tend to pursue sex promiscuously and to eschew spirituality almost entirely, we Mormons tend to repress or deny our sexual feelings out of fear and to live by strict codes of behavior which we equate with spirituality. Thus, the pendulum swings between rigidity and licentiousness.

What we need is a balance of these extremes, a balance suggested in the idea of godly temperance, which is the substance of the temple ceremony's admonition that we should keep our passions within the bounds the Lord has set. We usually think that we are being required by this exhortation simply to contain our passions. But, we think, it is also a call to expand them. Let us explain: Imagine two circles, one very large and the other very small. Let the small circle represent our human passions and the large one represent the passions of God. Picture the smaller circle overlapping slightly the larger one. Let this arrangement represent that our passions are like God's in some ways but not all. To bring our passions into the bounds the Lord has set does require us to bring our small circle into the circumference of God's larger one. But it also requires us break the circumference of our small circle so that it can be expanded and begin to approach the magnitude of divine love. We cannot do this until we come to terms with our sexuality, until we are able to see it as an extension and part of our spirituality and personhood. We must be sanctified beyond the shame that is the legacy of the fall and see our sexual desires in a new and blinding light, to see them as an essential part of our eternal nature, something to be magnified not feared.

Another valid objection to the doctrine of polygamy is that it encourages deviations from ethical behavior for anyone wishing to depart from ordinary ethical conventions. This is a genuine danger. But it is no more dangerous than believing that our moral constructs are identical to God's and should be inflexible. Neither of these possibilities is hypothetical. We have seen the results of moral certainty, and they can be appalling. In the church this often manifests itself in the form of judgment and condemnation. We know of one man who upon failing to follow the counsel of his stake leaders not to divorce his wife was excommunicated for his disobedience on grounds that he had committed adultery — in his heart. This could not have happened if his judges were not convinced that their own moral views were absolute and absolutely correct. We also know of others, who believing that they are free from moral constraints and that, to please God, they must prove themselves, have taken actions that contradict established notions of morality or that put themselves and others at serious risk. People who act in these ways are, in our opinion, not simply guilty of immorality. Their problem is a religious one — the problem of distinguishing revelations from temptations.

The question is, how do we do this? Again, we are not certain. Our answers can only be tentative. But it appears to us that the revelations of God could not be of human invention, self-concocted and self-imposed. They would probably be unexpected, unsought for, and simply endured. Their purpose would undoubtedly be to increase faith, love, and knowledge. Temptations, on the other hand, like those of Jesus in the wilderness, would more likely be in the nature of seductions to avoid the pain of enduring by the exertion of control. They would amount to enticements to assuage hunger by making bread out of stones, or to assuage vanity by jumping from the pinnacle of the temple and landing unharmed, or to assuage frustration by attempting to establish the kingdom of God by force. They could also involve attempts to assuage our sense of ordinariness by destroying the fragile fabric of our families and plunging headlong into some new marriage arrangement to show the Godhead that we are worthy of being their favorites, their elite. This is not to say that God will not sometimes call people to something new. But, it seems to us, that genuine revelation would require us to sacrifice ourselves rather than to oppress others, to acknowledge our sins and weaknesses rather than to prove our worthiness, to forgive rather than to seek revenge, to repent rather than to accuse, to reaffirm the equal dignity and value of every human being rather than to establish an elite entitled to special privileges and status. As we have seen, the Abraham and Isaac story illustrates these points.

Another objection is that polygamy creates an imbalance between male and female. Women rightly assert that a marriage relationship consisting of one man and many women puts the male in the power position and implies that it takes many women to equal the value of one man. Such a relationship can create competition among the women for the favors of the man and spur men to acquire more and more wives as a symbol of superior status, thus further reducing women to mere objects or property. We share these concerns and for this reason do not argue in defense of polygyny ("many wives"), but have sought in this chapter to better understand polygamy ("many marriages"). In our view, polygyny was not the pattern revealed by God. Our point in emphasizing the story of Yahweh, Sarah, Abraham, and Hagar was to show that in this foundational myth, the pattern revealed was that of plural marriages, not plural wives. The early Mormons, we believe, were required to be polygamous not merely polygynous. Support for this opinion is found not only in the story of Sarah, but in the story of Mary the mother of Christ, who, according to Brigham Young, was married both to Joseph the carpenter and to the heavenly father of Jesus (JD 11:268). Moreover, true polygamy, involving elements of polygyny and polyandry ("many husbands"), was practiced under Joseph Smith in Nauvoo and under Brigham Young in the early Utah period (Van Wagoner; Johnson). Finally, Doctrine and Covenants 132 implies that a married women in the new and everlasting covenant may have more than one spouse if it is appointed by God (vv. 41–42). Though polygamy may not answer all the moral objections that can be raised against it, it at least seems more fair and balanced than polygyny. Moreover, true polygamy encourages role reversals and thereby creates an experiential basis for one spouse's understanding of the other's jealousy of as well as love for others.

The last objection that many raise to polygamy is its impracticality. Even if we concede its divine origins, polygamy seems doomed to flounder on human jealousy, fear of rejection, envy, egocentricity, exhaustion — not to mention such mundane constraints as time and money. The conflict between Sarah and Hagar illustrates this problem well. This last and simplest objection may be the best. For most of us, one marriage is challenging enough. We live in a day and age when the prospects of multiple marriages is mind-boggling and, frankly, distasteful. However, the fact that people continue to have affairs and divorces may demonstrate that simple monogamy is not adequate to deal with the complex psychology of human beings.

Perhaps the most our generation can learn from the polygamy experience of the early Mormons is to have humility and charity, to reserve judgment, to remain open-minded, especially about matters we consider settled, and to be ready to reexamine our own attitudes about gender, sex, and marriage and our own prejudices against the notion that sexuality and spirituality are closely connected. Perhaps, the single conclusion that can be distilled from the complex and often competing concerns raised in this chapter is, predictably, a paradoxical one: Though there are good reasons to disagree fundamentally with the concept of polygamy, to heartily disapprove of the marriage practices of Joseph Smith and the early Mormons, to be committed to monogamy as the best arrangement for the promotion of fidelity in marriage and the development of healthy and happy families, nevertheless we of the late twentieth century have no basis to assume a morally superior posture toward those who for one reason or another have sought, through conventional or nonconventional means, the resolution of the tensions created by our enigmatic psycho-sexual natures.

CHAPTER TWENTY-TWO

RENDING THE VEIL

Some time ago we heard from two independent sources that in the Provo Temple some women refused to veil their faces at the appropriate point in the ceremony. One source heard this incident reported during a ward council meeting. A visiting stake high councilman, apparently relaying directives, advised the ward leaders that, though it was not essential for women to veil their faces as part of the temple ritual, any woman refusing to do so should be referred to her bishop for disciplinary action on grounds of insubordination to priesthood authority.

This incident and the official response to it capsulize for us a painful dilemma associated with the temple ceremony. On the one hand, it underscores how the endowment can be interpreted to validate male domination and female subordination. Here in Mormonism's most sacred ritual, traditional images of the veiled woman, which many people connect with the oppression of secluded Muslim women, are presented along with promises of female deference to males. Recent changes have softened the covenants women make to men, but have not eliminated the subordination altogether, making discussion of this issue even more pertinent.

What emerges from these associations is a view of women as spiritual inferiors of men, a sense that women must depend and rely upon men for their salvation and exaltation in the kingdom of God. This view is fortified by the fact that admittance to the temple and discussions of the temple ceremony and symbols are under strict control of the church hierarchy, which discourages the development and dissemination of alternative interpretations of the endowment perhaps more favorable to women. Because of the apparent subordination of the female in the temple ritual, some women have come to feel that the endowment is a principal source of their disenfranchisement from full participation in important aspects of the church. More specifically, many of these women have singled out the face veil, worn as part of their ritual temple clothing, as the chief symbol of their second class citizenship in Mormon culture.

On the other hand, other Mormon women, while admitting the negative impact of the prevailing interpretation of the endowment, also assert that the temple has been an important part of their spiritual awakening and maturation. They have been instructed and even transformed by its rituals. Many of these women feel that, historically, the endowment provides the most important basis for the claim that women are entitled, equally with men, to the priesthood and all of its rights, powers, keys, and privileges.

For us, the quandary caused by these "negative" and "positive" attitudes toward the temple ceremony, especially the face veil, derives from the interpretation that is currently given to these symbols. We believe, however, that another approach to the temple ritual in general, and the symbol of the face veil in particular, might not only circumvent the prevailing, male-oriented traditions, yielding an interpretation more favorable to women, but that a fresh approach may well prove more spiritually sound and illuminating. What we propose to do in the balance of this chapter is to apply the principles of interpretation from chapter 2 to the face veil in order to show alternative ways this symbol can be approached.

Ideas that are not paradoxical tend to be sentimental, incomplete, and dogmatic. According to psychotherapist Scott Peck: "[I]f a concept is paradoxical, that itself should suggest that it smacks of integrity, that it gives off the ring of truth. Conversely, if a concept is not in the least paradoxical, you should be suspicious of it and suspect that it has failed to integrate some aspect of the whole" (1988, 238). The same can be said of symbols. Because symbolism expresses complex truths about the nature of reality, the most universal and ancient symbols seem always to encompass simultaneously a variety of conflicting ideas. As we have already seen, the serpent can represent either death or resurrection, Satan or Christ. It may also represent either a male god or a female goddess. When the serpent is in an upright position, it represents the phallus, and when it is coiled in a circle, it represents the womb. It also appears associated with the earth, the sun, the moon, with water, or, when it is winged, with the air. Because the world itself is comprised of opposites (its yin/yang quality reflected in the Book of

Mormon notion that all things are a compound in one), effective and enduring symbols express and illuminate this dualistic aspect of reality. Symbolist J. C. Cooper puts it this way: "Much of symbolism directly concerns the dramatic interplay and interaction of the opposing forces in the dualistic world of manifestation, their conflicting but also complementary and compensating characteristics, and their final union" (1987, 8).

As with all profound symbols, the face veil, worn as a headdress by women throughout the temple and used to cover the faces of women during a ritual prayer, reflects this dualism. The veil is a paradoxical symbol evoking both positive and negative associations. However, for our modern age the negative side dominates. Of the two major sources for this negative view, the most immediate is the Islamic custom that requires women to veil not only their faces but their whole bodies. In that culture women are subordinated to men in every possible way. (It should be noted, however, out of respect for this religious tradition that these extreme customs are the product of Islamic fundamentalism and are not observed by all adhering to the Muslim faith. Many devout Islamic women do not wear the face veil at all, but simply a covering on their heads. They would argue that men are also required to cover their heads and that both forms of head coverings are signs of honor. There is also a small feminist movement among some Muslim women, who are looking for ways to liberate women while remaining faithful to their traditions.)

Though the veiled Muslim woman is to moderns a strong image of the subordination and oppression of women, it is unlikely that Joseph Smith was influenced by this source when he introduced the veil for women in the temple. Therefore, it seems historically unwarranted to apply this connotation to the temple headdress for women, although in our modern world, many are hard pressed to quell a strong psychological and even religious aversion to this symbol.

A more likely source for Joseph Smith's use of the veil is the biblical passage where Paul argues that a woman ought to pray with her head covered since she is the glory of man, whereas the man ought to pray with his head uncovered, since he is the glory of God (1 Cor. 11:3–15). This scripture has been used historically to keep women under the power of men. For example, in a 1968 biblical commentary on this verse, several noted Catholic scholars conclude that God has ordained both a natural and religious hierarchy in which the "subordination of the woman should be recognized in her behavior and dress. The veil is a symbol of this subordination" (Brown, 270). Other scholars, however, have noted problems with this interpretation. While admitting that Paul does subordinate women to men, they have pointed out that he almost seems to give back with one hand what he takes with the other. Whereas Paul says first that "the man is not of the woman; but the woman of the man," he also makes the following equalizing statement: "Nevertheless neither is the man without the woman, neither the woman without the man in the Lord. For the woman is of the man, even so is the man also by the woman, but all things of God" (vv. 11–12). Moreover, the passage in 1 Corinthians 11 centers on a discussion of how women should be attired when they pray or prophesy, implying that women are praying and prophesying in public meetings, something which was not done in the Jewish synagogues. This indicates that Christians were granting women greater status than they had been allowed previously. The congruence of evidence both of equality and subordination of women in this passage has led some to conclude that although the apostle "accepted the traditional social view of the status of women, he rejected the traditional religious view," for Paul saw that all were made free in Jesus Christ (Gal. 3:28; Orr, 126).

If so, St. Paul's argument in Corinthians 11 then would be an appeal to abide by the dress customs of his day, so as not to disturb more than necessary those who were offended by Christianity's new and more favorable treatment of women. This argument coincides with a parallel passage in 1 Corinthians 10, where Paul admonishes the Corinthian saints to refrain from eating meat sacrificed to idols in order to avoid offending weaker saints or possible converts. For these same reasons, Paul may have recommended decorum in dress to women who are praying and prophesying.

History provides another piece to the puzzle. Though the married women of Paul's time did wear veils or coverings over their hair, this was not always true throughout the Old Testament period. Sometimes women wore head coverings, and other times they did not. This was also so for men (Buttrick, 747; Douglas, 324–25). Of course, in most modern Jewish worship, it is the men who are required to cover their heads. Such changes in custom strengthen the position of those who claim that Paul was not attempting to state a universal truth in 1 Corinthians 11, but was addressing a specific problem in view of prevailing customs.

Some Latter-day Saints may wonder if 1 Corinthians 11 could be alluding to an early Christian endowment-like ritual, records of which have been lost to us. But there are problems with this view. If Joseph Smith was relying on this passage as authority for the use of the face veil for women in temple worship, he did not follow it very closely. Paul says that it is a dishonor to God for a man to cover his head while praying. And yet in the Mormon endowment and prayer circle, the man's head is covered the whole time. Also nowhere in the Corinthians passage does Paul talk about a woman veiling her face; he talks only of her covering her head.

If Corinthians was not Joseph Smith's source for the face veil, what was? There is no reliable and conclusive evidence to answer this question. Joseph Smith may have been influenced by sources as divergent as magical practices, Old Testament traditions, or obscure folk customs. And, of course, there is the possibility that the face veil comes to us as a result of the revelation of God without secular or sacred precedent. But identifying Joseph Smith's sources of the face veil, although useful and important, is not what this chapter is about. Our chief purpose here is to explore the possible meanings which this symbol may have for Mormons.

One way to further this exploration is to examine other scriptural texts for indications of the use of the veil in ancient biblical cultures. There are only a few scriptural examples of a person with a veil-covered face; and each example shows a different way the veil can function symbolically.

Tamar, the daughter-in-law of Judah, covered herself with a shawl or veil and concealed her face in order to trick Judah into thinking that she was a prostitute (Gen. 38:14–19). However, another reference indicates that it must have been not chiefly the veil which signalled prostitution, but the setting in which Tamar put herself, since the same word used here for veil (*tsa'ivph*) is also used in Genesis 24:65 without any suggestion of prostitution. In Genesis 24:65 Rebekah covered herself with a veil when she first met Isaac. Her veil apparently served a bridal function, whereas in Tamar's case it concealed her identity. The woman in the Song of Solomon also wore a face veil. But the word for "veil" in this verse is translated from the word *tsammah*, which most likely connotes an ornamental and erotic purpose.

In the Bible, men are also sometimes depicted as veiling their faces. For example, King David covered his face when he mourned for his dead son, Absalom (2 Sam. 19:4). This passage does not specify what David used to cover his face. It could have been his hands, or a shawl, or a cloak. The gesture, though, suggests mourning in this context. At another time, David wept and veiled (*chapha*) his head, as did the people who were with him. This was a sign of his grief at being forced to leave Jerusalem (2 Sam. 15:30). The prophet Ezekiel was commanded to cover his face so he would not see the land as he left Jerusalem, possibly to symbolize the spiritual blindness of his people who soon would be forced to leave the city (Ezek. 12).

Perhaps the most illuminating account of a veiled or covered face in the scriptures is found in Exodus 34:33–35, where Moses veiled his face when he came down the mountain from the presence of God. Because Moses was so full of the glory or light of God, the people could not look directly upon his countenance. When Moses went back to talk to God, he removed the veil (*masveh*) again. In this story, God is also depicted as being veiled, only the divine veil is a cloud which masks God's glory. Exodus 34:4 states: "And the Lord descended in the cloud, and stood with him [Moses] there, and proclaimed the name of the Lord" (see also Ex. 16:10).

This last account of a veil image accords with the myths of other ancient cultures, where deities were often portrayed as hiding their "dazzling brightness behind a mask or veil, both to protect humans from injury because of their glory and also to 'see without being seen' " (de-Vries, 485). In some of these cultures, veils were associated with earth and fertility goddesses. For example in one complex section of the *Hymn to Demeter,* a poem dating from the seventh century B.C., the Greek goddess Demeter is depicted as being veiled while seated on a sheepskin (Athanassakis, 7). The symbols of the veil and the sheepskin are believed to have had ritual significance in the Eleusinian mystery cult, in which the demi-god Herakles figured prominently. A bas-relief on a vase depicting a veiled-Herakles sitting on a ram skin (Kerenyi, 56) corroborates the significance of the ritual use of the veil, for it is well attested in myth and art that Herakles was initiated in the Eleusinian mysteries to prepare him for his descent into the underworld as part of a heroic quest. In this ritual context, the veil, which is thrown over the head of the initiate, serves as a symbol of rebirth (deVries, 485).

A similar ritual usage of the veil is found in the Gilgamesh epic. Gilgamesh, a hero like Herakles, while engaged on a heroic quest to find the plant of life, encounters Siduri, a goddess of wisdom and the patroness of wine merchants. Gilgamesh, clad in a skin garment, approaches the veiled goddess to ask her how he may find his way to a boatman to ferry him across some great waters. Here again, the veil and the skins are associated with the hero's rite of passage (Gardner, 209; see also Langdon, 210–13).

Another example is found in *The Odyssey*, where the shipwrecked Odysseus is swimming naked in a treacherous sea in a desperate attempt to reach shore. The goddess Leucothoe comes to his rescue and gives him her veil to tie around his waist, thus empowering him to reach land safely. This entire scene is replete with rebirth imagery, suggesting that Odysseus has ritually passed into a new phase of life. In this instance, the veil, tied around the hero's waist, represents an umbilicus connecting him with the divine powers protecting him (Homer, Book 5, 2:333–55).

In these examples, the veil is connected, not with women as inferiors, but with the goddess as keeper of the gate or mystery which the initiate (often a man but sometimes a woman), either naked or skin-clad, must penetrate in order to obtain knowledge of a new or unseen world. The veil is also symbolically connected with the hymen (Walker 1988, 317) and as such represents the covering over the holy place, the inner sanctuary of the temple, which was anciently thought of as the body of the goddess into which the god or hero or priest/king had to enter to obtain the hidden wisdom or power.

In some myths, the hero's acquisition of what is hidden or unattainable can be accomplished only by his becoming invisible by means of a cap or veil. In the story of Perseus and Medusa, the gods give Perseus a magic cap to render him invisible and thereby give him power over the monster Medusa. Thus, caps and veils may function as keys of access to the spiritual world by enabling their wearers to enter dangerous, sacred, or forbidden places without being noticed or harmed (Walker 1983, 617).

The veil also emerges then as a symbol of invisibility, mystery, and hidden power. And here, too, is another instance of how a symbol can function in both positive and negative ways: invisibility as we have seen can bring great power and knowledge, but it can also prevent a person from being known or having any direct influence. The positive and negative aspects of being veiled or invisible are reflected in the word *reveal*, which can have opposing meanings, both derived from its Latin stem. It can mean to unveil or to veil again. Thus, the veil, like symbols in general, can reveal or conceal what is hidden.

In the worship of both the Greek goddess Athena and Egyptian goddess Isis, the veil appears not as a covering for the face, but in the form of a curtain to separate these divinities from their worshippers. As described by Plutarch, at a certain point in the rituals of these goddesses, the curtain was pulled back so that their images could be revealed: "In Sais, the statue of Athena, whom they believed to be Isis, bore the inscription: 'I am all that has been, and is, and shall be, and my robe [veil] no mortal has yet uncovered'" (Plutarch, 2:24–25).

Similar descriptions are found about the worship of the goddess Isis. According to one historian, "In his Eleventh Book Apuleius gives a very interesting description of the manner in which Isis was worshipped in Rome in the latter half of the second century A.D.... At day break on the day of the festival of the goddess the priest went into her temple, and threw open the doors, leaving nothing but white linen curtains across the doorway to screen the interior. When the courts were filled with people, these curtains were drawn, and the worshippers were permitted to gaze upon the image of the goddess" (Budge, 2:218).

In some mythologies, when the veil appeared in the form of a curtain, it was symbolic of "the universe which the goddess weaves" or "the world of manifestation woven by the Great Goddess" (Cooper, 185). It is significant that Athena, the Greek goddess of wisdom, was also the goddess of weaving. Her robe or *peplos* embroidered with mythological symbols was "carried like the sail of a galley in public procession" at the time of her festival (Liddell, 621). In the Christian apocryphal Book of James, the Virgin Mary is chosen by the priests of the temple to weave the veil of the temple from threads of blue, scarlet, and purple. It is while she is spinning the thread that the angel appears to tell her she will bear the son of God (Hennecke, 1:379–80).

But whether manifest as a curtain, or as a face covering, or even as girdle, the veil represents the boundary between the sacred and the profane. In myth and ritual, the veil signifies the threshold, which must be passed to gain life or esoteric knowledge. Sometimes the initiate wears the veil, as in the case of Herakles and Odysseus; and sometimes it is worn by the deity, as in the case of Demeter or Siduri. Anciently, the wearers of masks or veils were identified as gods and goddesses, "at least for the participation in the sacred drama or procession" (Walker 1983, 617).

The image of a god or goddess behind a veil or embroidered curtain brings us back to the more familiar symbols of the Israelite and Mormon temple veils. The Israelite's ancient tabernacle and later their temple contained several sets of veils which covered the entrances to the various sanctuaries within them. In fact the walls of the tabernacle built by Moses consisted of curtains or veils; and a special, embroidered veil hid the holy of holies (Douglas, 1231–33). In the Mormon temple, what is called "the veil of the temple" actually consists of a number of identically embroidered veils, usually set side by side.

Within the context of the endowment, the temple veil is symbolically connected with the embroidered undergarment. Both the veil and the garment contain similar ritual markings, suggesting that our physical bodies constitute the veil or boundary which separates us from the spiritual realm. Thus to be lifted out of the body is to be lifted beyond the veil into the spiritual world. This connection between the veil and the body is echoed by the New Testament writer of Hebrews, who connects the veil of the temple with the flesh of Christ. This writer explains that, under Jewish law, only the high priest could enter the holy of holies in order to make a blood offering for the people. He then goes on to say that this ritual foreshadowed the sacrifice of Christ, which altered our relationship with God. According to this writer, Jesus is our "Great High Priest." Because he was sacrificed on the altar of the world and passed beyond the veil of his mortal flesh into the true holy of holies of heaven, he has opened the way to God for all of us. To this end the Epistle states: "Having therefore, brethren [and sisters] boldness to enter into the holiest by the blood of Jesus, by a new and living way, which he hath consecrated for us through the veil, that is to say, his flesh" (10:19–20).

This verse also seems to refer to the tradition in the Gospels that at the time of Christ's death, the veil in the temple at Jerusalem was rent in two (Matt. 27:51), symbolizing the teaching that Christ parted the veil of mortality so that all could freely enter into eternal life and the presence of the Most High. The identification of Christ's body with the veil also emerges in the legend of how Christ's countenance was impressed in blood on Veronica's veil. According to tradition, she used the veil to wipe the face of Jesus as he ascended the hill of Calvary. An associated usage of the veil in Christian ritual can be seen in the custom of veiling the cross during the Easter season to commemorate the three days when Christ's body was in the tomb. This Christian custom parallels the Babylonian new year rites in which the shrine of Nabu was veiled in memory of his descent into the underworld (Langdon, 160).

Keeping all of these associations in mind, how can we interpret the image of the veiled woman in the Mormon temple? First, we should note that in none of the sources we have examined has the veil been used strictly as a symbol of female inferiority. In each of these contexts, the veil expresses complex and even conflicting meanings. The most important of these meanings is associated with the rite of passage and with rebirth.

In the Mormon temple ceremony, rebirth is a predominant theme. The initiates are first washed and cleansed as if from the blood of birth and then clad in coats of skin, represented by the white, priesthood undergarments. Like newborns they are given new names. Thus they are brought out of the world of the profane into the world of the sacred and are sent on a spiritual quest. They are told that their models in this pilgrimage are their spiritual progenitors, Adam and Eve. The purpose of their search is to obtain the mysteries of godliness and to eat of the fruit of the tree of life. To do this they must receive instruction from angels, pass certain tests, and finally approach the veil, where they will receive final empowerment from God. On this spiritual journey the initiates are given, piece by piece, sacred clothing. This clothing symbolizes the bestowal upon them of grace, power, spirit, knowledge — in other words, it symbolizes the priesthood of God — that allows them to bring their quest to fruition.

It is important to note in this regard that from the undergarment to the outer robes, the only ritually significant difference between the temple clothing of men and women is the head covering. The men wear caps and the women wear veils. In our view this difference does not mean that women are inferior, but it may mean that the priesthood as vested in women has some manifestations and functions which distinguish it from those associated with the priesthood as vested in men. In other words, the different head coverings signify that priesthood has a female as well as a male modality. However, the differences overall in the priesthood robes of men and women, and by implication the priesthood functions of men and women, are few when compared to their similarities.

Furthermore, although the cap and the veil may symbolize subtle differences in priesthood, they also accomplish the same ritual function within the context of the endowment because they signify the crowns of glory, placed upon the initiates as symbolic of their anticipated status as kings and queens and priests and priestesses.

So, why is it the *woman* instead of the man who must wear the veil in the temple? One reason is that, in the scriptures, the woman frequently appears as a symbol for Israel, for the Christian church, for the world, and for the earth — each separated from God by a veil. When she stands as the symbol of God's people, the woman is also called the wife of God or the bride of Christ, which brings to mind the image of the bridal veil. In fact the gnostic Gospel of Philip calls the holy of holies the "bridal chamber"; it is entered by going through a veil. But the "bride of God" is not merely the earthly church. She is also a heavenly goddess. For this reason, the woman, in the temple ceremony, represents what is on both sides of the veil: the visible world, including all the people of the earth who are covered by a veil, and the invisible world, including the realm of hidden divinities and hidden power beyond the veil. Men too function as symbols in the temple. They also represent both humanity and divinity.

Although it is true that in ritual one person can play many roles, our culture has assigned symbolic roles to males and females which often link men with divinity and women with humanity. The recurrent use in our culture of the female as the symbol of the lower or material world and of the male as representation of the higher or spiritual world has reinforced the notion that women are inferior (Reuther 1983, 80). Though women have more often been connected with the lower realm, as indicated by Reuther, there have been notable exceptions, most likely influenced by images of the Virgin Mary as a female divine. Dante's Beatrice and Goethe's "eternal feminine" fall into this latter category. Romanticism's idealization of women also followed this tradition.

The connection of women with the lower realm has happened in large part because our Western religious tradition has been virtually stripped of all imagery of a female divinity. The Heavenly Mother or Goddess is missing. This is true in Mormonism as well as other Christian religions. We are so conditioned by her absence that even in the temple it is difficult to see how the woman also reflects an image of the divine. That is why we must stress that the veiled woman in the endowment represents the Goddess, the Heavenly Bride, who is hidden and who must yet be revealed. What the temple has been teaching us for years is what many feminists have been recently saying: It is the woman's identity and power which must yet to be unveiled in this dispensation.

But why does the woman veil her face in the prayer circle? To answer this question we must recall that the temple prayer ritual, like all prayer, is the means by which a person encounters God. In other words, in prayer an individual or a group approaches the veil to knock, ask, and seek what is hidden. In the prayer circle the veiled woman represents Israel, the church, the world, the earth, Eve, as well as the whole group of men and women in the prayer circle. Each of those in the circle is separated from God by the veil, but each is invited to pursue the spiritual journey to the veil, where the mysteries of God will be revealed. At the same time the woman represents the hidden divinity behind the veil, who, when the prayer is over, will unveil her face, so that all may look directly upon the divine glory.

But is it not demeaning for women to wear the veil, since it implies that they cannot view God directly while men can? This view of the veil does not hold up scripturally or symbolically. We are told that no man (or woman presumably) can see God and live unless they have been transformed by the spirit. Moreover, when men and women actually approach and pass through the temple veil or curtain, they enter with their faces exposed. If the face veil meant that women could not view God directly, then they would be veiled at the point of entrance into the celestial presence. Furthermore, as we have seen in our examination of veil imagery, what is veiled or hidden is not inferior but superior to what is unveiled: the divine presence, the sacred place, the holy of holies, the celestial world.

Yet, the scriptures talk about a veil of darkness or unbelief which covers the people. Here is the paradoxical aspect of the symbol. But we must remember that this veil covers all people, not just women. And, too, the veil of darkness has its positive meaning. It is a symbol of protection, the cloak of Christ's charity or mercy that protects us in this probationary state from the brightness of God's glory — which would destroy us — until we can be transformed to endure God's presence. Thus, the veil of Christ's charity covers a multitude of sins. In his mythic novel *Till We Have Faces*, C. S. Lewis uses the veil image in a similar way; the veil hides our sin, our ugliness, our facelessness. We cannot unveil the face of God until we first have faces ourselves. Then we will see as we are seen.

In the temple the association of the veil with Christ's sacrifice for us is profound and unmistakable. Both men and women embrace God through the veil before entering the celestial room. This symbolizes that our contact with God is made possible through Jesus Christ, whose body is represented by the veil. The marks in the veil represent his wounds, suggesting that our way to God is through Christ's sacrifice. Before God accepts us into the glorified presence, God feels to see if we have received the wounds of Christ in our bodies. Only after we have ritually received the imputation of Christ's crucifixion are we empowered to enter the most sacred place. Thus, the veil, the caps, the embroidered garments—the veil of the temple itself—are symbols not of inferiority, but of rebirth and initiation made possible through the atoning blood of Christ. By his sacrificial act, Christ the Bridegroom rent the veil, parted it, and opened the way into the most sacred place for all—male and female alike. For in Christ Jesus are all made free.

But who has dared to enter freely into the holy place? Or to look upon the bare equality of the heavens? It has been easier for us, we fear, to retreat into the comfortable confines of our darkness than to open ourselves to new possibilities. It has seemed more respectable to keep our symbols secret than to understand what they mean. For our part, we believe that the purpose of the temple is to enlighten and empower us to part the veil and see as we are seen and know as we are known. Though we cannot part the veil for ourselves, we can stand at the door and knock, with receptive hearts, waiting for God to open. But, as St. Paul observed, unbelief can keep us from seeing; for "the veil is upon their heart. Nevertheless," he promises, "when [they] shall turn to the Lord, the veil shall be taken away. Now the Lord is that Spirit: and where the Spirit of the Lord is, there is liberty. But we all, with open [unveiled] face beholding as in a glass the glory of the Lord, are changed into the same image from glory to glory, even as by the Spirit of the Lord" (2 Cor. 3:15–18).

Because we are not taught to read, reinterpret, and revitalize our religious symbols, we are in danger of losing them. We do not wish to lose the richness of any of our symbols, particularly the face veil. And yet, neither do we wish to see it used to justify the subordination of women. We frankly doubt that our complex interpretation of the veil will become generally accepted in the church. It is more likely that the veil will continue to be perceived and presented as a negative image for women and as justification for their continued disenfranchisement.

So because the face veil has become a symbol of oppression and subordination of women in our age, we wish it were possible to rend the veil in two and on the pieces write a "title of liberty" in memory of all those whose faces have been hidden and hearts broken behind a veil of spiritual alienation and oppression. We wish it were possible to write on it in memory of our Mother, the Goddess; in memory of our Father, Jesus Christ; in memory of the gospel which calls us out of bondage and fear, and sin to mourn with those that mourn, to comfort those that stand in need of comfort, and to bear one another's burdens that they may be light, until that day when with open faces we shall look upon the unveiled faces of the Most High.

CHAPTER TWENTY-THREE

THE MORMON ENDOWMENT

The Mormon temple endowment is a secret ritual. Those of us who have been endowed take a covenant of secrecy as part of the ceremony. For people who take it seriously, this covenant presents a formidable obstacle to any public analysis or discussion of the endowment. This problem, we feel, must be addressed first.

The covenant of secrecy is quite specific. In making it, we do not promise to avoid discussion or study of the ceremony. We promise only that we will not reveal the specific endowment acts, which Brigham Young in a public discourse indentified as "the key words, the signs and tokens, pertaining to the Holy Priesthood" (JD 2:31).

In our view the covenant of secrecy was meant to prohibit the unofficial administration of the endowment to the uninitiated rather than to prevent discussions of the ceremony. We find support for our view in the scriptures, which are public but contain much that is presented in the temple drama. And of course the ceremony itself was not only published in the early part of this century as part of the Congressional Record but has for some time been available in various forms through non-Mormon sources.

Nevertheless the covenant of secrecy is important to us, and we wish to abide by it and to honor as much as possible the tradition that forbids the public airing of descriptions of the endowment rituals or of the specific language of the ceremony. On the other hand, we also wish to defend temple worship against accusations that the endowment is merely a hodgepodge of rituals adapted from masonry and ceremonial magic, and, therefore, either meaningless or anti-Christian. And we wish to demonstrate to the growing number of Latter-day Saints confused or put off by the ritual that it has more than mere social significance — that it should be considered, in fact, a genuine Christian sacrament.

In this chapter we do not attempt to chronicle the history of the
endowment or to ascertain the meaning it may have had for earlier
generations of Mormons. Rather we wish to explore the meaning the
endowment has for us, a meaning we derive from the ceremony itself.
We propose to adduce its meaning from its symbols and structure. In
this process, we will be subjective. We feel comfortable with this approach because we are not attempting to create either a creed, a historical narrative, or an objective description. We wish only to set forth an
interpretation that some may find helpful, fruitful, or useful in arriv-
ing at a better interpretation for themselves.

This is risky business. We must, on the one hand, avoid presenting
details that would amount to a violation of our personal covenants and
that would offend those who, like us, take them seriously. On the other
hand, we wish to avoid, for those not exposed to the ceremony, a discussion so shot through with circumlocutions as to render it meaningless. If we do not succeed, we hope we will not be chastised for trying.
Our intention is not to write an expose for the curious, but to render
an interpretation for the bewildered.

We will begin with four general observations. First, the validity
and vitality of the endowment is, in our view, unrelated to its historical
origins. Perhaps the ceremony is ancient, going back to Solomon. Perhaps it was invented out of whole cloth by Joseph Smith and Brigham
Young. Perhaps it adapts masonic rites known and practiced in New
York in the early nineteenth century, rites whose beginning can be traced
back no further than the Enlightenment and no farther away than Europe. It doesn't matter. The historical origins of the endowment are
irrelevant to its ritual importance and its efficacy as an ordinance of
the restored gospel. Many if not all of the ordinances of the gospel existed in a secular or even profane form before they were adopted as
sacraments of the Christian church. This position may be surprising or
confusing to some, but a few examples may make our point clear.

The breaking of bread and drinking of wine as a covenant meal
were known prior to the time Christ established the eucharist. The washing of feet was a common hospitality ritual of the region long before
Christ invested the act with sacral significance. Baptism, too, was taken
from known practices and given new meaning within the context of the
gospel of Jesus Christ. The concept of making the profane sacred and
renewing the old is the centerpiece of the Christian promise of justification, sanctification, resurrection, and glorification. It should not, therefore, surprise us to learn that Christ could take a commonplace act or

event and invest it with new meaning and spirituality and thereby create an ordinance or sacrament of the church.

This process, we believe, occurred with the endowment. Either an old or a new collection of rituals was presented to the Latter-day Saints as something to help them transcend their own world and enter into a new and sacred world — a world of ritual whose principal purpose is to help reunite us with God. Even if the endowment ritual cannot be traced to ancient antecedents, its meaning can. The forms may be new, but the temple ordinances serve ancient sacralizing functions which appear in one mystery religion after another back into antiquity.

What can blind us to the mythic connection between temple worship and earlier mystery religions is the Mormon tradition that all the old "true" ordinances have been restored by revelation and are now precisely as they were in ancient times. In other words, we assume that the forms of the ordinances never change and that there is no connection between ordinances that serve the same function but take different forms. While it is undoubtedly true that the ordinance of baptism has remained the same, this is probably not so with the endowment, which may contain smatterings of ancient formulae, but which must also contain modern elements if modern Mormons are to understand it. With the endowment it is more likely that the form is new, but the function is old.

Our second general observation is that the word "endowment" is not derived from the word endow, meaning a gift or bequest. It is related to the word "endue" used in the King James version of Luke 24:49. "Endue" comes from the Latin "inducere," which is connected to the Old French "enduire," meaning to lead into or draw into. At the time the Bible was translated in 1611, "endue" meant to clothe and instruct or to invest a person with honors and dignities, with a power or quality or spiritual gift. The word "endowment," derived as it is from "endue," is apt in Mormon usage, for it refers to the ritual investiture of men and women with honors, dignities, and spiritual gifts, by enrobing them in priestly vestments, and inducting them into sacramental mysteries that are intended to give them access to greater light and knowledge.

Our third observation is that the endowment was, in our view, intended to restore to us the keys of the fullness of the priesthood. The church teaches that Joseph Smith received the Melchizedek priesthood from Peter, James, and John. But certain scriptures (D&C 2; 84:33–44; 124:47) suggest that this was meant as a provisional grant of priesthood power, sufficient only to administer the ordinances of rebirth, to organize the church, and to build the temple. A fuller priesthood was to follow. This priesthood, unlike those previously restored, is not conferred by the laying on of hands. Rather, it is transmitted through the temple rituals in three stages. First, the powers or keys of the fulness of the priesthood are vested in individuals through the temple endowment (105:11; 128:11, 14). Second, the endowed are initiated into the holy order of God through an ordinance called the second anointing by which they "come to an innumerable company of angels, to the general assembly and church of Enoch and of the firstborn" (76:67). And third, the initiates receive the promise of joint-heirship with Christ by an oath and covenant pronounced by the Most High (84:35–38).

Our fourth and final general observation is that though some Mormons feel that the endowment is strange and alien, we believe that neither its symbolism nor its structure departs from the teachings of the gospel of Jesus Christ. The endowment is, in part, the realization of Jesus' promise of further spiritual gifts, honors, and dignities to those who desire a fuller spiritual life. In the endowment, we are given Christian symbols of priesthood and royalty, conducted through rites of passage, and presented with a number of cosmogonical, cosmological, soteriological, and eschatological touchstones for our spiritual journey back to God.

One of Joseph Smith's important theological contributions to Christianity was his reassertion that the process of accepting divine gifts involves the acceptance of the ordinances of the gospel as well. The words "order," "ordain," and "ordinance" are obviously related. They all come from the same root "ord-," which means to commence, order, arrange, or prepare. Ordinances are mechanisms by which individuals prepare to meet God. They are points of contact with the divine through which God creates new spiritual arrangements. As such, ordinances memorialize those moments when new spiritual horizons are opened to us.

The endowment constitutes a series of interrelated ordinances through which we ritually reenact the work done by Jesus Christ for the benefit of humanity. Where faith, repentance, baptism, and the gift of the Holy Ghost are intended to effect in us a spiritual rebirth, the endowment is intended to facilitate in us spiritual maturation as a prerequisite to union with God.

With these general observations in mind, let us now turn to the issue of the structure of the temple endowment. The Mormon temple ritual is set within the mythic structure of the creation account, in which Adam and Eve journey from an unspecified initiatory stage, through the creation stage, the garden stage, the profane or telestial stage, the sacral or terrestrial stage, and back to the celestial stage in which God dwells.

What renders the endowment ritual somewhat obscure for many Mormons is the confusion that prevails from the outset of the ceremony about the unities of time and place. Where are we? And when is this? The temple drama, of course, can be interpreted as representing the past, the present, and the future simultaneously. In other words, it can be seen to take place in a mythic or timeless state. But we think it is more fruitful to assume that the drama is taking place in a future, celestial state — a point where a new creation is about to be launched. What we adduce from this assumption is the proposition that eternal life does not go on forever and ever as we supposed and that repeated resurrections are possible for the same individual. We have had some preparation for this idea in the Doctrine and Covenants, where we are told that endless punishment does not go on forever. Endless punishment is just another way of saying God's punishment. It follows that if eternal punishment does not go on forever, then eternal life does not go on forever either — at least not in the usual way we think. Eternal life refers to God's life. And what is God's life? What is the mystery of godliness? It is apparently an everlasting cycle through which an individual passes, going from time to eternity and from eternity to time. Or perhaps a less confusing way to say it is that Adam and Eve and we, their children, will move from the celestial world through the paradise of Eden, the telestial and terrestrial worlds, and back to the celestial. Then if we wish we may repeat the process again, in another eternity so to speak.

Joseph Smith seemed to have had this cycle in mind when he stated: "Here, then, is life eternal — to know the only wise and true God; and you have got to learn how to be Gods yourselves, and to be kings and priests to God, the same as all Gods have done before you, namely, by going from one small degree to another, and from a small capacity to a great one; from grace to grace, from exaltation to exaltation, until you attain the resurrection of the dead, and are able to dwell in everlasting burnings, and to sit in glory, as do those who sit enthroned in everlasting power" (TPJS, 246–47). What did Joseph Smith mean by the phrase "going from exaltation to exaltation until you attain the resurrection of the dead"? In Mormon theology, "exaltation" includes the resurrection of the dead. One cannot be exalted and remain unresurrected. We interpret this to mean that mortals are to progress from exaltation to exaltation (which includes repeated resurrections) until they obtain the power to resurrect the dead. It is in this way that we can eventually become like Jesus Christ.

The temple ritual, we believe, is rooted in this theology. Thus, at the outset of the endowment, initiates find themselves in the celestial kingdom as resurrected priests and priestesses, kings and queens, waiting to participate in a new creation. For this reason, the creation account of scripture becomes an important focus of the temple endowment.

Let us here observe, first, that we do not believe the creation story was intended to be taken literally. It was not intended to give us an accurate picture of how the world was brought out of chaos into nature. It is not meant to serve as an explanation of how the sun, moon, and stars were made, or how the globe was formed with the land thrusting up through the waters, the rains coming, and the rivers flowing. It was not meant to provide us with a scientific model of how plants, animals, and humans appeared on earth in their evolutionary order. Any resemblance between the creation account and modern scientific ideas of the creation is strictly coincidental.

Our Mormon creation accounts are probably sanitized versions of a story that was in its original form very like the ancient Sumerian or Mesopotamian creation myths. Thus, when the Genesis account tells us that God created heaven and earth, it does not speak from a scientific perspective, but a mythic one. As such, this phrase was probably meant to convey the idea that, in the beginning, God (a primordial deity like the god Chaos) created Heaven (Father Sky) and Earth (the Earth Goddess). The account then sets forth an antique pattern that communicates the notion that, through the union of these two deities, order and life was produced on earth. As the myth unfolds the sky god becomes associated with day and the sun, while the earth goddess becomes associated with night and the moon. The gathering together of waters in the heaven and in the earth represents the waters of life, the reproductive powers of these deities. The rain on the earth is an insemination symbol. And the earth bringing forth plants and animals is but a version — abstracted and sanitized, perhaps by later revisionists — of the old story of the earth goddess bringing forth life.

In the endowment drama of Adam and Eve, the role of Christ is central. After Adam and Eve partake of the fruit, they are told that all is not lost. God will not leave them comfortless. A savior will be provided who will assume the responsibility for their transgressions and the sins and frailities of their children. As a guarantee of this promise,

God provides coats of skin for Adam and Eve to solve the problem of their nakedness, which stands for their spiritual powerlessness. These skins represent the power of Christ to redeem them with an outpouring of his grace sufficient to protect them from the demands of justice urged by Satan.

Through the ordinances of the temple, initiates receive the greater light and knowledge about our purpose on earth. They also receive the full keys of the priesthood, by which they are empowered to come into contact with God through the mediation of Christ, whose symbols and signs are prominently featured throughout the ritual.

Many Mormons, upon first attending the temple, are surprised by the symbolic nature of the endowment rites. This is due, in part, to the fact that in Mormonism, ordinary church worship is as symbol-poor as temple worship is symbol-rich. Many are not prepared for this contrast, a problem exacerbated by the reluctance of members to discuss the endowment, even with the initiated. In what follows, we will set forth our own interpretation of certain of the symbols and types which Mormons encounter in our temple worship in an attempt to share the meanings we glean from our experience.

Symbols of Regeneration. We have mentioned before that the symbols of regeneration include faith, repentance, baptism, and confirmation. These, the first principles and ordinances of the gospel, are the ordinances of rebirth. Faith is a form of spiritual begetting. Repentance or a change of heart is our response to God's spirit and constitutes the embryonic recreation of a new, spiritual being. Baptism is birth out of the amniotic waters of an old life. And to receive the Holy Ghost is to take the breath of life, the spirit of God. The initiatory ordinances of the temple are a continuation of this rebirth imagery, even though they are administered to us years after we are baptized and confirmed. These ordinances symbolize our cleansing as spiritual newborns, by which vestiges of the old, profane world are washed away and all our bodily functions are rededicated to sacred purposes. Once ritually washed, we are, like newborns, anointed. The ritual unguent used for this purpose is olive oil, an important religious symbol, not only in the Mormon tradition, but in others as well. Joseph Smith referred to one of his revelations, Section 88 of the Doctrine and Covenants, as the "olive leaf" because it had been "plucked from the tree of paradise." Apparently, in his mind, the tree of life was an olive tree. This notion is echoed in the Book of Mormon account of Lehi's dream, where the tree of life is said to represent Jesus Christ, as the incarnate love of God (1 Ne. 11:8–28).

Extending this metaphor, the olive, as the fruit of the tree of life, represents Christ's spiritual gifts to humanity. And olive oil, as the essence of the olive, represents the spirit, power, or glory of God. This usage is enhanced by the fact that olive oil was an economic staple of the Near East and served as a cleansing agent, a preservative, a fuel for lamps, a condiment, an aid to cooking, and a fragrant ointment to condition and protect the skin. The New Testament contains the parable of the ten virgins of whom five had extra reserves of oil for their lamps as they awaited the coming of the bridegroom (Matt. 25:1–13). The Doctrine and Covenants clarifies that the oil in this parable is a metaphor for the holy spirit (D&C 45:56–57). This symbol resonates in the word "Gethsemane," which means "oil press," suggesting that Christ's atoning sacrifice consisted of a loss or withdrawal of his spirit or glory, a teaching asserted explicitly in D&C 19:20, where we are admonished to repent lest we suffer in a lesser degree the sufferings of Christ in Gethsemane, which sufferings "in the smallest, yea, even in the least degree you have tasted at the time I withdrew my Spirit."

Given these associations, it is not surprising that olive oil should be employed in the humblest and most common of all gospel ordinances, the administration to the sick, as well as in the most sacred and most guarded ordinances of the temple. In the blessing of the sick, the anointing of the head with olive oil signifies the outpouring of the spirit of God sought by the faithful in order to restore health or well-being. In the temple the initiatory anointings signify the outpouring of the power and blessing of God upon the individual. The anointing is an act of dedication and consecration. The use of oil in the initiatory ordinances not only signifies the bestowal of spiritual gifts granted as a help and protection, but it also establishes the individual as a candidate for the fullness of the priesthood, the full compliment of spiritual gifts and powers attainable by mortals.

Another symbol of regeneration is the act of naming. In the temple, we encounter the symbology of sacred names, which are not meant to function as names in the ordinary sense but are keywords. They point to differing spheres of being through which Christ and Adam and Eve passed and through which we too must pass if we are to be like them. The first keyword suggests that all of us came from a more ancient sphere of being, where we had names and identities and lives now forgotten, whose memory we must retrieve. From this other place, we, like Adam and Eve before us, come to earth. Here, travelling under our present names, we are isolated and must be reconnected with the other spheres of being. Like Adam and Eve we must pass into a kingdom prepared for us. In this journey we will be guided by Jesus Christ, in his role as the Son. We take his name as our name. Thus the interdependence of past, present, and future is symbolized by names that represent the different guises which a single soul assumes on this, the hero's or the heroine's journey. The fact that the names are given to us by Christ signifies that he is our initiator. The most sacred name is the name of God. It is not given in the temple, although initiates are taught how to ask for this name. It is not given because only Christ is to give it.

Sacred Clothing. In the temple, we are robed in sacred clothing, also symbolic of regeneration. This clothing serves two additional symbolic functions. First, it ritually confirms to us that righteousness must be imputed to us. We do not enter God's presence dressed in our self-righteousness, but clothed in the power and goodness of God. Second, the temple clothing represents the roles or personas we assume during the temple drama.

In the Garden, we are told, Adam and Eve were naked and unashamed until they partook of the forbidden fruit. Upon discovering their shame, God made coats of skin for a covering for them. This covering is now represented by a white undergarment. It symbolizes the skin of an animal slain in similitude of the sacrifice of Jesus Christ. The skin, then, represents the messianic priesthood of Jesus, the power that created and recreated the world. It is the symbol of his atonement. For this reason, it is embroidered with marks that represent the wounds, inflicted during his crucifixion, upon his palms, his wrists, his feet, and his side. By assuming the sacrificial skin thus adorned, we take upon ourselves the image of Christ and ritually assume his suffering and death as our own. And with Paul we can say that we bear the marks of the Lord's crucifixion on our bodies (Gal. 6:17). This is the mantle of God's love. It is the cloak of his charity. It is the covering of his righteousness. It reminds us daily that Jesus took our sins upon him as if they were filthy rags and, in return, he stands ready to clothe us in his own holiness. The garment is the symbol that Christ died as if he were as sinful as we so that we might live as if we were as sinless as he. We wear this symbol in secret to reaffirm that the grace of God is not to be used to obtain public admiration or social status.

In addition to the garment, as temple initiates we are introduced to other sacred clothing: the robes of the priesthood. It is through the process of ritual investiture that the endowed assume the roles and personas of Adam and Eve and of Jesus Christ. It is because of our identity with and connection to these beings that we become entitled to inherit eternal life and enter into the presence of God. The design of the robe is unusual because it can be draped over one shoulder or the other, allowing for the display of different symbols in the garment.

Geometric Shapes. In the temple, we encounter the symbols of the square, the compass, the arc, and the rule (or continuum). These symbols are never totally explained in the temple, although some interpretive suggestions are provided. It is important to understand that these symbols, though very possibly borrowed from Masonry, have a Christian meaning within the context of the temple ceremony.

In our view, the square signifies the justice of God in bringing order out of chaos. It is a symbol of creative power and of the primal organizing principle and is associated with Aaron's rod. The shape of the square suggests uprightness, law, order, strictness, exactness. In ancient Egypt the square was thought to be an abstract representation of Osiris's judgment seat, where he sat during the ritual weighing of the heart. This mark is preeminent during the lesser priesthood ceremonies, indicating that the primary purpose of this priesthood is to reveal the law of God, to create and maintain order, to make distinctions and to do justice.

The compass represents Christ's mercy—his purpose to bring not merely order out of chaos but also perfection, represented by the circle made by the compass. Medieval alchemists pondered the problem of turning the square into a circle and hit upon using the square as a compass to do this. By answering the demands of his own justice and taking upon himself responsibility for the transgressions of his people, God frees us from the exacting demands of divine justice. He turns the square into a compass. Thus, the perpendicular lines of the square, which suggest that mortals are at variance with God, become the legs of the compass, one active and one passive, working together to circumscribe all into one. The compass then represents the male and female divinities with their fullness of spiritual gifts and powers working in concert to produce the circle, the perfection that embraces everything in divine love. The compass serves additionally as a symbol of the fullness of the priesthood, which unlike the Aaronic priesthood, is exercised by males and females together. The square and compass are associated with the human breast in order to reinforce the teaching that the purpose of priesthood, both lesser and greater, is to nurture.

The arc no longer appears to be an arc, probably due to imprecision in its rendering over the years. Now it is represented as a straight, horizontal line or rule. In our view, the arc has a symbolic function similar to the arc of the rainbow in the story of Noah. It represents the power of Christ to break the circle of his perfection in order to lay down his life and take it up again. It represents the power of endless lives, the power to enter and to exit the body, to go from one resurrection and exaltation to another. It was believed by some early Mormons that our spirits entered and exited our bodies through the navel. Thus, the navel is associated with the power to enter and exit mortality. Because the navel is the aperture of nourishment for the body in its fetal stage, its associated symbol, the arc, reminds us that we humans are continually nourished by God — by the very body and blood of Jesus — through the medium of his incarnation, death, and resurrection.

The rule or continuum is associated with the knee. The knee in Mesopotamia and in other places was a euphemism for the genitals. The idea that every knee shall bow and every tongue confess that Jesus is the Christ is an apt statement to associate with the knee mark. The meaning is that the procreative powers rest in Christ, the central creative force of the universe. And that these powers in us are derived from him.

In sum, the square, compass, arc, and rule represent Christ's divine attributes: (1) justice, law, order, creation, distinction, and the necessary polarities comprising the paradoxes of the universe; (2) mercy, love, forgiveness, acceptance, union, transcendence, and perfection; (3) the power of God over mortality and immortality, over temporal life and eternal life; and (4) eternal progression, the continuation of the seed forever.

Other Signs and Symbols. In the temple, we also encounter certain symbols representing the four principle elements of the sacrifice of Jesus Christ: First, Christ ascended up on high. Second, Christ descended below all things. Third, Christ was pierced for the transgressions of the children of Adam and Eve, thus taking upon himself responsibility for their mortality and making possible their resurrection from the dead. And fourth, Christ was pierced for our individual sins, thus assuming the full weight of the sins of the world in order to redeem each person. This sacrifice lies at the heart of God's fellowship with us. It is the symbolic fulfillment of the promise made by God to Adam and Eve to provide a Savior for them and us.

Other symbols or signs are connected with Christ's role as the initiate's prophet, priest, king, and friend. A rod in the right hand, related to the symbol of the square as a sign of power over the elements, signifies that the fundamental attribute of God in the temporal world is justice. In a world where entropy reigns, the ordering power is the prime desiderata. An orb in the right hand represents the white stone or seer stone or Urim and Thummim into which we may look to obtain a higher vision for ourselves and others. Also an orb can be associated with the bitter cup Jesus drank to give us access to this better world. A scepter resting near the bowels (the seat of mercy) usually signifies a two-edged sword with which the sovereign may take life or raise an individual to knighthood. The sword near the bowels of the monarch indicates that if mercy is to flow unto others, we as kings and queens must be willing to lay down our lives for others.

The final representation of a dove in flight recalls an outpouring of glory or power, which transfigures, translates, resurrects, and glorifies. It represents the blessing of immortality and eternal life, the calling and election made sure as symbolized by the descending pillar of flame or tongue of fire of the pentecost. It represents the reception by us of the hand of God, laid upon the head to emblazon thereon the name of God. It represents Jacob's ladder, upon which eternal beings must ascend and descend from eternity into time and from time into eternity in a never-ending cycle in imitation of God.

Prior to April 1990, Mormons encountered in the temple certain symbols of justice and propitiation, called penalties. Some Mormons, particularly in the nineteenth century, assumed that in reenacting these rituals Mormons were agreeing to allow their lives to be taken if ever they violated any of their temple or other covenants. We assume that because this tended to be offensive to many modern Mormons, the penalties were removed. In our view, however, to the extent these rituals were interpreted to reinforce the concept of self-atonement, they were misunderstood.

There is no question that justice has a place in our religion and that the wages of sin is death. But, within the context of the temple ceremony, it is to be remembered that the death threatened is assumed not by the initiate but first by Adam and Eve and then, ultimately and infinitely, by Jesus Christ in whose persona each initiate stands. The ritual punishment seemed to mean that justice cannot be robbed and that punishment follows sin, but such a punishment may be suffered by a divinity who voluntarily assumes responsibility for us and thus becomes the author and finisher of our salvation. Thus, the penalties intended for us are suffered by God. The penalty ordinances were representations of the ancient blows of death suggested in the earliest Hebrew texts treating the Abrahamic sacrifice and are associated with covenant making. Abraham slit the sacrificial animal in three places, and God passed through the parts as a pillar of fire, saying in effect, "Abraham, I promise to bless you and I will keep my promise, even if it means that what happened to this animal must happen to me." And of course it did. We think the ancient Japanese ritual of seppuku is related to these blows of death, which constitute a revelation about the nature of the godhead — resurrected and glorified beings who have the power within themselves, as Christ declared, to take up their bodies and lay them down again as required for the benefit of their posterity.

The Veil. In the temple, we are also introduced to the symbol of the veil presented in two forms: a curtain and a face veil. At the veil or curtain of the temple, we encounter symbols that remind us of the seven wounds of Jesus: one in each palm, one in each wrist, one in each foot, and one in his side. The number seven is associated with God's wounds, which are also symbolized by the seven stars in the big dipper, the seven openings in the human head, and the seven stars in the Pleiades. The veil represents Christ himself. Its presence reminds us that access to the eternal world is through his sacrifice. In wearing the garment, we are actually covered with a veil, who is Christ.

At the veil we are not required to impress God with our knowledge of doctrine, or our worthiness, but with our allegiance to Christ. For if we are wounded with his wounds, we have received his grace and may enter into heaven as if we were Christ. The Lord is the keeper at the veil. It is he who draws us through into the celestial world, the place of first creation, the place of final maturation. This is where all things begin and end. We have come full circle and have greater light and knowledge as a result of our experience. We understand that eternal life is one eternal round.

By way of conclusion, we wish to make three points. First, our discussion is not intended to be exhaustive. We believe there is much about the temple which should be explored and analyzed: architectural symbols, the symbolic import of the movement of the initiates through the temple rooms along different points of the compass, the various arrangements which prayer circles may assume, the geometric position of certain physical symbols, the symbolic meaning reflected in the order for laying the temple cornerstones, and the significance of the entire temple as a calendar of mythic events. This catalog is far from complete.

Second, we do not want anyone to think that we are advancing our interpretations in a dogmatic or credal way. We wish only to show that the temple is more than a potpourri of plagiarized tropes. It has a meaning relating directly to Jesus Christ as God and Savior. Whether the true meaning of the temple resembles the interpretations we have advanced here is something each person must answer for himself or herself. And that is the only way it can be. It is the way of myth and symbol and continuing revelation.

Finally, although our interpretation is debatable, we think that Joseph Smith considered the temple endowment to be his crowning contribution to the church. The endowment is his greatest sermon, a sermon in symbols. The ceremony of the temple was given to lead step by step through rituals and robings to the point where endowed men and women might stand prepared to enter into the most sacred of all associations with God. This association is the *hieros gamos*, the divine marriage, where the creation and the creator are made one.

Union with the Most High is the fulfillment of the promise of the endowment, the promise that we should become the friends of God, to be sealed to the sacred personages who have assumed the chief responsibility for our eternal life and joy, so that with them we might be one and hold in common the fullness of the godhead.

BIBLIOGRAPHY

Allen, James B. "One Man's Nauvoo: William Clayton's Experience in Mormon Illinois." *Journal of Mormon History* 6 (1979): 37–59.

Allred, Janice. "Toward a Mormon Concept of Original Sin." *Sunstone* 8 (May-June 1983): 13–18.

Andrus, Hyrum L. *God, Man, and the Universe.* Salt Lake City: Bookcraft, 1968.

_____ and Helen Mae Andrus, eds. *They Knew the Prophet.* Salt Lake City: Bookcraft, 1974.

Ashe, Geoffrey. *The Virgin.* London: Routledge and Kegan Paul, 1976.

Athanassakis, Apostolos N., ed. and trans. *Hymn To Demeter.* In *The Homeric Hymns*, 1–15. Baltimore: Johns Hopkins University Press, 1976.

Barth, Karl. *Church Dogmatics: A Selection.* Ed. and trans. G. W. Bromiley. New York: Harper & Row, 1961.

Bethge, Hens Gebbard and Orval S. Wintermute, trans. "On the Origin of the World." In *The Nag Hammadi Library in English*, 161–79. Ed. James M. Robinson. San Francisco: Harper & Row, 1977.

Blair, Lawrence. *Rhythms of Vision: The Changing Patterns of Belief.* New York: Warner Books, 1975.

Bleeker, C. J. "Isis as Savior Goddess." In *The Saviour God: Comparative Studies in the Concept of Salvation Presented to Edwin Oliver James*, 1–16. Ed. S. G. F. Brandon. New York: Barnes & Noble, 1963.

Brock, Rita Nakashima. "The Feminist Redemption of Christ." In *Christian Feminism: Vision of a New Humanity*, 55–74. Ed. Judith L. Weidman. San Francisco: Harper & Row, 1984.

Brown, Raymond E., Joseph A. Fitzmyer, and Roland E. Murphy, eds. *The Jerome Biblical Commentary.* Englewood Hills, NJ: Prentice-Hall, 1968.

Budge, E. A. Wallis. *The Gods of the Egyptians or Studies in Egyptian Mythology.* Vol. 2. London: Methuen & Co., 1904.

Buerger, David John. " 'The Fulness of the Priesthood': The Second Anointing in Latter-day Theology and Practice." *Dialogue: A Journal of Mormon Thought* 16 (Spring 1983): 10–44.

_____ . "The Development of the Mormon Temple Endowment Ceremony." *Dialogue: A Journal of Mormon Thought* 20 (Winter 1987): 33–76.

Bullock, Alan, Stephen Trombley, and Bruce Eddie, eds. *The Harper Dictionary of Modern Thought*. Rev. ed. New York: Harper & Row Publishers, 1988.

Buttrick, George Arthur, ed. *Interpreter's Dictionary of the Bible*. Vol. 4. Nashville: Abingdon Press, 1962.

Bynum, Carolyn Walker. *Jesus as Mother: Studies in the Spirituality of the High Middle Ages*. Berkeley: University of California Press, 1982.

Campbell, Joseph. *The Masks of God: Primitive Mythology*. Vol. 1. New York: Penguin Books, 1976.

_____ , with Bill Moyers. *The Power of Myth*. Ed. Betty Sue Flowers. New York: Doubleday, 1988.

Cannon, George Q. "2 August 1883 remark." In Minutes of the School of the Prophets of 1883. Special Collections, Harold B. Lee Library, Brigham Young University, Provo, UT.

Collier, Fred, comp. *Unpublished Revelations of the Prophets and Presidents of the Church of Jesus Christ of Latter-day Saints*. Vol. 1. Salt Lake City: Collier's Publishing Co., 1979.

Concise Sacramentum Mundi. Ed. Karl Rahner. New York: Seaburg Press, 1975.

Cooper, J. C. *An Illustrated Encyclopedia of Traditional Symbols*. London: Thames and Hudson, 1987.

Corbin, Arthur L. *Corbin on Contracts*. St. Paul, MN: West Publishing, 1952.

Corpus Juris Secundum. St. Paul, MN: West Publishing, 1988.

Daly, Mary. *Beyond God the Father: Toward a Philosophy of Women's Liberation*. Boston: Beacon Press, 1973.

_____ . *Gyn/Ecology: The Metaethics of Radical Feminism*. Boston: Beacon, 1978.

_____ . "Why Speak About God?" In *Womanspirit Rising: A Feminist Reader in Religion*, 210–18. Eds. Carol P. Christ and Judith Plaskow. San Francisco: Harper & Row, 1979.

Dames, Michael. *The Silbury Treasure*. London: Thames & Hudson, 1976.

Day, Terence. "A Parent's Guide: Sex Education or Erotophobia?" *Sunstone* 12 (March 1988): 8–14.

Derr, Jill Mulvay. "Woman's Place in Brigham Young's World." *Brigham Young University Studies* 18 (Spring 1978): 377–95.

deVries, Ad. *Dictionary of Symbols and Imagery*. Amsterdam: North Holland Publishing Co., 1974.

Donne, John. *The Complete Poetry and Selected Prose of John Donne*. Ed. Charles M. Coffin. New York: Modern Library, 1952.

Douglas, J. D. *The New Bible Dictionary*. Grand Rapids, MI: North Holland, 1974.

Driver, Tom F. *Christ in a Changing World: Toward an Ethical Christology*. New York: Crossroad, 1981.

Dundes, Alan, ed. *Sacred Narrative: Readings in the Theory of Myth*. Berkeley: University of California Press, 1984.

Ehat, Andrew F. "Joseph Smith's Introduction of Temple Ordinances and the 1844 Mormon Succession Question." M.A. thesis, Brigham Young University, 1982.

Eiselen, Frederick Carl, Edwin Lewis, and David G. Downey, eds. *The Abingdon Bible Commentary*. New York: Abingdon Press, 1929.

Eliade, Mircea. *The Sacred and the Profane: The Nature of Religion*. Trans. Willard R. Trask. New York: Harcourt, Brace and Jovanovich, 1959.

Eliot, T. S. "Four Quartets" ("Little Gidding"). *The Complete Poems and Plays 1909-1950*, 117-45 (138-45). New York: Harcourt, Brace & World, Inc., 1971.

Engnell, Ivan. *Studies in Divine Kingship in the Ancient Near East*. Oxford: Basil Blackwell, 1967.

Ensley, Gerry L. and Bradd C. Hayes. "Letters to the Editor." *Sunstone* 8 (Nov.-Dec. 1983): 6-7, 42-43.

Evola, Julius. *The Metaphysics of Sex*. New York: Inner Traditions International, 1983.

Faulring, Scott H., ed. *An American Prophet's Record: The Diaries and Journals of Joseph Smith*. Salt Lake City: Signature Books in association with Smith Research Associates, 1987.

Fiorenza, Elizabeth Schussler. "Women in the Early Christian Movement." In *Womanspirit Rising: A Feminist Reader in Religion*, 84-92. Eds. Carol P. Christ and Judith Plaskow. San Francisco: Harper & Row, 1979a.

_____. "Feminist Spirituality, Christian Identity, and Catholic Vision." In *Womanspirit Rising: A Feminist Reader in Religion*, 136-48. Eds. Carol P. Christ and Judith Plasow. San Francisco: Harper & Row, 1979b.

Ford, J. Massyngberde. *Revelation*. The Anchor Bible Series. Vol. 38. Garden City, NY: Doubleday & Co., Inc. 1975.

Foster, Lawrence. *Religion and Sexuality: The Shakers, the Mormons, and the Oneida Community*. Urbana: University of Illinois Press, 1984.

Fraser, R. M., trans. & ed. *The Poems of Hesiod*. Norman: University of Oklahoma Press, 1983.

Frazer, James. *The Golden Bough: A Study of Magic and Religion*. 12 vols. New York: Macmillan, 1913-66.

Gardner, John and John Maier. *Gilgamesh: Translated from the Sin-legi-unninni Version*. New York: Vintage Books, 1984.

Gimbutas, Marija. *The Gods and Goddesses of Old Europe*. London: Thames & Hudson, 1974.

Glascoe, Marian, ed. *Julian of Norwich: A Revelation of Love*. Great Britain: University of Exeter, 1976.

Goldenberg, Naomi R. *Changing of the Gods: Feminism and the End of Traditonal Religions*. Boston: Beacon Press, 1979.

Gottlieb, Robert and Peter Wiley. *Americas Saints: The Rise of Mormon Power*. New York: G. P. Putnam's Sons, 1984.

HC. *History of the Church*. 7 vols, 2d ed. Ed. Brigham H. Roberts. Salt Lake City: Deseret Book Co., 1950.

Heimmel, Jennifer Perone. *"God Is Our Mother": Julian of Norwich and the Medieval Image of Christian Feminine Divinity*. Salzburg: Institut fur Anglistik und Amerikanistat, Universitat Salzburg, 1982.

Heller, Jan. "Der Name Eva." In *Archiv Orientalni* 26 (1958): 635–56.

Hennecke, Edgar, and Wilhelm Schneemelchs, eds. *New Testament Apocrypha*. 2 vols. Trans. R. McL. Wilson. Philadelphia: Westminster Press, 1963.

Hillers, D. R. *Covenant: The History of A Biblical Idea*. Baltimore: John Hopkins Press, 1969.

Homer. *The Odyssey*. Trans. E. V. Rieu. Baltimore: Penguin Books, 1946.

Hooke, S. H., ed. *Myth, Ritual, and Kingship: Essays on the Theory and Practice of Kingship in the Ancient Near East and in Israel*. Oxford: Clarendon Press, 1958.

Interpreter's Bible. Vol. 10. New York: Abingdon Press, 1953.

Janowitz, Naomi and Maggie Wenig. "Sabbath Prayers for Women." In *Womanspirit Rising: A Feminist Reader in Religion*, 174–78. Eds. Carol P. Christ and Judith Plaskow. San Francisco: Harper & Row, 1979.

JD. *Journal of Discourses*. 26 Vols. Liverpool: Albert Carrington, 1855–86.

Jensen, Richard L. "Forgotten Relief Societies, 1844–67." *Dialogue: A Journal of Mormon Thought* 16 (Spring 1983): 105–25.

Johnson, Jeffery Ogden. "Determining and Defining 'Wife': The Brigham Young Households." *Dialogue: A Journal of Mormon Thought* 20 (Fall 1987): 57–70.

Johnson, Paul. *Modern Times: The World from the Twenties to the Eighties*. New York: Colophon Books, 1983.

JST. *Joseph Smith's Translation of the Bible*. Independence, MO: Church of Jesus Christ of Latter Day Saints.

Juergens, Sylvester P., ed. *The New Marian Missal*. New York: Regina Press, 1950.

Katz, Jacob. "Traditional Society and Modern Society." In *Jewish Societies in the Middle East*, 35–47. Eds. Shlomo Deshen and Walter P. Zenner. New York: University Press of America, Inc., 1982.

Kenney, Scott, ed. *Wilford Woodruff's Journal*. 9 vols. Midvale, UT: Signature Books, 1983–85.

Kerenyi, C. *Eleusis: Archetypal Image of Mother and Daughter*. Translated by Ralph Manheim. New York: Pantheon Books, 1967.

Kikawada, Isaac M. "Two Notes on Eve." *Journal of Biblical Literature* 91 (March 1972): 33–37.

Kimball, Heber C. "Holy Order Minutes." Journal, 21 Dec. 1845. Special Collections, Harold B. Lee Library, Brigham Young University, Provo, UT.

Kirk, G. S. *Myth: Its Meaning and Function in Ancient and Other Cultures*. Berkeley: University of California Press, 1970.

Kirkland, Boyd. "Elohim and Jehovah in Mormonism and the Bible." *Dialogue: A Journal of Mormon Thought* 19 (Spring 1986): 78–98.

Kramer, Samuel Noah. *The Sacred Marriage Rite: Aspects of Faith, Myth, and Ritual in Ancient Sumer*. Bloomington: Indiana University Press, 1969.

Langdon, Stephen Herbert. *Semitic Mythology. The Mythology of All Races.* Vol. 5. Eds. John Arnott MacCulloch and George Foote. Boston: Marshall Jones Co., 1931.

Lewis, C. S. *Till We Have Faces: A Myth Retold.* Grand Rapids, MI: William B. Eerdmans, 1966.

Liddell, H. G. *An Intermediate Greek-English Lexicon.* Oxford: Oxford University Press, 1889.

Luther, Martin. *Lectures on Genesis.* In *Luther's Works.* 55 vols. Ed. Jaroslav Pelikan (vols. 1–30) and Helmut T. Lehmann (vols. 31–55). St. Louis: Concordia Pub. House, 1958–67.

MacDonald, George. *Lilith: A Romance.* Grand Rapids, MI: William B. Eerdmans Pub. Co., 1981.

Madsen, Carol Cornwall. "Mormon Women and the Struggle for Definition: The Nineteenth Century Church." *Sunstone* 6 (Nov.-Dec. 1981): 7–11.

————. "Mormon Women and the Temple: Toward a New Understanding." In *Sisters in Spirit: Mormon Women in Historical and Cultural Perspective,* 84–110. Eds. Maureen Ursenbach Beecher and Lavina Fielding Anderson. Urbana: University of Illinois Press, 1987.

Matthews, Robert J. *"A Plainer Translation": Joseph Smith's Translation of the Bible: A History and Commentary.* Provo, UT: Brigham Young University Press, 1975.

McCarthy, Dennis J. *Old Testament Covenant: A Study of Current Opinions.* Atlanta: John Knox Press, 1976.

McConkie, Bruce R. "Our Relationship with the Lord." *B.Y.U. Fireside and Devotional Speeches* (No. 83), 97–103. Provo, UT: Brigham Young University Press, 1981.

————. "What Think Ye of Salvation by Grace?" BYU devotional address, 10 Jan. 1984.

McMurrin, Sterling M. *The Theological Foundations of the Mormon Religion.* Salt Lake City: University of Utah Press, 1965.

Mendenhall, G. "Covenant Forms in Israelite Tradition." *Biblical Archeologist* 17 (1954): 50–76.

Millett, Kate. *Sexual Politics.* Garden City, NY: Doubleday, 1970.

Minutes of the School of the Prophets of 1883. Provo, UT. Special Collections, Harold B. Lee Library, Brigham Young University, Provo, UT.

Mollenkott, Virginia Ramey. *The Divine Feminine: The Biblical Imagery of God as Female.* New York: Crossroad Publishing Co., 1983.

Moltmann-Wendel, Elisabeth. *A Land Flowing with Milk and Honey: Perpsectives in Feminist Theology.* New York: Crossroads, 1986.

Morford, Mark P. O. and Robert J. Lenardon. *Classical Mythology.* 3d. ed. New York: Longman, 1985.

Mormon Doctrine. McConkie, Bruce R. *Mormon Doctrine.* Salt Lake City: Deseret Book, 1958.

MS. *Latter-day Saints' Millennial Star.* 132 vols. Manchester, Liverpool, and London, 1840–1970.

Neumann, Erich. *The Origins and History of Consciousness*. Trans. R.F.C. Hull. Princeton: Princeton University Press, 1954.

————. *The Great Mother: An Analysis of the Archetype*. Trans. Ralph Manheim. 2d ed. Princeton: Princeton University Press, 1963.

New Annotated Oxford Bible. May, Herbert G. and Bruce M. Metzger, eds. *The New Oxford Annotated Bible With the Apocrypha*. New York: Oxford University Press, 1977.

Newell, Linda King. "A Gift Given; a Gift Taken." *Sunstone* 6 (Sept.-Oct. 1981): 16–25.

Newell, Linda King. "Gifts of the Spirit: Women's Share." In *Sisters in Spirit: Mormon Women in Historical and Cultural Perspective*, 111–50. Eds. Maureen Ursenbach Beecher and Lavina Fielding Anderson. Urbana: University of Illinois Press, 1987.

————and Valeen Tippetts Avery. *Mormon Enigma: Emma Hale Smith Prophet's Wife, "Elect Lady," Polygamy's Foe, 1804–1879*. Garden City, NY: Doubleday & Company, Inc., 1984.

Nibley, Hugh. *The Message of the Joseph Smith Papyri: An Egyptian Endowment*. Salt Lake City: Deseret Book, 1975.

————. "Subduing the Earth." In *Nibley on the Timely and the Timeless*, 85–100. Religious Studies Monograph Series. Vol. 1. Provo, UT: Brigham Young University Press, Religious Studies Center, 1978.

Olsen, Donald P. "Understanding the Scope of the Grace of Christ." *Sunstone* 9 (Autumn 1984): 21–25.

Orr, William F. and James Arthur Walther. *1 Corinthians*. Anchor Bible Series. Vol. 32. Garden City, NY: Doubleday & Co., Inc., 1976.

Ostler, Blake. "The Mormon Concept of God." *Dialogue: A Journal of Mormon Thought* 17 (Summer 1984): 65–93.

Packer, Boyd K. "A Tribute to Women." In *Ensign* 19 (July 1989): 72–75.

Pagels, Elaine. "What Became of God the Mother? Conflicting Images of God in Early Christianity." In *Womanspirit Rising: A Feminist Reader in Religion*, 107–19. Eds. Carol P. Christ and Judith Plaskow. San Francisco: Harper & Row, 1979.

Patai, Raphael. *The Hebrew Goddess*. New York: Avon Books, 1978.

————. *The Messiah Texts*. New York: Avon Books, 1979.

————. *Gates to the Old City: A Book of Jewish Legends*. New York: Avon Books, 1980.

Peck, Scott. *The Different Drum: Community-Making and Peace*. New York: Harper & Row Publishers, 1988.

Pelikan, Jaroslav. *Jesus Through the Centuries: His Place in the History of Culture*. New Haven: Yale University Press, 1985.

Phillips, John A. *Eve: The History of an Idea*. San Francisco: Harper & Row, 1984.

Phipps, William E. *Was Jesus Married? The Distortion of Sexuality in the Christian Tradition*. New York: Harper & Row, 1970.

_____. *The Sexuality of Jesus: Theological and Literary Perspectives.* New York: Harper and Row, 1973.

_____. *Recovering Biblical Sensuousness.* Philadephia: Westminister Press, 1975.

Plaskow, Judith. "The Coming of Lilith: Toward a Feminist Theology." In *Womanspirit Rising: A Feminist Reader in Religion,* 198–209. Eds. Carol P. Christ and Judith Plasow. San Francisco: Harper & Row, 1979.

Plutarch. "Isis and Osiris." In *Moralia.* Ed. and trans. Frank Cole Babbitt. Loeb Classical Library. Vol. 5. Cambridge, MA: Harvard University Press, 1957.

Pope, Marvin H. *Song of Songs.* Anchor Bible Series. Vol. 7c. Garden City, NY: Doubleday & Co., Inc., 1977.

Pratt, Orson. *The Seer* (2 vols. in 1). Liverpool England, 1853–1854. Reprint. Eugene Wagner, Salt Lake City, 1960.

PWJS. Jessee, Dean C., ed. *The Personal Writings of Joseph Smith.* Salt Lake City: Deseret Book, 1984.

Quinn, D. Michael. "Latter-day Saint Prayer Circles." *Brigham Young University Studies* 19 (Fall 1978): 79–105.

_____. "LDS Church Authority and New Plural Marriages, 1890–1904." *Dialogue: A Journal of Mormon Thought* 18 (Spring 1985): 9–105.

_____. *Early Mormonism and the Magic World View.* Salt Lake City: Signature Books, 1987.

Rector, Daniel H. "Beyond Orthodoxy: Joseph Smith's Amplified Doctrine of Grace." Paper presented at the 1985 Salt Lake City Sunstone Theological Symposium. Copy in the possession of the authors.

Relief Society Manual. "Male and Female Created He Them." In *Relief Society Courses of Study, 1985,* 113–16. Salt Lake City: Church of Jesus Christ of Latter-day Saints, 1984.

Renault, Mary. *The Bull From the Sea.* New York: Pantheon Books, 1962.

Revelations. Revelations to Joseph Smith and Brigham Young, 1829–47 (Section 84). Newell K. Whitney Papers (1795–1850). Special Collections, Harold B. Lee Library, Brigham Young University, Provo, UT.

Revelations Not in the Doctrine and Covenants, 1830–43. Joseph Smith, Jr., Papers (1827–44). Special Collections, Harold B. Lee Library, Brigham Young University.

Richards, Franklin D. Miscellaneous Papers. Special Collections, Harold B. Lee Library, Brigham Young University, Provo, UT.

Richardson, Alan. *A Dictionary of Christian Theology.* London: SCM Press, 1969.

Ricoeur, Paul. *Hermeneutics and the Human Sciences.* Ed. and trans. John B. Thompson. Cambridge: Cambridge University Press, 1981.

Robinson, James N., ed. *The Nag Hammadi Library.* San Francisco: Harper & Row, 1977.

Robson, Kent. "Omnis on the Horizon." *Sunstone* 8 (July-Aug. 1983): 21–23.

Ruether, Rosemary Radford. *Sexism and God-Talk: Toward A Feminist Theology.* Boston: Beacon Press, 1983.

Sanders, James A. *Canon and Community: A Guide To Canonical Criticism.* Philadelphia: Fortress Press, 1984.

Scarf, Maggie. *Intimate Partners: Patterns in Love and Marriage.* New York: Ballantine Books, 1988.

Sebeok, Thomas A., ed. *Myth: A Symposium.* Bloomington: Indiana University Press, 1965. 1st ed. 1955.

Smith, Joseph Fielding. *Essentials in Church History.* Salt Lake City: Deseret Book, 1950.

————. *Doctrines of Salvation.* 3 vols. Salt Lake City: Bookcraft, 1954.

Stone, Merlin. *When God Was A Woman.* New York: Dial Press, 1976.

Talmage, James E. *A Study of the Articles of Faith.* Salt Lake City: Church of Jesus Christ of Latter-day Saints, 1977. 1st ed. 1899.

Taylor, Vincent. *The Names of Jesus.* London: Macmillan, 1953.

Teubal, Savina J. *Sarah the Priestess: The First Matriarch of Genesis.* Athens Ohio: Swallow Press, 1984.

Thompson, William Irwin. *Darkness and Scattered Light: Four Talks on the Future.* Garden City, NY: Anchor Books, 1978.

————. *The Time Falling Bodies Take to Light: Mythology, Sexuality and the Origins of Culture.* New York: St. Martins Press, 1981.

Tillich, Paul. *Systematic Theology.* 3 vols. Chicago: University of Chicago Press, 1951–63.

Times and Seasons. 6 vols. Nauvoo, IL, 1839–46.

TPJS. Joseph Fielding Smith, Jr., ed. *Teachings of the Prophet Joseph Smith.* Salt Lake City: Deseret Book, 1938.

Trible, Phyllis. "Eve and Adam: Genesis 2–3 Reread." In *Womanspirit Rising: A Feminist Reader in Religion,* 74–83. Eds. Carol P. Christ and Judith Plaskow. San Francisco: Harper & Row, 1979.

————. *God and the Rhetoric of Sexuality.* Philadelphia: Fortress Press, 1978.

Tullidge, Edward W. *The Women of Mormondom.* New York, 1877. Reprint. Salt Lake City, 1977.

Turner, Rodney. *Woman and the Priesthood.* Salt Lake City: Deseret Book, 1972.

Ulanov, Ann Belford. *The Feminine in Jungian Psychology and in Christian Theology.* Evanston: Northwestern University Press, 1971.

————. *Picturing God.* Cambridge, MA: Cowley Publications, 1986.

Van Wagoner, Richard S. "Mormon Polyandry in Nauvoo." *Dialogue: A Journal of Mormon Thought* 18 (Fall 1985): 67–83.

————. *Mormon Polygamy: A History.* Salt Lake City: Signature Books, 1986.

Voros, J. Frederic. "I Am Not Under the Law." Unpublished paper presented at the August 1987a Salt Lake City Sunstone Theological Symposium. Copy in the possession of the authors.

————. "Was the Book of Mormon Buried With King Follett?" *Sunstone* 11 (March 1987b): 15–18.

Walker, Barbara G. *Woman's Encyclopedia of Myths and Secrets.* New York: Harper & Row, 1983.

_____ . *The Woman's Dictionary of Symbols and Sacred Objects*. San Francisco: Harper & Row Publishers, 1988.

Warner, Marina. *Alone of All Her Sex: The Myth and Cult of the Virgin Mary*. New York: Pocket Books, 1976.

Weinfeld, M. "Covenant of Grant in the Old Testament and in the Ancient Near East." *Journal of the American Oriental Society* 90 (1970): 184–203.

West, Angela. "A Faith for Feminists?" In *Walking on the Water: Women Talk About Spirituality*, 66–90. Eds. Jo Garcia and Sara Maitland. London: Virago, 1983.

Wilcox, Linda P. "The Mormon Concept of a Mother in Heaven." In *Sisters in Spirit: Mormon Women in Historical and Cultural Perspective*, 64–77. Eds. Maureen Ursenback Beecher and Lavina Fielding Anderson. Urbana: University of Illinois Press, 1987.

WJS. Ehat, Andrew F. and Lyndon W. Cook, eds. *The Words of Joseph Smith*. Provo, UT: Religious Studies Center, Brigham Young University, 1980.

Wolkstein, Diane and Samauel Noah Kramer. *Inanna: Queen of Heaven and Earth: Her Stories and Hymns from Sumar*. New York: Harper & Row, 1983.

Woman's Exponent. 41 vols. Salt Lake City, 1872–1914.